A Whisper of Bones

By Rosanne L. Higgins

Copyright © 2014 Rosanne L. Higgins
All rights reserved.

To Bob, Max and Charlie, I love you always.

To Joyce, Doug and Jennifer, thanks for including me in such a great adventure!

Prologue

Ciara Nolan stood in the pouring rain vigorously rubbing her hands along her cold and wet arms to keep warm. Two equally drenched and shivering young men removed the casket from the wagon and tried to ease it into the muddy hole they had dug by the light of a single lantern. It was just dawn on Friday morning and the poor lads could barely see what they were doing. It was difficult to maneuver the large wooden box on the slick ground and the men were not timid about expressing their annoyance at having to bury the body so soon after death.

Part One

Chapter One

Maude Travers sat by the cash register, behind the long oak counter of her antique lamp boutique, counting the day's receipts. On days like today, when the profits of a single sale had most of the bills paid before they even arrived in the mail, she did not regret leaving her academic post in the Department of Anthropology at a major university to pursue a less demanding career in the antique business. After she made her evening deposit her time was her own to spend with her husband and two boys. There were no more late nights working on grant proposals, galleys or last minute additions to the syllabus. No more expensive trips to conferences for which the University no longer paid. No more last minute runs to the only post office open until midnight to assure the symposium abstract was post marked on that, the absolute last day it was due. (Well, to be fair, most submissions were via e-mail now, but years ago there had been plenty of those late night postal runs.)

Now, ten years later, Maude closed up the shop at six and was sipping a gin and tonic with her husband as they prepared dinner by 6:30 at the latest. When asked, as she often was, 'Do you miss it?' she always replied 'Not one single bit.' It had been hard to balance a demanding career in a town five hours from the one in which she lived, with two small boys and a husband who had a demanding career of his own, not to mention the expense of maintaining two households in addition to the nannies and the housekeepers. After six years of commuting from Potsdam to Buffalo, she decided family came first and left academia the year her tenure decision would have been made.

If she was being honest, Maude did miss parts of her life in academia very much. She missed the anthropology. The study of humans had always fascinated her. She had known in the 4th grade she would one day be an Anthropologist. It was not until later, as an undergraduate, that she found her passion in skeletal biology and chose Biological Anthropology as her field of concentration, but that part of her life was over. Maude had just filled out her deposit slip for the bank and was reaching for her keys when her cell phone rang.

"Maude, it's Jean. Do you have a minute?"

For Dr. Jean McMahon, Maude would always have a minute. She had kept in touch with her Ph.D. thesis advisor even after she had left academia. Jean had been there at her wedding and for the birth of her two sons. Maude hadn't spoken to her mentor in a while, so she put her keys down and took a seat. It would be more than a minute.

"Do you remember when you were working on your dissertation and you kept hounding me to let you excavate the almshouse cemetery?" In graduate school Maude had studied the impact of poverty on the human skeleton. The fact that the Erie County Almshouse and Insane Asylum had occupied the same piece of property as the University's Urban Campus currently used meant that her research would be local. By that time Maude was married and had given birth to her first child, so a local project suited her just fine. She had begged her mentor to seek approval to excavate the Erie County Almshouse cemetery, where thousands of Buffalo's poor had been laid to rest. After all, the general location on campus was known and it would be a substantial contribution to the discipline to have a collection directly comparable to the county poorhouse sample from Rochester, which was then housed at the university. What a dissertation it would have been! However, for many reasons, not the least of which was the understanding that you don't disturb a cemetery unless there is good reason (beyond scientific inquiry), her repeated requests were denied, though her doctoral dissertation turned out to be a respectable contribution to science nonetheless.

"Yes, I do, and I remember you telling me 'Maude, you can't just go around disturbing human burial grounds!' Why do you ask?"

"The University is making improvements on the road behind Michael Hall on the South Campus and they have uncovered a large sample of the cemetery."

"You're kidding!"

"Feel like getting dirty? It's a salvage project. We need to remove an estimated four hundred burials by September so the road improvements can stay on schedule. We can use all of the help we can get."

The excavation and study of human skeletal remains have always been tricky propositions in which scientists carefully balanced objective scientific inquiry with respect for the sanctity of eternal repose, and for the cultural traditions of those people they intend to study. The University had granted the Department of Anthropology permission to excavate and study the remains that had been disturbed by the new construction. However, as was usually the case in these sorts of salvage operations, both money and time were short. Whatever her involvement in the project, Maude knew it was strictly volunteer.

"Would I like to get dirty? Of course! How often does a person get a chance like this? Just tell me where to be and I'll be there, trowel in hand!" In the excitement of hearing the news that Maude would finally get to look at the bones of the people she had spent so many years studying through the historic record, the antique dealer had completely forgotten about her day job. Archaeological excavations took place during the day, often from the first light of dawn until the shadow of dusk, when the darkness endangered the removal of fragile treasures. Maude already had those hours filled with getting two tween age boys off to school and running her own business.

Reality finally dawning on her, Maude said, in a slightly less enthusiastic tone, "You know what, Jean, let me see what I can juggle around at work. I might not be able to help in the field, but I can definitely help in the lab cleaning and cataloging bones."

"Any help would be much appreciated. I'll tell the crew chief to look out for you if you can get away during the day. If not, I'll meet you in the lab on Saturday and we can start cleaning. It's a nasty mess of mud and clay out there with all of this rain we've been having. I was not kidding about getting dirty!"

"Looking forward to it!" Maude said and pushed the "end" button on her phone. Before she grabbed her keys she checked her purse for the emergency $20's she usually kept for gas or the unexpected trip to Hannah's Frosty Treats with her boys. She had just enough time to stop by Hertel Parker Liquors for a special bottle of Jameson - black label, the good stuff -before she picked up the boys from football. There would be some celebrating tonight.

Chapter Two

Maude left the lab late Saturday night smelling like embalming solution and wet clay. They had taken over the entire back room of the Wet Lab, generally used for the embalming of monkey cadavers used in the Primate Dissections course. Now the room was set up for the cleaning of bones which were coming in from the field site in large numbers every day. Jean had not been kidding when she said it was a muddy mess. Most of the bones were encrusted in clay, which made cleaning a long, tedious, and very dirty process.

The stainless steel tables were equipped with large plastic tubs and strainers so the bones could actually be placed in water for easier and faster cleaning. At first many of the grad students were appalled at the idea of using water to clean such delicate archaeological remains and looked on with some mixture of shock and disgust as Maude and Jean gently scrubbed the submerged bones with soft tooth brushes or placed the bones in strainers and rinsed them under the sink. Looking around at the expressions on their faces, Jean simply stated, "By the looks of that field site, these bones have been submerged in water more than once in the last hundred years. It won't hurt them to be wet a little bit longer."

"Besides, clay has a way of sticking to surfaces. If you try to remove it with a tooth pick or a dental instrument, it could very well take something valuable like a tooth with it." Maude added, "Better to dissolve the clay in water and be sure there is nothing valuable hiding in it."

"Oh, and be sure to look through the remains in the strainers very carefully before you discard the contents of your tub," Jean cautioned "We don't want any bone or tooth fragments to be thrown away by accident."

The graduate students began cautiously dipping a tooth brush into the water and gingerly scrubbing the clay from the surfaces of the bones. After a while, when they saw Drs. McMahon and Travers cleaning at twice their pace and with better results, they began in earnest to submerge the more robust bones. Before anyone knew it is was after nine o'clock. So engrossed with their work and the discussions of the different bone pathologies they had observed while cleaning, the group had worked through dinner.

Pushing back the sleeve of her latex glove to check her watch, Maude said, "Holy crap! I had no idea it was this late! I've got to get going." She finished cleaning the remaining bones from the burial she had been working on and placed them on the tray for drying, which she marked with the same burial number that was on the box from which she had taken the bones. She cleaned up her work station and headed for the door, turning back toward the group as she was half way through it to say, "I'll be back again tomorrow."

Maude had forgotten that it was difficult to receive or make cell phone calls in the Wet Lab, something about all of the computer equipment in the room directly above it interfering with the signals. So she winced just a bit when she found five missed calls from her husband. Guilt set in as she listened to the messages that ranged from "Maude, it's Don. Will you be home for dinner?" to "Maude, it's me again. I'm guessing you got caught up in your work. The boys and I ordered wings. There are still a few in the fridge if you are hungry. Love you."

From the time the boys were little, Saturday nights in the Travers household had always been "pull-out-the-bed-night". They ordered take out, pulled out the sofa bed in the family room and all piled on to watch a movie. It had always been the memories of those nights that reminded Maude that she had done the right thing by leaving academia. When the boys were small, they piled on the bed with their Dad, while she sat on a chair with her lap top, grading papers or working on her own research. For the past few years she had joined her family on the pullout bed to watch *Harry Potter* or *Lord of the Rings* for the millionth time. Now Billy was 11 and Glen was 12 years old. Pull-out-the-bed night had evolved into just movie night and Maude knew there would be fewer of those in their future as the boys entered their teenage years. She felt terrible to have missed this one.

Once home, she ate the remaining five chicken wings straight out of the fridge and stumbled upstairs. Maude was not surprised to see a warm bubble bath waiting for her in the master bathroom. Back in the grad school days, before they were married, Maude would return home in the evening, after teaching Comparative Primate Anatomy, to find a tub filled with fragrant foam awaiting her in the West Ferry apartment she shared with Don. At first, she thought it was the most romantic thing he had ever done. After a while, she realized it was his loving way of saying "Honey, you stink!"

She chuckled as she entered the room, shedding the long sleeved t-shirt and jeans as she walked across the hardwood floor toward the bath. "You remembered."

"I did." He replied.

She walked in the bathroom and immediately noticed the heavy crystal tumbler with a healthy dram of whiskey perched on the medicine chest that stood next to the claw foot tub. "Bonus!" she called out as she climbed into the pearly bubbles.

At the same time the following evening she sat in the tub, tumbler in hand, pondering the recent turn of events. In her wildest dreams, Maude never would have thought she would be back at the university and working on the Erie County Poorhouse Cemetery Collection. It was like getting a "do-over," a chance to do the project she had originally wanted. Do-overs were rare in life and this was the best one of all. Being no longer affiliated with any university, Maude was essentially a volunteer on the project, which suited her just fine. She was free to study the bones unencumbered. She had no budget to adhere to, no administration to deal with and nobody to impress. Those complications would be dealt with by others. Her thoughts were interrupted by a knock on the open door. It was Don with the bottle of Jameson and another glass.

"So what's the long term plan here?" he asked as he refilled her glass, then his, and took a seat on the edge of the tub. There had been no reproach for working all through the weekend and leaving both the care of the boys and the house to him. Don had always been supportive of her endeavors and she knew now would be no different. Still, he had a right to know where, if anywhere, all this time in the anthropology lab was leading. In his typical style, he asked a simple question and listened while she gave a long and complicated answer.

"This is a big deal, Don. They estimate they will

remove nearly 400 burials between now and September. All of the clay is making the cleaning very difficult. We are lucky if we get two complete burials cleaned each day. They really need my help."

He simply looked at her, knowing there would be more.

"You know I am loving every minute of this. I would give anything to be in the field helping with the excavation, but I could not justify paying anyone to work for me so that I can go volunteer, right?"

The blue eyes continued looking at her impassively, waiting for her to find a solution.

She continued. "I also know that I can't continue to work long hours at the lab on weekends. I appreciate you holding down the fort the way you did, by the way."

A nod this time.

"It's a shame I can't get some work done during the day. It's usually pretty slow after lunch. If I could get to campus for even a few hours to clean and photograph the skeletons, maybe, between the pictures and my notes, I work on some analysis back at the shop… I could clear off the work table in the back so that I have plenty of room to spread out. Do you think you could cover me for a few hours one or two days a week?"

Finally a comment from Don, "Do you think it would really only be a few hours? I know once you get started it will be hard for you to just stop when the clock strikes two."

"I will have to. Look, Don, I know that I am asking a lot of you, but I really want to do this. If my work on campus interferes in any way with our business, I will let it go with no argument. Will you let me try?"

Don got up and clinked his glass with his wife's and said "Here's to your triumphant return to anthropology!" As he left the bathroom, Maude detected a smirk on her husband's face.

"What's the look for?" she asked.

"Oh, nothing. I was just thinking your ghosts might have more to say about you working on this project than I do." He was referring to their assumption that the shop they rented was haunted. Over the years both Maude and Don had heard strange noises and voices that occurred without reasonable explanation. Twice when he was younger, Glen, their eldest son, claimed to have seen someone standing by the window when the shop was supposed to be empty. Their younger son, Billy, was still not comfortable being in the shop alone. "You better hope one of your almshouse inmates doesn't follow you home!"

She smiled "Well, the ghosts have been quiet recently so maybe they are bored with me. Perhaps some new people will perk them up a bit."

"Be careful what you wish for! You should get out of the tub, by the way. You're starting to prune."

Maude smiled and raised her glass once again in the direction of her husband. "Thank for this."

With a wink and smile, Don raised his own glass and left.

Chapter Three

Maude pulled her SUV into the alley behind her shop on Chippewa Street a little earlier than usual Monday morning. She had spoken to Jean the day before about her plan to spend a few hours a week in the lab. Maude was currently the most experienced skeletal biologist working on the project besides Jean, so her mentor welcomed the offer of help and met Maude early Monday morning to determine which skeletons would be worked on first.

The two-story building they rented dated from the mid-nineteenth century, when city merchants typically lived and worked in the same building. The second story apartment was rented by a truck driver who was seldom there. Maude had a key to his place and had agreed to check on his cat periodically when he was away. The ground floor consisted of the main shop area, filled just enough with brass, crystal, silk and fringe to make a potential customer strolling by stop at the large display windows and take a good long look.

While she and her husband were business partners, Maude seldom saw Don during the work day. He prowled around flea markets, estate sales and eBay locating and purchasing antique lamps to sell in their shop, while Maude managed the store with the help of one part time employee. The back room was used as an office for Maude and a workshop for Don, who often repaired and restored his precious finds before displaying them for sale. As she opened the back door, Maude was greeted by the aroma of Brasso and musty old building, with just a hint of WD-40. Toward the front of the shop, these industrious smells yielded to the gentle bouquet produced by the cinnamon and apple spice potpourri and lavender sachets also sold there.

"Good thing I got here early," she said to herself as she took in the piles of paper, scattered tools, pieces and parts that littered the back room. Modifying the office/workshop into a makeshift research lab would force Maude to organize the work space and purge it of unnecessary clutter. She often blamed Don for leaving his tools around and not cleaning up properly when a project was completed, but the truth of it was they were both slobs and sharing the same work space often resulted in the vast accumulation of things and stuff.

Maude stood in the back door of her shop with her keys precariously hung from her left pinky finger as she considered just how she would haul both the state-of-the art color laser printer and the largest computer monitor that money could buy into the shop. She and Don often sent and received digital photos of items for sale or purchase, and had outfitted their home office with computer equipment that would allow them to observe and evaluate even the most minute details of any antique lamp. The equipment she had transported from home would also be very useful for examining the pathologies of the bones she would photograph in the lab. Startled by a voice behind her, Maude maneuvered to prop the shop door open.

"Why is it a good thing you got here early? Let me help you with that," offered the tall women who worked in the shop next door.

"Oh, thanks, Christine, but I've got it," Maude replied as she slipped inside and quickly placed the boxes on the shelf by the door.

"Whatcha got there?" Christine asked.

This was not the person Maude wanted to run into right at this moment. Christine was a graduate student in the History Department and employee at Treasures and Trinkets, the antique shop next door. Both women were scholars of the early nineteenth-century United States and often chatted about their common interest in Buffalo's early history. When Christine learned that Maude was back in the anthropology department working on the Erie County Poorhouse Cemetery Project, as it was now known among the researchers involved, she would jump to the wrong conclusion that Maude was maneuvering her way back into academia. The two shops shared many patrons in a business where even the loss of one or two good clients could be financially devastating. If word got out that Maude was leaving the Antique Lamp Company to return to academia it could be very damaging to their business. She would have to keep her involvement in the project a secret for now.

"Just moving junk from one place to another," Maude said, casually closing the car door. Even the transfer of computer equipment would result in an assault of queries that Maude didn't want to answer. She was a terrible liar and thought the less said the better until she had time to think up a reasonable explanation for moving the expensive equipment from their more secure home office to the shop.

"You know what they say, 'one man's trash is another man's treasure.' Mind if I have a look?" Christine's curiosity and ability to sniff out anything even remotely interesting or valuable were definitely assets in the antique business, which is how she had been able to fund her ABD (all but dissertation) years on campus working in the antique shop next door. Those remaining years, when all the credits and various requirements were completed leaving the student free to research and write their doctoral dissertation, were typically lean, as students were limited to the number of years they could receive University or Department funding for their coursework. However, one or two good commissions on the sale of a particularly rare piece always seemed to allow Christine to register for just enough credits to keep the student loan police away for another semester. Maude suspected Christine was a professional student and would likely never finish her doctorate. There was no denying that the woman was incredibly bright, brilliant, even. Maude needed to respond to her request carefully or Christine would surely suspect something was up.

Maude's pulse quickened and she began to sweat, but somehow managed to reply casually as she started to close the door. "If you want, later. I've got a few things to get sorted out before the shop opens. I'll talk to you later." She shut the door before her friend could reply. When she heard the door to the other shop open and close, she locked her back door and breathed a large sigh of relief. Maude hated lying, even about small things, and was not good at it. She chuckled to herself after she opened the door as quietly as she could, exited the shop like a ninja and secreted the two heavy boxes back in undetected. *What have I gotten myself into*, she thought as she locked the door, confident that her secret was safe, at least for now.

After spending some time cleaning out the work area, Maude realized two very important things. The first was that, even after having cleared Don's space, she still had to leave enough room for him to work, leaving her very little room for spreading out the considerable number of photographs necessary to see an entire skeleton in anatomical position, not to mention close-ups of specific pathologies or trauma. The second thing was that materials and equipment would not be secure in this area during the workday because Christine often popped in using the back door to chat or have lunch. Maude needed some sort of visual barrier separating her lab space from the rest of the work area. But that would have to wait because there was a person already knocking at the door. Looking at the clock on her desk and realizing it was three minutes after ten, she left the boxes where they were and went to open the shop for the day.

The morning had been a busy one and by noon, Maude was ready for the break that typically came around then. The shop was the busiest in the late afternoon and she typically used the morning for bookkeeping, cleaning, and returning phone calls. The Hotel Lafayette was being renovated to its former glory and the owner was interested in period light fixtures for the lobby. It took the better part of two hours to show the man what was available from the 1940s and to negotiate prices for each item. Still, it was a big sale and she knew Don would be pleased when she told him at lunch. The couple seldom actually worked together, as Maude was anchored to the shop and Don traveled in pursuit of luminary treasures. Whenever it was possible, Don came by the shop and they had lunch together. It was one of the things Maude enjoyed most when they first opened. He would be coming by any minute, and the sale to the Lafayette would go a long way toward buttering her husband up when she asked him to help her move a large armoire up from the cellar.

The tall piece of furniture would be the perfect barrier between her work space and his, with the doors facing in towards her desk. There was enough shelf space to house the printer and monitor on them and easily hook them up to her laptop. Also, they would not be seen by anyone passing through the back of the shop. Although the piece was old, it was a common piece and in terrible shape and so would be of no interest to Christine, who had seen it before. If she needed to, Maude could close the doors and the equipment would be concealed from prying eyes. The drawers below the shelves were deep enough to store all her photographs, notes and binders when they were not in use. It was perfect. Big, heavy, and clunky, but perfect.

Chapter Four

Over the next few weeks, Maude had established a good working routine. The early morning hours were spent, as they always had been, with the day-to-day details of recordkeeping, cleaning and maintenance. Two days each week, during the slow part of the afternoon, she would shoot over to the University and work on the skeletons until it was time to either pick up the boys from school or head back to the shop. She was careful only to lay out what bones could be cleaned in a finite period of time. The long bones of the arms or legs, which were smooth and easy to clean, could completed in about an hour or so. The bones of the vertebral column, with all of their protruding points (or "processes") took longer, so she would only do a few at a time. The underside of the skull, with all of its foramina and fissures, would have to be done over several days.

As it turned out, Christine and her incessant curiosity were at bay because she was busy working on a grant from the National Endowment for the Humanities to fund her dissertation research, so Maude was able to get two burials cleaned each week without worrying about how she would explain her departure from the shop for a few hours at a time. She took detailed photographs of each bone from several angles, which she printed out back at the shop. From the photos, specific details were observed and recorded for further analysis or measurement when she was back in the lab. The system allowed her to stay on track and use her limited hands-on time in the lab more efficiently.

On Friday, after a quick lunch she began to sort through the latest box of bones. The burial was complete, meaning all of the bones that make up the human skeleton were present and in very good condition. At first glance, burial number 116 (the burial number was assigned by the archaeologists in the field based on the order in which it was excavated), looked to be female and, judging by the degree of dental wear, on the older side of forty. She would have to wait for further analysis of other bones in the skull and pelvis to confirm age, as dental wear could be deceiving depending on the individual's diet. Still, Maude liked to have an idea of who she was working on and what life may have been like for them. She felt it was more respectful, after having disturbed a person's permanent place of rest (however necessary it may have been), to become acquainted with them.

"What do we have here?" She asked out loud as she examined the right, then left, femora. This woman had bony projections at both ends of the bone that were typical of arthritis in both the hip and knee joints. Maude surmised the woman had worked hard at tasks that involved repetitive bending and lifting, perhaps as a housekeeper or a laundress. A more detailed examination of the muscle attachment sites on her bones might help narrow down her occupation. "Ouch, that had'ta hurt," she suggested, noting a few healed fractures on the woman's ribs. Perhaps she fell, or was beaten. Jean had always said that bones were like books and had a story to tell to those who knew how to read them. While further study would reveal more details of this woman's existence, it was a fair assumption that, in the later years of her life, she likely experienced considerable pain every day.

This woman represented by burial number 116 had not had an easy life. That much was evident with just a cursory examination of her clay-encrusted skeleton. They would know much more when all of her bones were completely cleaned and studied. A team of researchers would meticulously examine and measure all of her bones. They would know how tall she had been, if she suffered certain nutritional deficiencies or chronic infectious diseases, or whether she experienced other traumas in addition to her broken ribs. Examination of her teeth would answer questions about her diet and whether she experienced periods of extreme nutritional deprivation early in her life.

"It is interesting that one of the biggest things to come out of the Industrial Revolution in the United States was large scale poverty," Maude told burial number 116. "As students of American history, we learned about the building of the Erie Canal and the great railroads. We learn about the powerful men like Vanderbilt and Rockefeller. But what about you?"

It was the goal of Maude and the members of the research team to use a combination of meticulous skeletal analysis and exhaustive documentary research to bring the story of these largely forgotten people to light. The condition of this skeleton (all of the skeletons, for that matter) would be interpreted based on what was known about almshouses during the period. The early nineteenth century marked what was known as the Asylum Movement. Several policies during the early decades of that century were enacted to remove various problematic subgroups from the general population, including the poor, the mentally ill, the sick, the orphaned and the aged. Almshouses were established in an attempt to reduce the costs for relieving the rapidly growing number of individuals and families who were unable, for reasons such as illness, injury, intemperance and apathy, to provide for themselves. These institutions were not designed to provide long-term relief, and very quickly became overcrowded with massive waves of immigrants, a shift from agriculture to manufacturing and epidemic diseases produced large-scale urban poverty. Living conditions in these asylums were typically appalling and not much of an improvement over those available to the impoverished masses on the outside, short of a roof over their heads. Many almshouses provided no facilities for bathing and the sick were housed with other healthy inmates, even children, who were ever present and in large numbers.

"What's your story?" Maude asked. This woman was more than burial number116. She had lived and worked in the city of Buffalo. At some point she became desperate enough to seek refuge at the Erie County Almshouse. Perhaps she was a widow, and, with her ailments, unable to care for herself? Had she become ill? Had she been picked up on the street as a vagrant and taken there by the constable? These questions would not be answered by examining her skeleton. The numbered wooden stakes that marked individual burials were long gone, leaving the thousands of graves from the almshouse cemetery unmarked and largely forgotten. It was unlikely that her individual identity would be revealed, thus making it impossible to link burial number116 to any set of records that might have shed light on her story.

"Let's see what you've got to tell me." Maude decided to start with the long bones of the arms and set them on the tray for cleaning. She took the plastic washtub over to the sink and filled it with water. When she returned to the table she noticed another of the ribs with a healed fracture was sitting out among the long bones.

"Strange, I don't remember taking you out," she said as she picked up the rib to place it back in the box. As she touched the rough surface of the bone where the fracture had healed she was overcome with a vision of a woman on the wide planks of a hardwood floor, crouched in the fetal position as a large and angry man kicked mercilessly at the side of her rib cage. At the same time she felt a searing pain in her chest, which took her breath away. In an instant it was over, and the power of it left her hunched over and clutching her chest. Only when she caught her breath again did she realize the rib had fallen back into the plastic bag from which it had come.

Maude was astounded by how real it all seemed. One minute she was sitting at the table in the lab and the next she was in what she assumed to be a kitchen, and an old one at that. The details were so clear, the oak floor boards scrubbed smooth, dried herbs hung from the ceiling, and the smell of boiling oats with notes of whiskey and tobacco. What had just happened? With her heart still racing, she reached again for the bag that contained the broken rib. Just as she was working up the nerve to reach in the bag, the phone rang. Taking a deep breath, she walked away from the table to retrieve her cell phone.

Twenty minutes later, Maude pressed the "end" button on her phone, put on another pair of latex gloves, and returned to the table. She was a bit surprised to find the same rib still out. "Huh. I could have sworn I put you away." Tentatively she reached out and picked up the bone to take a closer look, feeling foolish when nothing happened. It was the fifth rib on the right side. Putting it down on the table, she opened the box and grabbed the large plastic zipper bag that contained the rest of the ribs. After another ten minutes of carefully disentangling the ribs from the bag and picking off the larger globs of clay, she had the 3rd, 4th, 5th, 6th, 7th and 8th ribs from the right side out on the table. Although they were still not entirely clean, she could see that the trauma to this woman's chest had started with the fourth rib and extended down, along the curvature or angle, to rib number seven. "What happened to you?" Maude asked out loud.

After cleaning all of the ribs, Maude laid them out in anatomical position as if the deceased were lying on his or her back on black felt and took a series of pictures: first the rib cage as a whole, then all aspects of each individual bone, and finally close-ups of the healed fractures she had observed. When there were enough images to fully examine the ribs back at the shop, she cleaned up her work station and left for the day.

Back at the shop, she wasted no time printing off the images and began laying them out on the large work table. Looking again at the healed fractures of ribs four through seven, she again said out loud, "What happened to you?" Her thoughts were disrupted by the familiar ringing of the bell that hung at the very top of her front door. "Ugh! I'm never going to get these sorted today. Just a minute," she called out as she hastily gathered up the photos and placed the pile face down on the table. Coming through the curtain covered doorway that separated the retail area from the workshop, she was surprised to find nobody there. "Hello," she called, feeling foolish for doing so when it was obvious there wasn't anybody there. Looking toward the door to see if anyone was walking away from the shop, she saw not a soul on the street. It was odd to have heard the bell when someone had entered the shop, but not to have heard the same noise when that person left. Turning to go back into the work area, she noticed one of the photos she had just scrutinized was sitting on the counter by the cash register. Looking closer, Maude realized it was the picture she had taken showing the lateral aspect of the entire rib cage, focused on the healed fractures. *How did this get here?* She wondered. "Hmph, I guess I had it in my hand when I walked out here," she said aloud. "Yikes, I don't remember doing that! That's enough skeletal biology for today."

It would not be until the end of the week when Maude was able to return to the lab. This particular skeleton was proving to be more of a chore to clean than the others had been. Thick clumps of clay stuck to the bones of the forearm, obscuring the long thin shape of each radius and ulna. It was not until the bones were thoroughly clean that Maude noticed another healed fracture on the right radius. Called a Colle's Fracture, this trauma usually occurred when an individual held out their forearm to break their fall. "Oh, you poor woman, what must your life have been like?" Maude asked, removing her gloves and reaching for her digital camera.

Placing the bones of the forearm on the black felt, she snapped the usual pictures. Before putting the bones back on their tray, Maude ran her finger over the healed fracture on the distal radius. She felt the immediate sensation of someone shoving her hard from behind and water splashing on to the floor. Falling forward, she reached out her arm to break her fall. When her hand made contact with the stone floor of the washroom, she felt a searing pain traveling up her arm. As she curled up on the floor, clutching her wrist, she had the vague sense of a man yelling and shaking soaking wet clothing at her. Maude closed her eyes and shook her head. When she opened them, she was on the floor of the laboratory. Gingerly flexing her right wrist, she was surprised to have full mobility and absolutely no pain.

What the hell had just happened...again? she thought as she got up and stared at the bone she had just touched. Had it been a vision? Her imagination? She felt like she had just experienced the events that had resulted in the fractures observed on the bone. How was that possible?

A Whisper of Bones

Maude looked at the clock, it was 2:30. She briefly considered the notion that she had nodded off and had dreamed the whole thing. Not likely, since she had been working steadily since after lunch. "It is definitely time for a break," she said out loud, prepared for the time being to attribute the experience to fatigue and an overactive imagination.

Attempting to push all thoughts of the experience from her mind, she cleaned up her work station and headed back to the shop to meet the late afternoon shoppers, but burial number 116 remained in Maude's thoughts for the rest of the day. She recalled examining the inmate records for the Erie County Almshouse when she had been working on her dissertation. Each record contained the name, age, birthplace, occupation and reason for seeking relief at the almshouse. Additionally, there were notes specific to some individuals describing other aspects of their personality or circumstances. Sometimes they were short like "with child" or "surly". Other times they were lengthy explanations jammed in the margins of a person's persistent abuse of alcohol or the need to stay long-term at the almshouse due to a chronic illness. Maude thought she had a sense of what life might have been like for those unfortunates who were desperate enough to seek relief there, but after having just briefly examined the few bones of burial number116, she realized that the impact of poverty had on these people was far greater than she had previously understood.

Seeing the healed wounds that had disrupted this woman's life and caused so much pain, likely emotionally as well as physically, connected Maude to this person and the almshouse in a way the records had not. This was dangerous ground for a scientist and Maude knew it. There was a fine line between understanding that each skeletal specimen had been a living, breathing person and having sympathetic feelings for a research subject that could inhibit the ability to form objective conclusions. It is an issue with which many scientists struggled. Scientific inquiry demanded objectivity, but were results also biased if they were not filtered through the subjective lens of humanity?

"What are you trying to tell me?" She asked out loud to the photograph of the healed Colle's fracture. "I hope you will keep talking, because I am most willing to listen."

Maude locked the back door to her shop a bit later Friday evening because she ran into Christine as they both were leaving. The two women had not seen each other in weeks and took a few minutes to catch up. Christine had met the deadline for her NEH grant on schedule and had some time to breathe again. They agreed to meet for coffee on Monday morning and said their goodbyes.

Chapter Five

OMG!!! Get over here ASAP! read the text on Maude's cell phone on Monday morning. She had known it was from Christine before she even read it from the specific ring tone for her top ten contacts (Christine was number eight). Every time her phone played the first few bars of the theme from The Mary Tyler Moore show, she knew it was Christine (something about her sense of fashion screamed Rhoda Morgenstern). She texted *'back in 5, have to check on the cat'* and then climbed the fire escape to the apartment above her shop. Ten minutes later she was standing at the counter of the shop next door while Christine lugged a box of old leather bound books from the back. "I was just looking at this box of old books that came in over the weekend when I stumbled across this," she said taking a small leather journal from the top of the box and waiving it invitingly toward Maude.

"What's this?" Maude asked taking the book from her.

"Open it and find out," Christine replied with a sly smile.

"Holy crap! Where did this come from?" Maude exclaimed after carefully opening the book and examining the first few pages. "This is the journal of the very first Keeper of the Buffalo Orphan Asylum! How on earth did it end up here?" As a scholar of the Erie County Poorhouse, Maude had observed the Keeper, Ciara Sloan Nolan, mentioned in various historic records associated with the institution's history.

"I know. Can you believe it? I have not even been through the rest of the box. I texted you the moment I realized what it was. Who knows what else might be in this box? It came in with the rest of the stuff from that clean out on Delavan Ave. The new owners sold us the entire contents of the attic. The clean-out must have been over the weekend. There are more boxes of stuff in the back. I knew the first orphanage in Buffalo was part of the county almshouse so I thought this would interest you."

"Can I buy it from you?" Maude asked, still carefully turning pages.

"Let me talk to the boys," (Christine casually referred to David and Tom, her bosses, as "the boys") "and see if they will just let you have it. They'll likely end up donating most of these books to the Buffalo History Museum, anyway."

"Will they mind if I take it next door and have a look? You know I'll be careful with it."

"I don't think they'll mind. David should be in today so I'll tell him you have the book and he can work out the details with you himself."

"This is unbelievable. I can't wait to get into it!"

Maude left the shop through the front door, holding the journal as if it were a sacred religious text. She entered her own shop through the unlocked front door and placed the book on the front counter. There were bills to pay, but those could certainly wait. There was a temptation to lock the front door to insure no interruptions, but she had made a promise to Don that this project would not interfere with the running of their business. Deciding against taking notes, she would read the journal all the way through and then go back and focus on specific details. A veteran of historical archives, Maude had a pair of white cotton gloves handy to prevent the oils on her fingers from damaging the delicate pages.

Before reading, she carefully flipped to the last entry on the last page. It was dated November 4, 1841. The first entry was dated September 3, 1840. It was just over one year of entries. That was not much in the grand scheme of things, but it was still an extraordinary source. Up until now they had only inmate records and other municipal documents like the Keeper's Annual Reports to shed light on the lives of those who sought refuge at the poorhouse. This was the journal of someone who had actually lived there. Ciara Sloane Nolan had been an inmate at the Erie County Almshouse and served as a nursemaid for the children who lived there. She married Dr. Michael Nolan, one of the physicians who served the poor in addition to maintaining a private practice. The newly married Mrs. Nolan became the Keeper of the Buffalo Orphan Asylum when it opened in 1836. Maude had read her name in both the inmate records from the almshouse and then again in The Report of the Supervisors and Managers when the Orphan Asylum had been built. It was quite an accomplishment and a bit of a shocker for a former inmate to marry a doctor and then be appointed to such a position. Maude could not believe she was about to read about a year in the life of Ciara Sloane Nolan!

September 3, 1840

The summer sun continues to shine and although the days grow shorter, the children are still able to enjoy considerable time outside. The five Houlihan boys have been taken in by cousins in Syracuse, and their two sisters by an aunt in Albany, leaving the number of children on the ward to 45. Even with five less, the boy's dormitory is full to burstin'. The wee ones are sharin' cots and two of the oldest boys are on the floor. 'Tis not much better in the infants ward. Four births last week alone and two of poor souls who bore them dead from child bed fever! That makes twelve babes under six months of age. Sure enough Mr. Proctor will not be pleased to send another of the women over to help in the nursery.

"I beg yer pardon, Mrs. Nolan," came a small voice accompanied by a gentle knock on the office door.

"Is that you, wee Sean?" The Keeper asked.

"Yes ma'am." The young lad stood in the doorway

of the simply furnished office looking down at the polished oak floor as he spoke.

"Come in lad. What is it yer after?"

"Miss Patricia says Mr. Proctor's sent a man to fetch ye," the little boy replied.

"Mr. Proctor knows fine where my office is if he wishes to see me. You may tell Miss Patricia to remind the gentleman of that."

"Yes ma'am," he replied. As he turned to leave the office he stood on tip toes so he could reach the handle to close the door behind him.

"Of all the cheek," she said to herself. "Expecting me to come runnin' all the way to the Big House every time he sends a man." (Those at the orphan asylum referred to the almshouse, which was located on the same parcel of land, as the Big House.)

Although Ciara and William Standish Proctor were both Keepers of their respective asylums, which in theory made them both subordinates under Alfons Pratt, the Superintendent of the Poor, Proctor was from a respectable family, and treated Ciara like he would his servants. Although now the wife of Dr. Michael Nolan, Ciara and her sisters were once inmates at the Erie

County Almshouse. They had lost their parents and their youngest sister on the voyage from Ireland to America in 1835. With no family who would take them in, they sought refuge at the almshouse, where Ciara (then 17 years old) took on the task of caring for the children who lived there.

"I've a job to do, the same as him. To be sure I've no time to be runnin' all the way over there," she continued complaining to herself.

Ciara and her sisters, who were just children themselves, lived at the almshouse until the Buffalo Orphan Asylum was built the following spring. With the help of Dr. Nolan, who gave generously of his time to help the sick children, and Mrs. Colleen Farrell (wife of the late Cain Farrell, one of the Founding Fathers of Buffalo), the unofficial leader of the Christian Ladies Charitable Society, Ciara transformed the children's ward on the third floor of the almshouse from a place of dismal despair to a place of joy and hope. She created an environment where the children could thrive and aspire to a life outside of the institution. Her efforts so impressed Mrs. Farrell and the other Christian Ladies that they argued passionately and successfully for Ciara to become the Keeper of the new orphanage.

Somewhere in the middle of all that she fell in love with Michael Nolan, whose commitment and compassion for those children was as strong as her own. The couple currently lived on North Street with a large extended family, including Ciara's sisters, Patricia and Martha, and Big Johnny, an orphaned lad who had worked his way into both of their hearts. Also residing at the Nolan farm were former almshouse inmates Alex Hanley, Charlie Edwards, and Karyn Friedlander, who had been Ciara's loyal friends, and Karyn's two children Bruns and Ellie.

Ciara's grumbling was cut short by another knock on her door, this time it was her younger sister, Patricia. "Mr. Proctor will not be happy to hear that," she said, not waiting to be invited in. Now sixteen, Patricia had finished school. She had begged Ciara to let her come and work in the nursery and had become a valued member of the orphanage staff.

"Ach, it would not be the first time and it will not be the last time he is cross with me. The man's got legs strong enough to carry him to the pubs and the whorehouses; he can walk over here if he needs to see me. To be sure I cannot spare a moment to be going over there today. There's twelve babes in the nursery, and at present only you and Mrs. Wilmar to care for them. If I'm to see anyone, it'll be Mr. Pratt to ask about sending a few more women to help out up there."

"Would you not fare better by speaking to Mr. Proctor about the matter?"

"No, I would not. He'll come up with some excuse about not being able to spare any able-bodied woman from their chores at the Big House."

"Well, Mrs. Nolan, it appears that you are more intelligent than I had thought. It is true, we can spare no able-bodied women at this time," said William Proctor as her entered her office.

"Mr. Proctor, whatever are you doing here?" Ciara asked.

"As it happens, I was waiting outside. I thought we might have a bit of a chat as my carriage continued on to the Big House, but my driver informed me otherwise."

Ciara was not the least bit concerned if Proctor had heard any or all of her conversation with Patricia. She would have never been rude to his face, but she would make no apologies to someone who had obviously been eavesdropping outside her office. "What is it that you need?" she asked as Patricia left to return to the nursery.

"I understand you have spoken the farmer, Mulligan, about a recent burial." (In this case the farmer was the person in charge of the burial ground.)

"Yes, I wanted to put a posy on Mrs. Lutz's grave. I was ill when she passed and could not attend her burial. Mr. Mulligan told me that stake number 45 marked her grave, but when I went there, I could not find number 45. The highest marker was 43, so I went to ask him if he had given me the wrong number."

The system of burial, such as it was, consisted of a numbered wooden stake to mark the interments of individuals who had passed within the year. That number corresponded to a death record in a ledger kept in the Keeper's office. Burial records were spotty at best, and during epidemics, when deaths occurred fast and frequently, few, if any, were listed in the record. Not that it mattered, as few inmates were ever claimed by relatives or friends and exhumed for a proper burial elsewhere.

The recently deceased were kept in the death

house, a small area in the back of the barn that served as a morgue, for up to three days during the warm months, longer during the cold months, to give time for friends or relatives to arrange for burial elsewhere. Those who were unclaimed were buried in the almshouse cemetery without ceremony or even a headstone. Most of the dead were unclaimed, as few but the rich could afford a decent burial. At the end of the year the stakes were pulled up and reused the following year, leaving the existing graves all but forgotten.

"Mulligan was mistaken. The woman was taken by relatives," Proctor informed her.

"But she had no kin. Mrs. Lutz and her husband came here from Germany. He died years ago. She was alone," Ciara argued. Elke Lutz was one of the women that Ciara had met when she lived at the almshouse. The woman had been there since she lost her husband to tuberculosis six years ago and had come to the orphanage at different times over the years when it was overcrowded and they were in need of more help. She had been working in the kitchens for about the last year and had tripped on the stairs carrying one of the large pots up from the cellar kitchen to the dining hall for supper. The poor woman was scalded over most of her body and died about a week later.

"Then I am mistaken. She must have been taken by friends, I do not recall the specific details," he said, not even pretending that he cared enough about any of the inmates to even remember their first names. They were paupers, not worthy of respect in life or in death.

"I don't recall her having any friends outside of the almshouse," Ciara insisted.

"Mrs. Nolan, trickery and lies are the tools of the indigents. They often claim there is nobody they can turn to for support when they come here. It is of no matter to me who claimed the woman as long as the almshouse was relieved of the expense of her burial."

* * *

At the end of each day, Dr. Nolan left his clinic on Niagara Street and drove the short distance to the orphanage to pick up his wife and sister-in-law. The habit served the dual purpose of allowing him to check on any ailing or injured children, for there were always a few, one last time before he went home, and it insured that Ciara would leave at a reasonable time. She knew firsthand the hardships many of the children had endured and felt guilty returning to her happy home at the end of each day. There were always one or two children that needed just that little bit more love and comfort that she felt only she could give.

Michael knew that his wife would have them all at the house on North Street if she could. Although the house was already full, the Nolans had no children of their own. Ciara had been severely beaten while at the almshouse and had sustained injuries that she suspected had left her unable to bear children. It did not take long to come to terms with this revelation, as she was doing God's work, and having children of her own would prevent her from giving these desperate, parentless children the attention they needed and deserved .

"What's on yer mind?" Michael asked wondering why his wife was uncharacteristically quiet as they rode home.

"I had a visit from Mr. Proctor today," she replied.

"What was so important to bring him away from his card game?"

"That's just it. He made a point of stopping by the orphanage on his way to the Big House, so he said, to talk to me about Mrs. Lutz."

"What about Mrs. Lutz?"

"I went to place a posy on her grave, but when I got there, I could not find her grave marker. Mr. Mulligan said it was number 45, but there was no number 45. Mr. Proctor came all the way over to the orphanage to tell me Mrs. Lutz had been taken by relatives. When I told him she had no family in America, he told me she had been taken by friends. Michael, I am certain she had no friends outside of the almshouse. She's lived there for six years and did not know many folk before her husband got sick."

"Well, there must have been someone. To be sure Proctor would not have cared who as long as the county did not have to pay for the burial," Michael said.

"That is exactly what he said," she replied.

"Be happy the poor old soul had someone to give her a decent Christian burial," he said, putting an arm around her and kissing the top of her head.

"Aye, I suppose."

"Did ye convince him to send over a few of the women for the nursery?" Michael asked.

"He claims there are no able-bodied women to spare," she reported. "I plan on speaking to Mr. Pratt myself first thing tomorrow. I'll have some help by the end of the day or he'll be dealing with Mrs. Farrell. I don't like the idea of Patricia spending all day in the nursery and all night there as well."

"Ach, she's just like you! You'd be livin' there as well if I didn't drag you away each night."

"Aye, I'm glad of it," she said looking into his eyes.

"Glad of what?" he asked meeting her gaze.

"I'm glad you drag me away each night. I hate to sleep alone" she said, tilting her head slightly so her lips could meet his.

"I'm glad of it as well!" he said. Letting go of the reins and trusting the horse to pull the carriage a few yards without guidance, Michael pulled her closer for a proper kiss.

* * *

September 10, 1840

It took some doing, but we finally got some help in the nursery. Mrs. Farrell has continued to be an ally in this battle for the children's survival. My request for additional help to Mr. Proctor was denied, but her request to Mr. Pratt was not. Lord knows what words were exchanged between those two men, but we've got two older women to give a much needed helping hand.

Too old, Mr. Proctor thought, *to be of use in the almshouse kitchen, the sick ward or the laundry. Mrs. Kaiser is a widow who had recently sought refuge at the almshouse. I have seen more than my share of widows over the years. She seemed relieved to be there, rather than scared, like the rest. She's a kind woman and has a way with the babes, like dear Patricia does. Mrs. Olsen is a bit stern but has thus far kept the nursery spotless. They seem happy to be away from the almshouse and will stay in the nursery at night. Both women have been a God send, and Patricia can finally come home at night, although I think she would prefer to stay at the orphanage. I worry about her. She is so focused on the babes that she forgets she is a beautiful young woman who has so much to offer the world. I want so badly for her to find happiness, as I have.*

Mrs. Twichel, the newest member of the Board of Directresses, came by with 12 skeins of yarn today and has offered to teach the older children to knit their own stockings and hose. It is a grand idea and will most certainly keep idle hands busy during the winter months, with the added benefit of providing the children with warm winter stockings. We still need boots, though. We had no new donations last year and four pairs of the smaller boots are worn through and quite beyond mending. I shall ask Mrs. Farrell if the Board can help in that regard as well.

"Oh, you're still workin'. I won't keep you," Michael said as he opened the door to their shared study.

"Oh, I'm just finishing up," she replied. "I am trying to keep a journal at least once a week, but I confess so far I have not been terribly compliant."

"I thought we might take a walk before supper," Michael told her.

"Aye, 'tis a fine night," she said as she walked out from behind the desk and in to his arms.

"I might just reconsider the idea of a walk now that I have ye here in my arms," he said as his hands took full advantage of having the women he loved in his embrace.

"I am thinkin' the loft in the barn is very private," she replied taking his earlobe gently between her teeth.

"Why Mrs. Nolan, had I known it was privacy you desired, I would have interrupted you earlier," he said, letting his lips on the angle of her jaw say the rest.

The Nolans had chosen to spend their modest income supporting their large extended family and so occupied a small farm house on the edge of the city rather than a home in one of the more fashionable neighborhoods. It was not easy for them to find time alone between both of them working long hours. At home, they were often busy with the four young ones and four other adults always coming and going. In addition to Patricia, there was Karyn to run the house. They also hired two other former almshouse inmates to keep up the property and the livestock. Alex Hanley and Charlie Edwards had looked out for Ciara when they were living at the almshouse and had saved her from that monster, Angus Mclean, who beat and nearly raped her. The two men shared a one room cabin just beyond the barn. They pretended not to notice Ciara and Michael's occasional trips to the loft.

"Do ye mind much?" He asked later, limbs entwined and clothes scattered on bales of hay.

"Mind what?" She asked.

"This," he answered, gesturing with the sweep of his arm to their clothes strewn about the loft.

"I can't say as I ever mind this," she said, kissing the spot just above his navel.

"No, I mean sneakin' off to the barn to make love. I can't think of the last time I had ye in a proper bed."

"That's boring," she replied, gently swirling her

finger around the spot where her lips had just been.

He was amazed after what they had just done that he could be aroused at such a simple gesture and it took all of his self-control to lift her hand off of his abdomen. "I wish it could be different," he continued.

"And just how would things be different? Would we give up our family? Would ye give up your patients? Would I give up the children? Ye know well the answer to all those questions is No."

"Aye, I just love ye so. Ye deserve better than this."

"Have ye ever heard me complainin'?" she asked as her wandering hand began exploring the inner part of his thigh this time.

"Never," he managed to groan, rather than speak, as her hand continued up further. "Karyn will be callin' us for supper soon." As the words came out of his mouth, he wondered why on earth he felt the need to say them.

"I'm not hungry," she replied.

Chapter Six

"Well?"

Maude looked up, startled to see Christine standing in front of the counter in her shop. "Did you come in through the back? I didn't hear the bell ring," she said trying not to look worried that she had forgotten to lock the back door.

"No, I came through the front door, been standing here for a few minutes."

Doing her best not to show relief, Maude put the book down gently on the counter, marking her place with a special bookmark made of acid free paper, meant to mark the place but not damage the page. "What time is it now?" She asked, straining to see the clock that had become obscured by the stack of lamp shades on the top shelf that were listing to the right. "I started reading as soon as I came from your shop."

"It's nearly noon. So, have you learned anything interesting or juicy?"

"It's fascinating; slow reading, though. You would think I would be used to reading nineteenth century handwriting," Maude said.

"You're out of practice. David was in briefly. I told him about the journal and your interest in it. He said you can borrow the book and any others in the box you might find useful. He thinks they should be donated to the History Museum when you are done."

"Agreed. Thanks, Christine. Were there any other books or documents related to the poorhouse or the orphanage? Where did you say they came from again?"

"No, I don't think so. I spent the morning going through them. They are from a house on Delavan Avenue. I think the original owners must have owned a shop or something back in the 1850's because there were lots of ledgers, old catalogs, correspondences to and receipts from various dry goods suppliers in New York City and Boston, but nothing more about the almshouse or the orphan asylum," Christine reported.

"I wonder what a shop owner on Delavan Avenue was doing with Ciara Nolan's journal?" Maude asked, more to herself than to Christine.

"You should go through the boxes yourself. I don't recall the mention of any specific names, but maybe you will see a connection that I didn't. Should I bring them by and put them in the back?" Christine offered.

"No!" Maude said rather abruptly. Seeing Christine's eyes narrow ever so slightly she hastily added, "I don't want to be responsible for anything that valuable. You've seen it back there. I could just see Don putting his power tools, or worse yet, an oil can or turpentine on top of one of the boxes.

"Oh God, you're right. Better to keep them where they are," Christine agreed. "I'll keep them on the shelf by the office in the back. Come by when you can. Our back door is not locked," she said with a raise of her brows.

Oh crap, Maude thought, *I'm busted*. "Thanks I will." Before she could explain away the issue of the locked back door, the bell on the front door rang, announcing the arrival of a potential customer.

October 18, 1840

A family of six has come to the almshouse; a mother with a babe on the way, her husband and four wee ones. They are simply destitute. I have already received a request from Mr. Pratt and an order from Mrs. Farrell to go over and collect the children. How am I to break up a family? It would be one thing if the father was too fond of the drink, or the mother a whore, or a drunk herself, but that is not the case. These folk were brought low by misfortune. Mr. Pratt tells me that Mr. Fontaine, the father of this unfortunate brood, had worked at Gardner's tannery, in the Second Ward. He was taken with the summer complaint and missed a full week of work and was let go by the foreman upon his return. They struggled to make ends meet until they just couldn't do it anymore. I am daily pressured by Mrs. Farrell to remove the children from the almshouse, but have put her off for the time being owing to the lack of space in the young lads ward (as three of the youngest of the children are boys).

"Come in," she called through the closed door.

It seemed to be harder and harder for Ciara to keep her journal. Every time she found a moment to write in it at the orphanage, she was interrupted by someone, and at home it was impossible. Today, the workday interruption was from Mrs. Farrell. Ciara could tell by the knock on her office door, all four knuckles, three times in rapid succession.

"Good morning to you, Ciara."

"And to you, ma'am."

"Ciara, please do not call me ma'am. You are practically family. Will ye never call me Colleen?"

"Good morning, Colleen. What can I do for ye this fine day?"

"I've come with good news. Sean is to be married." Sean Farrell, the only son of Colleen and Cain and heir to the Farrell Seed fortune, had become like a brother to Ciara as their daughters, Maeve and Evelyn, had become like sisters. Ciara knew this was a bitter sweet moment for her mentor, who was pleased to see her son settled and with a good wife, but sad that his father would not be there to see it. Cain had died two years ago from a heart attack, leaving the Farrell Flower and Seed Company to his very capable son. Ever the good son, Sean was reluctant to court any of the available young ladies in Buffalo, taking his responsibility as the head of house very seriously. His sister, Evelyn, had married the son of a prominent physician before her father's death, but Sean still had young Maeve, who was 20 and betrothed to an attorney from Rochester, and his mother to look out for. The right girl for Sean would have to understand and accept this as well as put up with his rigorous and demanding work schedule. Ciara was as thrilled as Mrs. Farrell that the right girl had finally come along.

"That's wonderful news!" Ciara said, rising from her desk to give Colleen a hug.

"Aye, I'm that pleased," Colleen beamed.

"Would I know her?" Ciara asked.

"I don't think so. Her name is Anke Metz. They met in Albany when Sean was making his rounds. You know, since we started selling flowers, he insists on making all of the deliveries himself, even the ones outside of Buffalo. Anke's father is a physician in Albany. He buys all his plants and seeds from us for both his home and his clinic. The two met in the spring and he has found every excuse to go to Albany ever since.

"Metz, a German lass?" Ciara asked.

"Aye, she is," Colleen replied, not at all bothered by the fact that her future daughter-in-law was not

Irish. "I've not had the pleasure of meeting her or her people yet, but if she can turn the head of our Sean, I'm that sure she is a lovely girl," Colleen informed.

"When are they to be married?" Ciara asked.

"In June, her people are coming to Buffalo in four weeks to meet us. We shall have a grand party to celebrate and would be that pleased if you and yours were in attendance." By that Mrs. Farrell had meant all of the residents of the Nolan household: Ciara, Michael, the children, Charlie, Karyn, Alex and Michael's parents, Katherine and Daniel. She had grown to love them all and thought of them as an extended family, like the one she missed so much from the old country. However, she knew only Michael, Ciara, the older girls and Johnny would actually come. The senior Nolans, although well-to-do merchants and always pleased to have Colleen for tea, would find a polite excuse not to attend, finding society just a bit overwhelming. The others, although considered by Michael and Ciara to be family, knew their place and thought it inappropriate to attend any gathering of the upper class.

Still, Ciara sincerely accepted for the entire clan. "We shall be glad to attend such an important event!"

"Good, I shall send word to the house with all of the particulars. Now, we must discuss the Fontaines."

Ciara had expected the topic of the newly arrived family at the almshouse to come up at some point, and only hoped that Mrs. Farrell's joy for her son would buy Ciara some bargaining power. Mrs. Farrell was now the chairwoman of the Board of Directors for Indoor Poor Relief, the board that oversaw the almshouse and orphan asylum. It would not be easy to argue against her wishes.

She thought she might just try to reason with "Colleen", her mentor, woman to woman. "Those children belong with their parents. I've looked into the case. The father fell briefly to the summer complaint (a catch all category that summarized any and all gastrointestinal ailments that occurred during the warm months when food and milk spoiled easily and water was more vulnerable to contamination). He only lost his job because of that. They are good people who have just had a rough time of it."

"Ciara, surely you know by now that it is not their parents I seek to separate the children from. The influences at the almshouses continue to be unacceptable for young, impressionable minds. If those children are to have a chance, they need to be removed from the devious habits of the drunks that flock there, rather than seek work, and the wretched existence of the sick, who have no choice but to spend the rest of their miserable lives there." While Colleen Farrell genuinely cared about those less fortunate than her, she sometimes succumbed to the common misunderstanding that hard work, temperance and piety could cure everything. Having seen firsthand just how fast bad things could happen to good people, Ciara was always the advocate for those individuals and families whose misfortunes were not their own doing. While the women did not always agree, they did respect each other, and from there could always find a middle ground.

"I've spoken to Mrs. Fontaine. She keeps the children to the third floor and she is hopeful that her husband will find work. He goes out looking every day. Can we not give them a bit more time?" Ciara asked.

"One more week, and not one day longer or I shall go and collect them myself."

"Yes, ma'am. I mean Colleen," Ciara replied.

Later, at the end of the day when the Nolan's carriage pulled into the long drive that lead up to their small house, the three passengers observed Karyn and Charlie outside the barn. From their posture, it was obvious that the conversation was strained, ending abruptly at the sight of the carriage, with Karyn returning to the house, and Charlie to the barn.

"Ach, what are those two on about now?" Patricia commented, rather than asked anyone in particular.

"Whatever do you mean?" Ciara asked.

"You'd have to be blind, a fool, or both not to see that they love each other. They should have been long since married. It seems that every few months one is cross with the other about something foolish," Patricia reported, matter-of-factly.

Ciara and Michael looked at each other for some explanation as to what the girl was talking about. They had a kind and loving home and were concerned with the health and happiness of all who lived in it, however, they spent a considerable amount of time working and missed a lot. The two of them were aware that there was a special affection between Charlie Edwards and Karyn Friedlander, but were not exposed to, and thus did not understand, the subtle dynamics of their relationship. Patricia, however, never missed a thing; and they relied on her to inform them when circumstances arose within the family that required their attention. Their confusion lay in the fact that they were unsure if this particular situation required their attention.

"Whatever are ye talkin' about?" Michael finally asked.

"Ugh! Sometimes I wonder about you two. They've been in love since we lived at the Big House. All you have to do is watch how they look at each other, especially when they know the other isn't watchin'."

"So, what's the problem, then?" Ciara asked.

"That's just it, I have no idea and neither does Karyn."

"You have spoken to Karyn about this?" Michael asked in disbelief.

"Not in so many words, no, but she makes the odd comment about him not knowin' what he wants and I've heard her more than once grumbling to herself," Patricia reported.

Ciara and Michael again exchanged looks of confusion. They sat in silence for a moment, processing all that Patricia had told them. Leave it to her, once again, to have her finger on the pulse of the household. Finally, they said at the same time, "I suppose I could talk to him/her."

At the supper table, where they all ate together, there was no evidence of tension between Karyn and Charlie. Whatever was between them, they kept between them. Ciara and Michael both felt relieved to know that there were no outward signs of tension between the two that they had failed to notice.

Later that night when they prepared for bed Ciara sat at her dressing table brushing her hair, knowing that after four or five strokes with the brush, Michael would take it from her and finish the job himself. "I wonder if the problem between Karyn and Charlie is us."

"How so?" Michael asked as he abandoned the brush and gathered her hair from behind, and began gently rubbing the base of her neck.

"Well, if they married, they might want a home of their own with Bruns and Ellie. Maybe one or both of them does not want to leave," she suggested.

"Surely they know by now they'd be welcome to stay," he replied.

"I would hope so, but I could not say for sure. Patricia would know," Ciara said.

"Aye, she appears to know a whole lot more than we do," Michael replied dryly. "Sometimes I think we are just boarders in our own rooming house."

"Now, don't ye fret," Ciara said as she turned to face him. "Whatever is between Karyn and Charlie will work itself out. The children are all well, and scarcely children, come to that. Patricia is practically a grown woman, and Johnny would leave school and work for your father if we let him. Martha, sweet Martha, is happy and well, God bless her."

"Patricia will be needin' a husband soon, Johnny needs to stay in school another two years before he can go work for my father, and wee Martha will be a woman before you know it," he replied. "I just want to do right by them and sometimes I think we have put too much on Karyn by asking her to run things while we are away. Maybe that is why she and Charlie have not married. Maybe she feels she can't leave here yet."

"Well, we said we'd talk to them and we will. We'll let them know that they are both free to leave and welcome to stay, as they wish. That's all we can do," Ciara said.

As she rose from the table he asked her, "And what if they choose to leave?"

"We'll manage," she said with a confidence she did not feel. It was true, they would manage, but Ciara would be heartbroken if they decided to leave.

Chapter Seven

Maude was finishing up with some bones around lunchtime, waiting for Don, who had called to say he would be back in town after noon and was bringing Dinosaur Bar-B-Que for lunch. That had to mean he was also bringing home some good news and a few new treasures. He had gone to Syracuse to meet an elderly couple that was moving to a condo in Florida and looking to sell some of their family heirlooms. Among the many prized possessions wasan1880s rose brass Victorian parlor lamp and a winged mermaid sconce, gas-burning, circa 1880s.The special lunch treat must mean that Don had done better than he had hoped. It had taken a bit of persuading, but Maude managed to talk her husband into meeting her at the lab for lunch

Hurrying to clean up from her work area, Maude had to stop again and stare at the long bones of the feet, the metatarsals, she had been cleaning. There was yet another healed fracture, this time on the fifth metatarsal, the long bone of the foot closest to the pinky toe, one more indication of the pain and suffering this woman must have endured. As she carefully placed the small bones of the foot and ankle on the trays to dry she said, again, "What the hell happened to you?"

Just then she heard a knock on the door. Don, preceded by the savory aroma of molasses and vinegar, entered carrying two large containers of smoked perfection. "How ever did you make a two and a half hour drive with that smell in the car? Weren't you tempted to gnaw on a few ribs along the way?" she asked.

"Yes, I was and I did," he said as he kissed her soundly on the mouth. She tasted the barbeque sauce on his lips. "I only have half a rack left. Yours are on the bottom. Dig in while I grab a box from the truck," he said as he handed her the bag and turned back toward the door, "I don't want to leave my new acquisitions in the parking lot."

Maude finished cleaning up and sat down at a desk on the other side of the room to enjoy the feast of ribs, coleslaw and corn bread from one of the finest barbeque joints in Western New York. As she was happily licking sauce from her fingers, Don brought in a box containing what looked like three lumped up towels. He carefully unpacked the box; patiently unwrapping multiple layers of terrycloth and Maude was reminded of how he had been with the boys when they used to come in from the cold after an afternoon sledding in Delaware Park. Don would stand in the back hall patiently unwinding scarves, unzipping jackets and boots and removing multiple sweaters to reveal the treasure that was each child. Now he was humming while he worked, an indication that he was particularly pleased with himself. Finally, with a reverence that could have been taken for awe, he held up the best of the days' find. "This baby will go a long way towards funding that trip to Scotland you have been talking about." It was the rose brass Victorian parlor lamp with a brass overlay font and shade cover containing glass jewels of all colors.

"Oh, it's beautiful! Casey will love it." Casey Lee was a longtime client whose love of fine antiques was absolutely infectious. Don often saved particularly rare items to give her "first dibs" before he put them out in the shop for sale.

"Yes, she will. She has exquisite taste. She will love the sconce just as much; take a look at this detail! It's made of cast brass, you can see every scale and hair on her!" Don's appreciation for fine craftsmanship was as enthusiastic as Casey's and the two had become good friends. Taking in the trays of drying bones just beyond his wife, Don commented, "I see you have been hard at work today," as he leaned forward to sneak a rib off of her plate. "Using the bones as bookmarks now, are you?" He asked as he nodded in the direction of her desk.

"What are you talking about?" Maude asked.

Don wiped his hands casually on his jeans and then reached over her to point to the metatarsal that lay between the open pages of Ciara Nolan's journal.

"What the…? How on earth did that get there? I put all of the bones on the tray when you went back out to the truck and I have not looked at the journal yet today.

"Well, it did not walk over there on its own," Don said, pleased with himself for his witty remark. Seeing the startled look on her face, he continued more seriously, "Hey, you have been working pretty hard between the business and the South Campus project. Why don't you go home from here and let me take care of things at the shop."

"I know I am tired, but I think I would know if I had used one of the bones of the foot for a bookmark. Besides, I would never do anything so disrespectful to the skeleton or the journal," she argued, still looking at the bone. After a minute, she continued, "I'm fine. Go call Casey. I know you are dying to tell her about the lamps."

When her husband left the lab to make his phone call, Maude again looked at the small bone nesting between the two pages of the open journal. "How the hell did you get over here?" She said as she reached for the bone. Before thinking better of it, Maude ran her finger along the healed fracture on the protuberance at the end of the small bone. Somewhere in her head she heard a scream and she felt more than saw a large hand grabbing at the shoulder of a woman, who was trying desperately to get out the door. With a final lunge, the angry man clutched her shoulder like a vice and jerked her toward him. Staggering, she turned her ankle and stumbled over a single stair. Then he shoved her down the remaining three stairs and slammed the door as she lay on the ground.

"Maude! What the hell?" She was breathless as she came back to herself and noticed Don hovering over her. She had collapsed on the floor. The small bone had spilled out of her hand and lay just beyond her fingertips. It had all seemed so real. She had felt the woman's fear and the pain in her foot as she landed on the ground and collapsed like a rag doll. "What on earth just happened?" he asked as he helped her up.

"I don't know. I just sort of felt dizzy and the next thing I knew I was on the floor with you looking over me." In truth she had some idea of what just happened, but until she was sure she would keep it to herself rather than worry Don. "My blood sugar is probably low. I skipped breakfast this morning and I have yet to finish my lunch."

Taking in the nearly full plate still sitting on the table, Don had just the slightest twinge of guilt for showing off his treasures when she had not yet finished her lunch. Placing his arm firmly around her shoulders to guide her to the door, he said, "You're exhausted and starving, and you need to go home. Let me pack this up and then it's off to bed for you."

"Ooo, that sounds like a plan," she said with a smile she hoped would convince him that all was well.

"Alone. You need your rest."

"Stop looking so worried. I am fine, really I am. I just need to eat."

Maude sat in the passenger seat of Don's truck (for he didn't want her driving in her condition) and considered what had just happened, again. Could it be that she had some connection to burial number116, such that touching a healed trauma with her bare hand allowed her to see and feel how it really happened? While a possible connection to the bones was unsettling, it did not frighten her, as it might have frightened someone who did not believe such things were possible. Maude believed in ghosts. She believed in the idea that people who left their physical bodies could still have some connection to the living world. It was just part of her overall world view. She was not particularly religious or spiritual, but she was open minded and accepting of unorthodox ideas if they made sense in her mind.

While the idea made sense, she was still trying to wrap her head around why these things were happening to her specifically. She had been helping clean the skeletons for a few weeks now and did not have these experiences with any of the other burials. She had touched many of the bones that made up the skeleton of burial number 116, but only the ones with healed traumas seemed to cause her…visions? Is that what she was having? What was this woman trying to tell her? Maude was so deep in thought she did not hear her husband speaking to her until he gently nudged her shoulder.

"Maude, you can hardly keep your eyes open. You're not planning on reading that journal when you get home, are you? He motioned with his head toward the small leather book that was peeking out of her bag on the floor of the truck.

"It's not even 2 o'clock in the afternoon. I am not planning on going to bed for the night. I will finish my lunch and try and take a nap, alone, per your request, but I have too much to do to spend the rest of the day in bed…by myself, that is."

"I hate to break it to you, my dear, but you are not in grad school anymore and there is no reason for you to push yourself so hard. You are only a volunteer on this project and it will do you no good to work yourself into a state of exhaustion," Don replied, ignoring the last part of her remark.

"I appreciate the concern, but I just stumbled a bit and I am fine now, really."

"Maude, you did more than just stumble. You collapsed like a house of cards! What if I hadn't been there?"

His last comment unsettled her more than just a bit. It would not do for her to collapse or worse yet, lose consciousness while she was alone at work. She needed some time to think things through. Maybe she had just imagined a connection with this woman. Maybe she really was just overtired and in need of some food. "Okay, I will take it easy, I promise. I would like to do some reading later this evening, but I won't stay up all night, I swear."

Later, feeling pleasantly full Maude drew the blinds closed and attempted what she knew would be a futile effort. She had never been able to sleep during the day. Her mind just wasn't wired that way. Even back in the old days when she worked on her research into the wee hours and didn't get to bed until two or three in the morning, she would be up as soon as the sun came up.

Darkening the room made no difference because her body knew it was still daytime. When she rolled over to turn on the lamp beside her bed she noticed her bag was laying on the floor, right beside the nightstand. She smiled as she reached in and grabbed the journal. Don knew her so well. All of that talk about getting some rest, but he knew she would be unable to sleep during the afternoon and had brought up her bag so she could read in the few quiet hours before the boys came home from school.

Chapter Eight

October 25, 1840

I am reminded to give thanks to the good Lord this night for hearing my prayers. Mr. Fontaine has found work at Schoellkopf's leather goods shop on Mohawk, and will send for the rest of his family by week's end. I'm thinkin' 'tis not too much to ask should I say a small prayer for their continued good health. Colleen seemed not at all surprised to hear the news and I am left wondering if she did not have a hand in the family's good fortune. Sure enough it wouldn't be the first time.

Even as I write this I hesitate to put the thought on paper for fear that, if I do, things will most certainly change. However, it is such a rare occurrence that it bears recording for posterity. Right now all is well. The children all have their health and are content such as can be expected in this place. The staff is pleasant in their attitudes and diligent in their efforts. There is neither disease nor weather conspiring against our efforts to provide for these children, who have been forgotten by everyone else. My superstitious nature prevents me from continuing to comment on our current prosperity for fear that such comments could lead to its demise…

Ciara put her quill down and pushed the open journal aside. She was, indeed, afraid to write more about how well things were currently going at the orphanage. During the years since the Buffalo Orphan Asylum first opened not a week went by when there wasn't some crisis or another to deal with. Sadly, there was always a steady stream of homeless infants and children in need. The building was occupied to capacity within the first year it was built. If it wasn't sickness or injury that left these children orphans, it was depravity, apathy or drink. There was always the risk that children would bring sickness in with them. During the winter months they had to manage enough warm clothing, coats and boots for the children. It was the constant threat of the summer complaint, a catch all term for stomach ailments, in the warmer months. The lack of competent help was a year round problem. However, none of these issues was pressing at the moment. Ciara had tempted fate by acknowledging it and could not bring herself to add any more details. It was just as well.

A Whisper of Bones

Michael would be by soon to take her and Patricia home.

Rising from her desk, Ciara began the process of gathering her things to leave for the day. Making her way down the hall, she heard Patricia's voice coming from the back door. Ciara wondered who her sister could be talking to. It was too late in the afternoon for any deliveries; milk and other necessities always came in the morning. She pushed open the door to the back hall and stopped short of entering when she saw that her sister was talking to a young man.

"…and so you see, Miss Sloane, we've been able to purchase new primers thanks to a generous donation and I thought you might find a use for these," the young man said as he held out the battered school book. "They're a bit worse for wear, but I could repair the damaged bindings if ye find ye can use them."

"That's kind of ye, Mr.…." The tall young man had caught Patricia off guard with his dark eyes and his warm smile and she could not remember his name, although he had just spoken it minutes before.

"Mr. Thomas, Rolland Thomas," he reminded her.

"That is very kind of you Mr. Thomas. We would

be happy accept your generous offering," she said.

From where Ciara stood, she could see the two young people, though they were unaware she was watching them. She smiled to herself while she listened to the young man begin to stammer as he made arrangements to return next week with the rest of the primers and his assurances that he would see to the repairs himself. Patricia became shy of him during the course of the conversation, Ciara saw it happen. Her sister's head dipped, just a bit, and she was unable to meet his eye, although she nodded and smiled, agreeing to his plan. There was a moment of awkward silence when their business was concluded but neither wanted the conversation to end. Ciara took a few silent steps back and then called out for her sister before moving forward again to enter the hall.

"Oh, beggin' yer pardon. I did not realize there was someone at the door. I've come to fetch ye for home. Michael will be here soon."

Relieved to have something to say, Patricia turned toward Rolland and introduced him to her sister. "Mr. Thomas, may I present Mrs. Nolan, the Keeper of this asylum. Mrs. Nolan, Mr. Thomas is a teacher at the

Goodell Street School. He has come to offer us some primers for the children."

"I am at you service, Mrs. Nolan. I was just telling Miss Sloane that I will need a few days to repair some of the rougher books, but I should be back early next week if it pleases."

"I thank ye Mr. Thomas. It is most kind of you to think of our children."

"Not at all, ma'am, I shall look forward to seeing you next week," he said and Ciara could not help but notice that he was looking at Patricia. "Good day to you ladies."

"Good day to you sir," Patricia replied with a smile that Ciara had never seen before; shy but intrigued and maybe just a wee bit smitten.

During their evening meal, Ciara remarked to know one in particular, "That was a nice lad from the school."

"Who's that?" Michael asked.

"Mr. Thomas, a young teacher from the school came by just as we were getting ready to leave with a lovely donation of primers for the children. He was a nice enough lad. Good manners and handsome, wouldn't you say, Patricia?"

At this Michael raised a brow and looked from his wife to his sister-in-law. When it became evident Patricia had nothing to add, he said "Ah, Mr. Thomas, he is recently arrived from Albany, I think. He is meant to be a replacement for Mrs. Flannigan, who by the way, was delivered of a son just yesterday. Isn't that right Johnny?"

As Johnny had a mouth full of food so it was Martha who answered. "You remember Ciara, we told you about him last week."

"Ah, now that you mention it, his name did seem familiar. How do you like him?" Ciara asked the younger children.

"Oh, we like him just fine," Martha said.

Through another mouthful, Johnny added, "I think he fancies Patricia."

"What!" Patricia, who had remained silent until this last remark, began to turn red. "Ye know better than to tell tales, Johnny," she chastised.

"But it's true!" He claimed. "He asked me about ye last week, the day after ye walked us home from school. He asked your name and if ye had any suitors."

"Johnny! I'll thank ye to stop this right now!" Patricia's face grew a darker shade of red as embarrassment turned quickly to frustration. She hadn't even had time to consider her encounter with Rolland Thomas and now it was the topic of dinner conversation.

"All right, that's enough," Michael said, ending the conversation with a stern look at both of them.

Patricia was uncharacteristically quiet for the duration of the meal. Had Rolland Thomas noticed her and asked about her? Johnny was always teasing, it was his way. Surely he was just telling tales again. Besides, what did she care one way or the other?

The next day Ciara arrived at the orphanage to find Mrs. Kaiser struggling to climb the stairs to the nursery with a basket of freshly laundered clouts. With 14 babes in the infant's ward (two more had been surrendered to the asylum in the past week) who were fed and changed several times throughout the day, laundry was a chore that saw no end. Ciara draped her coat on the banister and hopped up the steps to lend a hand. "Mrs. Kaiser, let me help ye with that."

"No need, Frau Nolan, I can manage," she stated.

"'Tis no bother. As it happens I am on my way up

to the nursery for a wee visit," Ciara said as she took the basket. It was a part of her regular morning routine to visit each of the wards and spend some time with the children. Mrs. Kaiser looked relieved to be free of the burden and leaned heavily on the banister as she continued up the stairs.

"I am grateful to you, ma'am. The cold is not kind to these poor old bones," she said looking down as she gingerly tested her foot on the stair before she placed her full weight on it and lifted the other foot.

"Just ye ask one of the lads to fetch the clean wash," Ciara told her."No need for you to climb up and down these stairs all day. The exercise will do them good."

Mrs. Kaiser's pace quickened as she heard the sound of an infant crying. Although Patricia already had little Michelle cradled in her arms, she could do nothing to comfort the fussing newborn. Without a word, Mrs. Kaiser took the baby from Patricia and held her close so that her tiny head rested right over the widow's heart, one hand stroking her fuzzy hair, and the other carefully supporting her little bottom. After a few endearments murmured in German, the tiny girl was content. "This little one needs to be held close," Mrs. Kaiser told Patricia. "She likes you to sing to her as well." Without another word, she walked over to the rocker, crooning softly, giving baby Michelle her full attention. Ciara smiled as she saw the wee babe relax in the widow's arms and drift off to sleep. Mrs. Kaiser seemed more at ease too. It was as if all of her pain melted away when she held a child in her arms.

Later that day, after their evening meal, the women of the Nolan house were scurrying around the kitchen clearing, washing, sweeping and wiping. Ciara was relieved when the younger girls insisted she and Karyn sit down and they would finish up the cleaning. The kitchen was the heart of the house and it was built with plenty of room for the extended family who spent so much time there. Ciara had always liked the design of her mother-in-law's kitchen, and her kitchen was simply a larger version of theirs. The kitchen proper was at one end of a large room, separated by a long counter from a sitting area near the hearth. Each area had a window looking out to the back toward the barn, brightening the room with natural light. Her mind began to wander as she relaxed and listened to the comforting noises of dishes being stacked and counters being scrubbed while the girls chatted about their day. Thinking of her earlier encounter with Mrs. Kaiser, she said to Patricia "Tomorrow would ye see to it that the older lads are sent on errands down to the kitchen and laundry to save Mrs. Kaiser from runnin' up and down the stairs."

"Aye, I have been meanin' to speak with ye about just that," Patricia answered."She nearly fell the day before last on her way up from the kitchens. I asked did she need help but she was determined to carry the tray up herself."

"Ach, the poor old soul was havin' a time of it climbin' the stairs this mornin', and her with a full basket of clouts," Ciara replied. "She wouldn't take my help either, but I insisted and took the basket right out of her hands."

"I imagine she doesn't want to appear a bother for fear we will send her back to the Big House," Patricia remarked.

"Would that be Old Mrs. Kaiser, from Cherry Street?" Karyn interrupted.

"Mrs. Frederika Kaiser, recently widowed. Do ye know her?" Ciara asked.

"When Karl was alive we lived not far from the Kaisers for a time. If she is widowed now, God has finally granted her some peace. Her husband was as mean as they come. He worked down on the wharf, doing what, I never knew. When he came home he was always angry and drunk. More nights than not you could hear her screaming and him yelling. It does not surprise me that she struggles with her tasks. I would guess he has broken every bone in her body."

"He beat her, you mean?" Patricia asked.

"He was a brutal man. Old Mrs. Kaiser has seen death's doorstep more than once, I should say," Karyn replied.

Ciara found that words could not express her emotions. Mrs. Kaiser was not the first abused woman who had sought relief at the poorhouse, but there was something about her that Ciara had connected with. Maybe it was her way with the children; she loved them so and seemed to understand without being told what each child needed. Perhaps it was the way she struggled through her day without complaint. Now that Ciara thought about it, she had seen the woman wince more than once as she bent to lift one of the babes from their cribs and noticed the relief on her face when she sat in the rocker to feed them. Whatever happened to Mrs. Kaiser in the past, she still felt the pain of it today. For so many women, their time at the poorhouse represented the most desperate time in their lives. Ciara got the feeling that Mrs. Kaiser welcomed this new chapter in her life and felt only relief to be rid of her cruel husband. There were no words to express her anger and grief at that."The poor dear," was all she could manage to say.

"'Tis a blessing that she ended up with us," Patricia noted. "She has a peace about her when she's holdin' one of the babes and rockin' them to sleep."

"She did not have any of her own," Karyn commented. "I think she was unable to carry a child after all the beatings she took." As the words were coming out of her mouth, Karyn realized the impact they would have on Ciara, but was unable to stop them. To have done so would have been to acknowledge what none of them had ever said out loud. Only Ciara and Michael knew the truth of why they had no children of their own, but Karyn had suspected her brutal encounter with Angus McLean was to blame. Before she left the almshouse Ciara had been brutally beaten and nearly raped by one of the other inmates. It was something of which they never spoke.

"Well, if the babes bring her a bit of joy, then leave her to them. The washin' and the other chores can be managed by Mrs. Olsen and Mrs. Wilmar."

Chapter Nine

November 1, 1840

Mr. Thomas came by yesterday to bring the primers. It was cold and he had walked all the way from the school carrying the books in a sack on his back. I thought Patricia would have an apoplexy on the spot when I invited him in to warm himself and have a bit to eat before he set off again. She is fearfully shy of him and sat with her head down and her hands folded in her lap at the table while I put together a plate for the poor lad. When the silence was more than I could bear, I sat down to see what could be done about it. By way of getting a discussion going, I explained to young Mr. Thomas that we had no budget at the orphan asylum for a teacher, but we would be ever so grateful if he could come by some time and explain how best to progress the children through their lessons. He is such a kind lad and agreed straight away.

Marta Richter passed the day before last at the Big House. The poor girl was not yet twenty and had delivered three babes there in the last five years, two were stillborn and this time both she and the babe died in childbed. Many called her a whore, but I saw a kindness about her. Most of the lasses that earn their living on Canal Street have little choice in the matter and so many of them end up here anyway. The ground is not yet frozen, so the burial should be Monday unless someone comes to claim her. I intend to say a prayer at her grave to mark her passing, although I fear that, once again, I will be the only mourner.

Ciara was sitting at the desk in her study at home that morning and found she could write no more about poor Marta. She looked out the window at the bleak landscape that had come with the frost. The leaves had fallen from the trees and the grass had taken on the brownish color typical of late autumn. Unable to think of any more events that were worthy of recording, she closed the small leather bound book. Karyn was out in the yard, struggling toward the clothesline with a basket of wet laundry. She would hang the wash outside even in the dead of winter, claiming she disliked the smell of things dried indoors by the hearth. Ciara suspected that she recalled the foul smells typical of the almshouse in winter. With so many people relegated to the indoors, the stench of unwashed bodies, smoke and chamber pots was ever present. Ciara saw the steam rising from the basket of wet clothes. Karyn's fingers would be frozen by the time she was through outside. Without another thought for her journal, Ciara headed off to help her friend. At the back door the sound of voices stopped her in her tracks. Charlie had come up from the barn and taken the basket from her and the two of them were chatting companionably as they walked out to the clothes line.

"You missed your breakfast," Karyn said as she took the shirt he handed her from the basket.

"The doctor rode his mare hard to get back from Williamsville this morning. It took some time to cool her down."

"I will make you a plate as soon as I am done here," she said. "Now be off, I will be in shortly." Charlie ignored her directive and continued handing her the wet clothes.

Ciara found herself again standing unobserved and spying on members of her family. She knew she should return to her office, but could not help but watch the couple as they worked together. He did not touch her, but there was an intimacy between them, a comfortable familiarity, really, and Ciara felt she was intruding on their privacy. Turning to walk away, she ran right into Michael. She noticed he had shaved and changed his clothes but he still looked exhausted from his late night call to the Abernathy hunting lodge in Williamsville. It was one of the grandsons who had nearly severed his foot while chopping wood in an effort to prove his superior strength to his younger cousin. Michael had ridden out last night and Ciara had not expected to see him back this morning.

"Ah, I've caught you spyin' Mrs. Nolan," he teased.

"I've done no such thing. I was on my way out to help Karyn with the wash but as you can see she already has help," she argued in her defense. "Look at them, they seem happy. Do you think they have settled things between them?"

"I doubt it. A man doesn't help a woman hang the wash in the freezing cold if things are settled between them." That earned him a poke in the ribs. "Ouch! What was that for?"

"For catchin' me spyin'. Now let's leave them to their work. Where were ye off to anyway? We should be leavin' soon," she asked.

"Oh, to have a quick word with Alex." Glancing in the direction of Karyn and Charlie, he continued, "I find myself wondering if he might not be more comfortable movin' up to the house for the winter. He's getting on in years and the winter promises to be a harsh one. Besides, it will give Charlie some time to sort things through," he said with a knowing smile as his gaze was still fixed on the couple outside.

"Michael Nolan, just what are you up to?" Ciara asked.

"Well it seems to me that if I were a man interested in a woman, I might be troubled by the fact that I had little to offer her. We've space enough in the house now that young Alec has gone back to Inis Mor." Some years back, the Nolans had taken in Ciara's cousin Alec, who had lost both of his parents to influenza (and whose mother had turned Ciara and her sisters away after they had lost their own parents on the voyage from Ireland). When Alec turned 16 he went back to Ireland to live with family there and work the land that had been left by Ciara's parents when they came to America."With Alex cleared out of the cabin, Charlie will have a place to call his own, a place big enough for a family."

"Yer a fine man," she said, leaning forward to kiss him. Never one to waste an opportunity, Michael pulled her in and kissed her properly.

A few minutes later Michael found Alex preparing the horse and carriage for the Nolans morning commute to the city. "Looks as though you rode hard this morning," the older man said glancing at the mare, whose head peeked out of her stall at the sound of her master approaching. "I'd say 'tis safe to give her oats now, if you've a mind to," he continued, shifting his glance to the feed bucket that was outside the mare's stall waiting for her to cool down enough to safely eat.

"Aye, she earned them this morning sure enough," Michael replied as he lifted the bucket with one hand and the latch on the stall door with the other.

"Why the rush to get back?" Alex asked.

"I see little enough of my family as it is. Besides I was hoping for a quick word before we're off," he said as he watched his horse tuck into her oats. Alex turned from his task to give Michael his full attention and followed the other man's gaze out to where Charlie and

Karyn were walking back toward the house. The two men watched the couple in silence until they had disappeared into the house.

"How would it be if you moved up to the house for the winter?" Michael asked.

"I won't deny I'd welcome a proper fire at day's end for these old bones," Alex answered. "Sure enough Charlie'd be well pleased to be rid of me and my snorin'!"

"I should think the study will do fine for now," Michael continued. "Give me a day or two to clear it out." Alex nodded and just like that, it was settled, and without any discussion of the real issues at hand. Each man knew what the problem was and what had to be done to solve it. They'd give Charlie a place to call his own and the rest would be up to him, at least as far as they were concerned.

As the carriage pulled up to the back door of the orphan asylum Michael was surprised when Ciara told her sister to go on in without her. She watched Patricia enter the building then turned to her husband. "If ye can drop me off at the Big House I can walk back when I am done," she said.

"I can," he answered. "What business have ye up there?"

"Marta Richter, passed yesterday, and the babe as well, and I just want to make sure the lads fetch Father Mertz when they put her to rest. I can't bear the thought of their poor souls leaving this world without so much as a wee prayer."

"You don't think anyone will come to claim them?" Michael asked as the carriage began to roll slowly in the direction of the almshouse.

"No, I don't. She's no family that I am aware of and to be sure the Godless creature who owns the whorehouse she worked in will not pay for a decent Christian burial. I doubt she even knows the name of the man who fathered her child. No, she had nobody, I'm certain of it."

As the carriage pulled up around the back of the Almshouse, the Nolans noticed Tom Mulligan walking toward the house from the barn. Michael was helping his wife down from the carriage, so neither of them noticed the brief look of alarm flash on the other man's face as he saw them. The expression they saw when they turned to greet him was one of welcome. "Good

Morning, Mrs. Nolan, Dr. Nolan. What brings the two of you here?" Mulligan asked.

"Good morning to you, Tom. I'm just dropping Mrs. Nolan off to have a brief word with Mr. Proctor."

"Mr. Proctor's away just now," Tom informed them.

"Mr. Mulligan, I'd be pleased if you would remind Mr. Proctor to call Father Mertz before Miss Richter is laid to rest. She must have a proper burial. If you'd be so kind as to send one of the lads to fetch us, Dr. Nolan and I would also like to attend the burial," Ciara said, knowing that Father Mertz would, indeed, be called if Mr. Proctor knew she and Michael would be in attendance.

Tom took a moment to consider the name and then replied, "Richter? She was the whore who died in childbed?"

Before he could continue his comment, Michael cut him off with a stern warning. "I'll thank you to be respectful of the dead and of the woman present!"

"I'm that sorry ma'am. There will be no burial here for Miss Richter and her babe. They were taken away just this morning."

"What? She only died two days ago. She had no kin, who claimed her?" Ciara asked.

"Don't know, Mr. Proctor told me to prepare the bodies for transport and that he would deliver them himself. He didn't say to where," Tom said, anticipating the unasked question.

"Is Mr. Proctor expected back today?" Dr. Nolan asked.

"I couldn't say," Tom said. "Ye can leave word wi' Mrs. Rowan if ye like."

"We'll do just that," Ciara started to say but then stopped when Michael placed a hand casually on her arm and moved slightly in front of her. "No need," he said as he steered his wife back toward the carriage. "As long as the woman's got someone who will see to a decent burial for herself and the babe, that's all that matters."

Ciara was a bit put out at being taken away before she had completed her business, but she waited until they were headed back to the orphanage and well out of earshot before she spoke. When she turned to face him, he was miles away, his expression a mixture of shock and disbelief. "At present I am less concerned with our abrupt departure than I am with the look on yer face. Tell me your thoughts," she said.

Michael considered how much to tell her. The thought had only just occurred to him and he had not yet had a chance to think it all the way through. On top of that, what he had to say was not pleasant and would likely upset her. However, she knew he had something on his mind and would insist on hearing what it was and how it related to the business at hand. There was no stopping Ciara when she was determined, and she was more than determined now to find out where Marta Richter had been taken. The carriage rolled on for another minute before he answered her. "I remember back when I was at the medical college. I wondered where the bodies came from, the ones used for dissection. It was a question no one dared to ask, but we all wondered."

With a look of utter horror, Ciara processed what her husband had just said. "Do ye mean to say that ye studied the dead? Ye opened them up and looked inside?" At her husband's nod she made the sign of the cross, for fear that the mere conversation they were having was a sin. She had never thought about his medical education. She had never seen a doctor in her life before she came to America. On Inis Mor, the island she grew up on in Ireland, there were no doctors. The women passed down what they knew about healing fevers, birthing babes, and binding wounds to their daughters and their daughter's daughters. Ciara found the idea of denying a poor soul of his eternal place of rest bad enough, but cutting them up for study was the worst kind of sacrilege.

Michael immediately regretted saying anything. It was too much to ask of any decent Christian to understand. Unless you truly felt the calling to heal, it was difficult to understand and accept many of the less pleasant aspects of learning medicine. Michael had immediately recognized the value of studying the human body and had long since reconciled himself with God. He only hoped that Ciara would think no less of him now that she knew what he had done. He watched cautiously as her expression turned from horror to absolute disgust. He could think of nothing to say and waited for her to speak first.

It seemed like an eternity before she turned and looked at him straight on. Her words could hardly find their way out, so choked up was she at the thought of what she was about to ask. "Do you think that Mr. Proctor is bringing Marta and her wee babe to the medical college?"

"It is possible, and I would not put it past him. This is not the first time you have inquired about the death of an almshouse inmate and found things to be amiss. Remember Mrs. Lutz and now Miss Richter. Both women were paupers with no family and no one to miss them after they passed."

Words failed Ciara. There were too many emotions swirling around in her head like a hurricane: anger and disgust at William Proctor, profound sadness for Mrs. Lutz, Marta Richter, and who knew how many others, confusion and disillusionment that such a thing could happen in the first place. Both of those women had lead difficult lives and now were denied peace even in death. It just was not right.

She was quiet for the rest of the short ride back to the orphan asylum. Michael knew he could not leave her without some words of comfort, but he could think of nothing to say. They sat in the carriage for a few more minutes and finally he pulled her in and kissed the

A Whisper of Bones

top of her head. "I may very well be wrong. I hope to God that I am," he told her. She did not have a reply and her expression was unreadable as she climbed down from the carriage.

Chapter Ten

November 2, 1840

'Tis just after midnight and I am reconciled that sleep will not find me this night. I fear for the immortal souls of Mrs. Lutz and Miss Richter. I can only pray that the wee babe was spared the atrocities experienced by these women. Stolen from their final place of rest and denied a Christian burial, then desecrated for study, 'tis an assault on their very souls....

Ciara sat back in the chair, she could no more write about what Michael had told her about than she could talk about it. She turned her chair around to look out into the night. It seemed like an hour or more had passed when she heard the door of the study open behind her. She did not turn around when Michael spoke, she had found a peaceful place staring out into the darkness and she was reluctant to part with it.

He came up behind her and sat on the edge of the

desk, looking at her reflection in the window. Ciara had been quiet on the way home and again at dinner, although no one else noticed with all of the plans to move Alex up to the house. She had complained of a headache and gone to bed early; for the first time without him. Michael did not know if she was upset with him and the things he had observed learning medicine or with the possibility that the poorhouse keeper might be involved with selling the bodies of dead inmates to the medical school for dissection, or both. He could not take back what he had told her and he could not deny the things he, himself, had done. He could only try to make her understand his reasons, but he did not know how.

Michael was afraid he would not be able to make her understand, and of what that might mean. He had come to bed and slipped in silently beside his wife, knowing she was still awake. He could feel her thinking things through, trying to understand and thought it best to leave her to her own thoughts for the night. After a while, he heard her get up and go downstairs, but he was afraid to say anything or go after her. He lay in bed and cursed himself for a coward, trying to figure out what to say. Finally he realized that he should just ask her what was troubling her mind. He sat up for another quarter hour working up the nerve to go downstairs and say his piece. "I wanted to come down earlier, but I don't know what you need from me, I don't know what to do. Do ye think me a monster?" The last bit slipped out and he was furious with himself for sounding so desperate.

She turned from the window and looked at her husband. Her expression was a mosaic of confusion, sorrow, anger and frustration. She decided to start with confusion. "Why on earth would I think ye a monster? You're the kindest man I know."

Relief flooded through him and he pulled her close and kissed her forehead, then her temple and finally her lips. She could feel him trembling. "What's this about?" she asked.

"When I spoke of my studies at the medical college, I thought I scared you. I didn't know what ye must think of me," he said, uncertain if he should bring up the subject again.

She had been so horrified at the idea that Mrs. Lutz and Marta Richter might have been stolen from

A Whisper of Bones

their graves and sold for dissection, that she had not even stopped to think about the fact that Michael had been one of the people who had participated in the very activities that appalled her. "I hadn't even though t of that," she started to say, but stopped when she saw the wary look on his face.

"I became a doctor because I wanted to heal people. I wanted to help wives keep their husbands and mothers keep their sons. What we observed, in the anatomical theater, it was with the knowledge that we were learning so that we could be better doctors. I always said a silent prayer over the body…"

She held up her hand to silence him. She did not want the images of what he was about to describe in her head. The look on his face broke her heart and it only took a moment for her to understand and accept what he was trying to say. "Michael, ye don't need to explain yourself to me. I don't want to think about what ye did, but I know why ye did it. You're a fine doctor and a fine man, nothing ye could ever do will change that."

He looked deep into her eyes before he kissed her with such admiration and affection, that she could hear something so shocking about him and still love him for the man she knew, he did not deserve such a woman but he was glad to have her.

After a few minutes she asked "Do you think they were all, the ones ye studied, taken the way Mrs. Lutz and Marta were?"

Michael blew out a deep breath before he answered her. "I don't think so, but I don't really know. We assumed the dissection specimens to be convicted criminals sentenced to death, but we were never told where they came from, and we did not ask. Most of us were uncomfortable with what we were doing so we focused on what we could learn to make us better doctors." He did not dare push things by telling her the whole truth. When a body was on the table it became a specimen, not a person. They were students, detached and unemotional. The stench of blood and decomposing flesh made the experience somewhat unpleasant and so they approached the theater as professionals, there was no room for the faint of heart. He did not tell her that there were students, like him, who did not struggle much with the moral aspect of what they were doing. They saw the beauty of the human body and were excited by what it could teach them. It was that very notion that had fueled his fear after he had witnessed her strong emotional reaction to what he had told her the previous morning. The very activities that had horrified his wife had excited and intrigued him. There were times, back then, when he did think himself a monster and said as much to a few of the other students. They had decided that what they did, they did for the greater good. There was no room for other thoughts after that, just the pursuit of knowledge. He was so deep in his thoughts that he did not realize Ciara was speaking until she tapped him gently on the shoulder.

"You were far away. Is there more you are not telling me?" she asked.

"Not that you would want to hear." That was an honest reply in what was becoming a more difficult conversation than he had anticipated, although for very different reasons. He had never lied to his wife and although he had not done it now, he was not at all comfortable continuing this talk.

She accepted his answer and did not want to know any of the details of what was done in the anatomical theater. "I was saying I wonder what it is we should do.

I can't just stand by and let William Proctor sell people, people I knew and cared about, to be cut open and put on display, no matter how noble the cause."

Again there was a long silence. He had no real answers. Ciara's silence the previous evening had also given him time to think this issue through. Even if they were certain that Proctor was selling the bodies of unclaimed paupers for dissection it would be difficult to do anything about it. William's family had used their influence many times to get him out of trouble. Now would be no different. Michael's former mentor, and William Proctor's uncle, Dr. Reginald Standish, was the professor of anatomy at the Geneva Medical College. Between his influence and the wealth and power of the Proctor family, any involvement by William in selling dead inmates could easily be covered up. Michael knew Ciara did not want to hear that. Instead he shared some of his other thoughts. "Well, we've no proof that is what he is doing. All we have now is two inmates who were supposed to be buried in the potter's field, but were not. If these two women were claimed, I need to find out by whom. Make no mistake, this could be dangerous business we're getting into and I'll no' have ye putting yourself in harm's way over it. I will make a few inquiries and see what I can find out but ye need to stay out of it."

Ciara looked at him the way she always did when he tried to order her to do anything (although in the beginning he would argue that he was not ordering her, but merely asking her to comply with a reasonable request). She had learned to nod in agreement rather than argue and then devise a plan of action of her own. She would find out herself what William Proctor was up to and see to it that he paid dearly for his sins.

Chapter Eleven

On Thursday morning Maude had her keys in hand and was about to enter the shop when the cell phone in her back pocket began to ring. She put the key in the bolt lock and reached around to her pocket with the other hand. She did not check the caller ID because the ring tone (the theme song to the old sitcom, Murphy Brown) told her it was Jean. She was returning Maude's call from the previous night. Still standing outside the door, she pushed the green button and said hello. "I'm just getting in, so give me a minute," she said, placing the phone on the work table and returning to shut and lock the back door.

"I got in too late last night to call you back," Jean said. "I have to admit, I was tempted to anyway. You sounded so excited, what's up?"

Maude went through the door way to the front of the shop to turn on the lights. It was still early and she would not have to unlock the front door for another half hour, and so took a seat behind the counter. "I found something interesting in Ciara Nolan's journal. Do you remember those two burial locations where they found big logs in the coffins instead of human remains? I think I might have an explanation."

Jean listened without interrupting while Maude relayed Ciara's Nolan's suspicions that the Keeper of the almshouse was selling unclaimed dead inmates to the medical college. "It became legal eventually, in 1854, I think. I know that the almshouse hospital mortality registers record removal of some individuals to Niagara University's medical school or UB's medical school by the mid 1890s," she reported.

"What year was this, 1840?" Jean asked. "That would have been too early to be selling cadavers to UB or Niagara University. It was likely Upstate Medical, I think they called it Geneva Medical College back then," she said.

"What's that, about 90 or so miles from here?" Maude asked. "That is a long way to travel with a corpse."

"Over land, maybe, but don't forget that Geneva is

on Seneca Lake, which was connected to the Erie Canal in 1828 by the Cayuga Seneca Canal. It would have been a much shorter journey in good weather that way," Jean told her.

"Well then, perhaps that's one mystery solved," Maude said.

"Perhaps. I doubt we'll know for sure as the man who buried the caskets containing logs is long gone! What other mysteries are you working on?" Jean asked.

Maude's mind flew immediately to burial number 116 and the strange things that were happening when she touched the healed traumas on that poor old woman's bones. Her voice sounded more evasive than she had intended when she answered. "Who, me? I'm not working on anything. I mean there's no mystery here. It's just me and the bones, and the journal, nothing unusual happening." *Oh, God, shut up Maude, she thought, just shut up!*

Jean chuckled because she had no other response for such a bizarre reply. "Okay, then, on that note I'm off to the lab. Let me know if you find out anything more."

Maude pressed the end button on her phone and

cursed herself for carrying on like such a fool. She did not dare tell Jean about her experiences with burial number 116. Jean would think she had finally gone insane. Putting the idea of otherworldly skeletons out of her mind, she looked at her watch and went to unlock the front door.

Later that day Maude sat at the work table in the anthropology lab with the vertebrae of the lower spine drying on a cardboard tray. She had just the sacrum and coccygeal vertebrae (the tail bone) to clean and the vertebral column would be finished. This was a long and tedious job that had taken several days. There are more than 30 segmented bones that protect the spinal cord. Twenty four of these vertebrae, from the neck to the lower back, have a dense body separated from the one above and below by a fibrous shock absorbing disk, a large hole for the passage of the spinal cord, and bony projections (called processes) for the attachments of the muscles and ligaments of the back and neck. When attached together, or articulated, they looked like a segmented insect. The lower five vertebrae of the sacrum, were different in that they were fused together into a triangular shape, with holes along the inner and outer surfaces for the passage of nerves, rather than a canal down the center. At present, the holes were obscured by globs of clay. Maude worked past noon meticulously picking clay out of the holes, or foramina, with a wooden pick and using a soft brush to remove the dirt and clay from the surfaces of the bone. She held the bone at its broad edge and very gently brushed away the dirt from the lower, narrower end. As she cleaned the lower most point, where the last sacral vertebra was fused with the smaller vertebrae of the coccyx, she stopped and put the bone down. The bone was clean enough that she could easily tell that the lower sacral vertebra and coccyx had been badly broken and poorly healed. Instead of being aligned with the bone above, the last sacral vertebra was misshapen and the fused coccygeal vertebrae could not be distinguished as individual bones.

Maude knew better than to touch the bones, but she badly wanted to know how this injury had occurred. She took off her gloves as she considered her options. She could just touch the trauma. Maybe nothing would happen. She looked at her watch. It was just twelve thirty. Don would be at the Lafayette Hotel delivering the lighting fixtures for the lobby. She made a quick decision, stepped outside the lab and shot him a text. *Can you stop by the anthro lab before you head home to pick up the kids?*

She was not surprised when the phone rang. "Hey, what's goin' on? Are you feeling ok?" he asked. Don had been attentive to the point of annoyance since her collapse in the lab a few days earlier. He would drop everything and go to her now if she needed him. It was about time she told him what was going on. Of all the people she knew, Don would not think her completely crazy when she told him about her unusual connection to this particular skeleton. He may not agree, but he would listen, and even offer alternatives to her theory that this woman was trying to tell her something. Most of all, she wanted him here with her when she touched the bone. If nothing happened, he would not think her foolish. However, if something did happen, he would be there. He could watch her and at the very least make sure she did not hurt herself. Beyond that he would know if she said anything during the experience or if she did anything unusual.

"Yes, I'm fine. I wanted to talk to you about what

happened in the lab the other day, and I have something to show you."

She could see the look on his face through the phone, so well did she know this man. Don knew there was something she was reluctant to tell him the other day when she collapsed at the lab, but rather than insist on an explanation, he had chosen to wait until she was ready to tell him. "Okay. I'll be done here by one. Can it wait 'til then?"

"Yeah, sure. I'll leave the door unlocked for you," she told him.

Shortly thereafter, Don was walking from the parking lot behind the Social Science Complex when he saw Christine headed toward him from the other direction. "Fancy meeting you here." Her greeting was accompanied by a suspicious arched brow. The part time antique dealer/history grad student had not been so distracted by her own work that she still didn't wonder what was going on in the back of the antique lamp shop. "Have you decided to go back to school?"

Don knew that once Christine was on the trail of something suspicious, unusual or valuable there was no stopping her. If she knew that Maude had turned their

A Whisper of Bones

work space into a makeshift laboratory for analyzing human skeletal remains she would blab it all over the city. Maude was so much better at deflecting her than he was. He would have to answer this query carefully, so he started with a smile. Although Don was basically clueless about his good looks, he knew that his smile could go a long way toward getting him what he wanted when it came to women. "Hey, Chris, coming back from lunch? Whatcha got there?" he asked nodding toward the Styrofoam container sticking out of her large purse.

The smile had worked and she returned a silly grin. "Half of a roast beef sub, are you hungry? I won't finish it and I'd hate to throw it out."

"I could eat. Mayo or oil?"

"Oil, lettuce, red onions and banana peppers," she answered.

"Sold, thanks. Hey, I gotta run, I'm meeting Dr. Rinkledardt about a restoration he's doing on Franklin Street," he said taking the container she offered and slipping through the door before she had a chance to say anything else. Opening the container as he walked down the long corridor toward the anthropology lab, he said, "Dodged a bullet and got lunch for my efforts. Not bad!"

"Do tell," his wife said as he came through into her work area.

"She wanted to know why I was on campus," he reported, knowing he did not have to identify who *she* was.

Maude rolled her eyes and laughed. "You ran into Christine. What are the odds? If only she was as determined to finish her dissertation as she is to uncover the mysterious goings on at the Antique Lamp Company!"

"Laugh if you want, but you know what will happen if she finds out what's hiding in that armoire of yours," he said, pulling up the other chair.

"I know, I know. I probably should not have asked you to come here, but I never imagined you'd run into her. What did you tell her?"

Don knew Maude was stalling. He looked at his watch and then took a seat. "I told her I was meeting a client. Listen, I'll need to get the boys in an hour, you gonna tell me what's on your mind?"

Maude blew out a deep breath. "Okay, here it goes."

Don never took his eyes off of her while she told him of the unusual experiences she was having with burial number 116. He casually munched on his roast beef sub and then sat quietly for a minute when she was done speaking.

"You're killing me. Say something," she said.

"Well, it is a little weird, but I don't think you are nuts if that's what you're worried about. I would ask why you think you are connected to this woman in such a way but not to any of the others?"

"I don't know. I have been wondering that myself. I feel like weird things have been happening since I have been working on this burial. I mean, how on earth did a metatarsal bone jump from a tray on one side of the room to an open book that I had not yet removed from my bag on the other side of the room? The other day I heard the bell ring at the shop. I went out to find nobody there, but one of the photographs I had taken of her skeleton, the one with the broken ribs, was lying on the front counter by the register. Don, I had no recollection of having carried the picture out there, or of putting it on the counter. Maybe you were right; maybe one of the inmates followed me back to the shop."

Maude's whole body language indicated how insecure she was about having this conversation, even with her husband. She was sitting in the chair, shoulders hunched, arms folded across her chest and her head bent just a bit. She mostly spoke to the floor and only occasionally looked up at her husband.

He rolled his chair closer to her so that their knees were touching and took both of her hands in his. "You could have told me this at home later on, why did you want me to come here now?"

She blew out another deep breath. This was the hard part. She had to admit that, intrigued though she was, she was more than just a bit wary to touch the healed fracture of on the sacrum. "There's another healed fracture, a pretty bad one at the very base of the vertebral column."

"Did you touch it?"

"Not with my bare hands, no. I cleaned it but I don't get any…any visions with gloves on or through the tools. I figured I'd wait for you just in case anything unusual happens."

Don let go of her hands and sat back for a moment to consider what she was saying. "You say that during these visions you feel actual pain in the area where the woman was injured?" Maude nodded. "Do you feel any pain or any other sensation after the vision has passed?"

"No. It scares the crap out of me and I am usually out of breath, like the other day, but I am fine after a few minutes."

"How long do these visions usually last?"

"A few seconds, maybe a minute, I don't know."

"So…you want me to be here when you touch this bone and do what?"

"I want you to be here just in case anything happens and I want you to tell me if I say or do anything, you know, unusual."

Don stood up and pulled Maude up and into his arms. They were just about the same height and fit perfectly together. He kissed her forehead and then held her face in his hands. "Are you sure you want to do this?" She nodded."What if nothing happens? You have considered the possibility that nothing will happen, right?"

"Hell, I am hoping that nothing happens."

He kissed her again, this time on the mouth, for

luck he said. "Okay, go for it. I am here to observe and report, and call 911 if necessary." He jumped aside and narrowly missed a poke in the stomach.

She walked around the other side of the table and reached for the bone.

"Wait! Maybe you should sit in the chair or better yet on the floor in case you fall over again," Don suggested.

"Good idea." Maude took the sacrum, being careful to only touch the top of the bone until she was seated cross legged on the floor. "Here goes." She held the vertebrae in her right hand and dramatically raised the other, index finger extended, and ran it across the rough surface of the fused and mangled bone.

She inhaled sharply and then began to tremble. Her eyes were open, but unfocused. She was mumbling, no whimpering, but Don could not make out what she was saying. She fell on to her knees and bent over, with her arms held protectively over her head. Then she screamed, tried to roll away. With eyes still unfocused, she began to yell, "Stop. Please, please stop!"

Don wasn't sure what he should do. Less than a minute had passed, but the anguish on her face was unbearable. Finally, he could stand no more and dropped to the floor and took her by the shoulders. "Maude, that's enough. Come back Maude, come back to me."

Her eyes opened and she was frightened to find Don so close. "Get away from me!" she screamed as she slapped at him to force a retreat.

Don jumped back and pushed himself even further until he was sitting on the floor about three feet from his wife. "Maude, it's me, Don. I am not going to hurt you. Maude, do you see that it's me?"

The calm in his voice helped to soothe her raw nerves and she came back to herself. Breathing heavily, she responded slowly. "Yes. Yes, I see that it is you. Are you alright? Did I hurt you?"

He maintained his distance, although the urge to go to her was strong. "I'm fine, what about you? What the hell just happened?"

"Gimme a minute," she said as she sat up and leaned against the desk, trying to catch her breath. She took a minute to look around for the bone she had been holding just a few moments before, located it within arm's reach. She picked it up, carefully avoiding the healed trauma, and examined it closely.

She sat for just another minute with the bone in hand, until her breathing became normal, and then she spoke. "There was a man, a very angry man. It's always that man. We were in the same kitchen as before. He didn't like what I served him for supper, only I wasn't me, I was her. I got the sense there was nothing else, that there wasn't money for anything better. He smacked me, I mean her, in the face and then pushed her to the floor. She started to cry and begged him to stop, but that just made him angrier. He started beating her with something, a fire poker, maybe, in the back of the legs." She looked up at Don, waving the bone. "That's how this happened. I could feel the poker strike the back of her legs, then, when she tried to roll away, he kicked her right at the base of my spine. He's kicked her before."

Don noticed the change in her voice. There was less emotion, less fear, more clinical detachment. Maude the scientist was speaking now. This had been an experiment to her. She was nervous about it, but she had been after information, data. He looked at his wife, his expression somewhere between wariness and interest. "You are thinking that each vision you have been witness to is showing you how all of these healed traumas came about?" he asked.

"Yes, I think so. I think she is trying to help me understand what happened to her. So you believe me? Do you think I am right?"

"It would be hard to argue any differently after what I've just seen. Maude, don't do that again. I won't help you do that again. I mean it. You have no idea what you are dealing with here."

Maude was surprised by both the tone of his voice and the expression on his face. Don believed her, of that she had no doubt. He believed her and it scared the hell out of him. "Okay, just calm down. Nothing bad happened. I was a bit shaken, but now I am fine. After, I am always fine."

"You did not experience this from my perspective. You asked me to be here so that I could tell you what was happening to you while you were…focused elsewhere. Maude, you felt her pain. I could see it on your face. You felt her emotional pain as well as her physical pain. You have no idea what the long term effects of this could be if you keep doing it."

"I think you are overreacting. This woman is trying

to tell me her story. I don't know why she chose me, but I have to be receptive to this, whatever it is."

Don considered her words before he replied. "Do you know how this woman died? I mean you don't know what the impact of these visions might be on your long term mental and physical health. What if that brute beat her to death? You have no idea how that will play out in your vision. This is dangerous Maude. You have no idea what you are dealing with. I don't like the idea of you doing this again."

Maude knew better then to promise she would not do it again. The temptation to understand the trauma she was seeing in this poor old woman's bones was too great. So often skeletal biologists could only make educated guesses as to how people in the past lived or died. She had the opportunity to witness events in this woman's life first hand and she could not pass it up. "Look, there is not much more to clean. I have the skull to do and then I am done. In a few days this skeleton will be finished," she said, trying to avoid the real issue.

He was not fooled by her vague response. "Will you consider taking a break from this for a week or, better yet, a few weeks?" Seeing her about to argue, he put his hand up, "I know that they need your help but just hear me out. Maude, like it or not, you are not a graduate student any more. You have a husband, two children and a business that are also in need of your attention. What you are becoming involved in goes way beyond what we discussed a few weeks ago when you began working on this project." She knew by the expression on his face it was useless to argue that thus far her work on the project had not interfered significantly with either their home life or the business, so she just listened. "I am only asking you to step away from this for a little while and consider how this twist in the path will affect the other responsibilities in your life. What if you are injured the next time? You and I are a team and there is no room in our lives for either one of us to be on injured reserve."

He was right and she knew it. She would have argued if he had said that he would never forgive himself if she were hurt. He knew better than to tell her that, although it was true. He knew the only way to get through to her was to remind her of how much he needed her. They were partners, in business and in life. They shared equally and without complaint all of the chores and responsibilities of running their business, raising their children and running their home. "Okay, you are right," she conceded, "I will take a break."

Later that night after they had finished a delicious dinner of roast pork and all of the gravy-covered trimmings (it was Don's night to cook), Maude considered whether it would be cheating on her agreement with Don if she spent the evening reading Ciara Nolan's journal. She had promised to take a break from working on the bones. The journal was something entirely unrelated, so it could hardly be considered breaking her word if she were to read for a few hours. More than once while she finished up the dishes she found her gaze wandering to the canvas bag by the back door. This time she was jolted out of her thoughts by her youngest son's voice. "Mom are you ready now?"

"Ready for what, Billy?"

"My science project is due next week. We have to build a diarrhea."

Maude held back the smirk as she always did when the boys tried to inject potty humor into every aspect of life. "What is the subject of this *diorama*?"

"The habitat of a polar bear. I already found a shoe

box," he said proudly waving a Nike box in her face. "I chose the box from Dad's sneakers 'cause he has bigger feet, so there will be more room."

"Good thinking," she told him as she dried off her hands, cast a last longing look at her canvas bag and headed toward the "Projects" cabinet in the pantry. The lower shelves of this cabinet contained empty egg cartons, paper towel and toilet paper rolls, shoe boxes, magic markers, scissors, glue and a variety of other crafty items that might come in handy for a school project. On the two highest shelves was an assortment of cake and brownie mixes, frostings, sprinkles and birthday candles. Maude felt that this was one of her most impressive maternal accomplishments. In the early years of her boys' education she was forever running to the store at the last minute or baking into the wee hours because one (or both) of the boys would tell her that they needed a dozen cupcakes or an igloo made of sugar cubes for school by the next day. The Projects cabinet had saved her many trips to the store and countless sleepless hours since its establishment when Glen started middle school.

Maude and Billy spent the next two and a half

hours gluing cotton balls onto toilet paper rolls and fashioning aluminum foil into ice floes until they had a respectable shoebox diorama depicting a polar bear in the frozen tundra. When they parted, Billy headed for the television and Maude headed for her bedroom. The door to her bedroom was slightly ajar and she could hear the hockey game on the TV, Buffalo and Toronto. Don wouldn't notice if she ran in naked and screamed that the house was on fire. She pushed the door open and immediately spotted the small leather bound journal lying on her side of the bed. She slid quietly next to her husband and began to carefully open the journal to the page she had left off on.

Without taking his eyes off of the screen, Don said "I couldn't help but notice you eyeballing your bag all through dinner." No reply was needed. She kissed his cheek and settled in to read.

Chapter Twelve

November 18, 1840

Mrs. Ramsdell donated 13 pairs of boots today. Donations of wool for hats and mittens as well as a few second hand coats continue to come in. The children will have plenty to get through the winter. Mr. Curtis brought forty pounds of cheese and Mrs. Davis donated several pounds of dried beef. I am most pleased, however, about a donation of a blackboard from School number 15 over on Goodell Street.

I have invited Rolland Thomas to tea today in the hopes of asking him to donate some of his time to teaching the children. Patricia is doing a very poor job at feigning indifference to both my request and my invitation. She has pressed the good linens three times already and has enlisted Karyn and Martha to help her sweep, scrub or polish every surface of the house. Karyn and Charlie have agreed to take the younger children to Ma and Pa Nolan's for the afternoon....

"What are ye doin' sittin' there writin' in yer book?" Patricia scolded her sister. "Did ye forget we are havin' company for tea? I can't be settin' the table with you sittin' there, and if you've left so much as a smudge of ink on it I'll <u>throttle</u> ye! Yer no' wearin' that are ye?"

Ciara knew better than to say a word with the mood her sister was in. She closed the journal and retreated up to her chamber, although for what reason she did not know. She was already wearing her best dress. Perhaps it would be wise just to stay up there, she thought, until Mr. Thomas arrived. She opened the door to find Michael assessing the appropriateness of his appearance in the reflection of the window. "Your sister does not approve of my attire," he said with a hint of sarcasm.

"Nor mine. We'd be wise to stay up here until Mr. Thomas arrives. I've never seen her in such a state."

"That was my plan. So she fancies him, do you think?" Michael asked as he sat down on the bed.

"I should say so, and he her. Neither of them can seem to complete a sentence in the other's presence. It's all stammerin' and red faces."

"He'll need to ask permission if he intends to court

A Whisper of Bones

her."

"Oh Michael, let's just have tea for now. They hardly know each other. There will be plenty of time for courtin'." Ciara's thoughts were interrupted by the panic stricken shout from down stairs.

"Someone's at the front door! Michael, he's here. Mr. Thomas is here, at the front door!" Patricia shouts could be heard over the pounding of her boots up the stairs. Ciara feared they could also be heard outside the front door. Without bothering to knock, Patricia burst into the chamber with a final exclamation of the obvious. "He is here! Quick, come down. He's here!"

"Calm yourself, lass," Michael ordered.

"But…the front door!" Before Patricia could say it again, Michael held up his hand to signal silence.

"Whatever has gotten into you?" Michael asked. "Now just ye calm down and go answer the door. Your sister and I will be right behind ye."

Patricia ran down the first few stairs before Michael's firm grasp on her shoulder forced her to slow down. When she got to the door she turned and appealed to her sister with a look somewhere between panic and confusion. Ciara made a shooing motion with her hand and mouthed the words 'open the door!' Patricia shook her head 'no!'

As this non-verbal communication continued with the shooing of hands and the shaking of heads, Michael stepped in front of his sister-in-law and opened the door. "Mr. Thomas, so sorry to have kept you waiting. Please do come in.

"Good day to ye, Dr. Nolan, Mrs. Nolan, and to you, Miss Sloane." Rolland stood there smiling at Patricia for a minute before Michael cleared his throat and insisted that the lad come inside. "Oh, right, sir, yes, sir, I mean, thank ye, sir."

"Patricia, won't you take Mr. Thomas' hat and coat. Mr. Thomas, won't ye come into the parlor and warm yourself by the fire. You're chilled to the bone. Michael, see that Mr. Thomas is settled and I'll bring in the tea."

Rolland stumbled through the process of removing his hat and coat and clumsily handed them to Patricia before following Michael into the parlor. The truth was he rode into the biting wind the entire way from Mrs. Cornish's Boarding house on Beak Street and he was glad of a chair by the fire. "Are the children no' about?"

he asked.

"They've gone to my parents for tea. It's just the four of us today," Michael informed him.

Patricia went to the kitchen to join her sister. She paced the floor while Ciara assembled the necessities for tea on a tray. "You'll wear a hole in the floor if ye don't calm yerself," Ciara told her.

"I don't know what yer talkin' about. I am perfectly calm," Patricia retorted as she began to absently rearrange various items on the tray, carefully inspecting each dish before putting it back down.

Taking the spoon from her sister's hand, Ciara said, "Patricia, tell me."

"Tell ye what?"

"Tell me why you are carryin' on so."

Patricia looked as if she was about to explode. Finally she blew out a deep breath and told her sister. "I don't know what to do." With that admission, all of the tension drained from her face.

Ciara held her smile in check. "Ye don't have to do anything different. Just be yourself. He already fancies you." The last comment made Patricia turn the color of a beet. "Patricia, you've grown into a fine young lady.

Men will fancy you. I've seen ye turn a few heads already. There is no harm in becoming acquainted wi' the lad. We're no' trying to marry you off." That comment brought back the look of panic on her sister's face. "Just have tea with the lad. If he wants more, he'll ask Michael and Michael will ask ye before he gives the lad permission to court ye."

"I'd like that," Patricia said quietly.

"Well, there's the tea to get through first. They'll be wonderin' where we've gone off to." Ciara picked up the tray, and with a big smile on her face, lead the way out of the kitchen to the parlor.

"Mr. Thomas, I hope you've thawed a bit. 'Tis bitter out today. We're that grateful you've endured such foul winds to join us," Ciara said as she placed the tea tray on the sideboard.

"'Tis my pleasure, ma'am, and please call me Rolland."

"Well, Rolland, we're happy for such pleasant company on such a dreadful day." Turning to her sister, Ciara said, "Isn't that right, Patricia?"

Caught off guard at being drawn into the conversation, Patricia replied, "'Tis a dreadful day indeed."

Then, as an afterthought she immediately wished she had not expressed out loud, "A person would have to be daft to come out in this weather. I mean…What I meant to say was…" Patricia continued to stumble over her words, desperately trying to express that she was glad that he had come, but utterly failing. Finally Michael cleared his throat in an attempt to rescue her.

"Are you well pleased with your position at the school?" he asked.

"Aye. I am that," Rolland answered. "Your Martha is a bright young lass, if you don't mind me sayin'. She'd be a fine teacher one day."

"Aye, she's a rare lass, is Martha," Michael said, with a hint of pride in his voice. "Truth be told, she'd make a fine doctor," he said with a smile that revealed just how sincere his comment was. While good manners would have prevented Rolland from making any comment regarding how foolish it would be for Martha to become a doctor, he realized that Michael was right, she would make a fine doctor, and why not?

"Do ye have a classroom at the orphan asylum?" he asked Patricia.

Reluctant to participate in the conversation after

her initial debacle, Patricia was relieved to discuss something she was both knowledgeable and passionate about. "Aye, such as it is. We're pleased for the blackboard, and the primers ye gave us. 'Tis no easy task to get the children to settle into a routine in the classroom, though."

"Why is that?" Rolland asked.

"The poor wee souls come to us for so many reasons and none of them good. Many's lost their parents to sickness or to drink. They need arms to crawl into more than they need primers."

Ciara watched her sister become a different person when she spoke of the difficulties teaching the orphaned children. She no longer tripped over her words or blurted out random statements. She was able to collect her thoughts and rationally discuss the children's needs. For the remainder of the afternoon Ciara and Michael participated very little in the conversation as Rolland and Patricia devised a plan for accommodating the emotional needs of the children into their lesson plan, which included time for play and stories as well as time for primers.

Looking out the window at the late afternoon sky,

Rolland saw a carriage coming up the road towards the house with Charlie at the reins. "Ach, I've gone and taken up yer whole afternoon. I best be getting back while I've still got the sun to light my way."

"Nonsense, we've enjoyed havin' you and we are that pleased your willin' to help with the children," Ciara replied. "Patricia, fetch Rolland's coat and I'll just wrap up a few things for him to take along for later."

Ciara returned a few minutes later with a lumpy cloth sack filled with bread and cold meat, which she handed to a grateful and always hungry Rolland, and a plate of the same, which she handed to her sister along with a small pot of tea. "Patricia, walk out with Mr. Thomas and see that Alex gets something to eat. He's been puttering around in that cold barn all afternoon. He must be fair starved and nearly frozen.

As they walked down to the barn to retrieve Rolland's horse, Patricia picked up the pace, eager to be inside the barn and out of view when Charlie pulled up with the children in tow. She was enjoying her visit with Mr. Thomas Rolland, and the last thing she wanted was to be subjected to the taunts and teasing of Johnny and Bruns.

Rolland was unsure how to interpret the brisk walk down to the barn. It was cold, to be sure, and she was right that only a fool would be out in this weather. Did she think him a fool? Was she rushing to complete her task so she could sooner be rid of him? He had enjoyed talking with her and admired her commitment to the orphaned children. He was looking forward to working with her and getting to know her better. He thought she had enjoyed herself too. Was he mistaken?

Alex must have seen them coming from the house, because he had the horse tacked up and ready to go. Although he now lived in the house and would have been welcome for tea, Alex had deliberately stayed away, thinking it inappropriate for him to join the Nolans when they had guests. Now he was cold, and anxious to get to the warmth of his room. "I don't envy ye yer ride home, lad," he said. Taking the plate and tea pot from Patricia he said, "I'm chilled to me bones. If you'll not be needin' anythin' else, I think I'll take this back up to the house."

His expression implied that Alex had no intentions of leaving the two young people in the barn alone and so Rolland took the cue to depart with haste. "Yes, of course, sir, thank ye, sir. Miss Sloane, I thank ye for a most pleasant afternoon." Confused and not wanting to take the time to walk his horse to the mounting block, he hoisted himself into the saddle and took off at a trot as the gelding left the barn.

Disappointed in Rolland's abrupt departure, Patricia turned on Alex. "Could ye not give the man a moment to say a proper goodbye before ye rushed him off?" Before Alex could reply, she turned and stormed off in the direction of the house. She did not even acknowledge the carriage as it pulled up and she continued to the back door.

Karyn waited while Charlie helped the younger children down from the wagon. "Come along, Bruns, there's a good lad, down ye go. That was a fine jump, sir, yer a brave lad to be sure. Now, for my sweet Ellie." Charlie beamed as she fell into his arms and he spun her around before gently placing her on the ground. "There ye go, lass, off with yer brother."

Karyn's heart filled with joy at the sight of her daughter's face when she had jumped into Charlie's arms. It had been such a lovely afternoon with all of them together and she didn't want it to end. It was almost as if they were a family taking the children to Michael's parent's home for tea. Neither she nor Charlie had any family in Buffalo and they both enjoyed the visit to the senior Nolans. Karyn helped Katherine set the table while the men talked of hunting and livestock. The ride home was quiet. The children were stuffed with cakes and scones to exhaustion, while Karyn and Charlie were lost in their own thoughts. To Karyn it was a glimpse of how their life could be.

The magic of the afternoon was not lost on Charlie, however, a glimpse of how their life could be terrified rather than delighted him. With Alex moved up to the house, he began to think there might be a future for him and Karyn. He was still a young man and a hard worker. Why couldn't they build a life together? The more he considered it, the more it frightened him. He had learned the hard way not to plan for the future. It had been his goal to spend a few more years at the livery on Miller Street and then, with luck, he would move on to manage the stables for one of the families on Pearl Street. He would earn enough money to support a family, not on Pearl Street, but they could live comfortable enough in one of the tenements in the First Ward.

Those dreams turned into his worst nightmare when he ended up an inmate at the poorhouse, the result of a terrible accident that left him crippled and without a job. He searched for nearly a year for a job, but with his bad leg, nobody would hire him. It was the kindness of Dr. Nolan that allowed him to leave the poorhouse. What if something happened to Dr. Nolan? Charlie would never be able to find a job with his lame leg. If it were just him, he might be able to pick up odd jobs here and there, enough to keep himself fed, maybe. However, he would be in no position to support a family. Karyn deserved better. She deserved someone who could provide for her and the children.

He was came out of his thoughts and extended a hand to help Karyn down from the carriage. She was smiling at him. She had said something and was repeating herself. "It was a cold ride home, come up to the house when you are finished with the horses and have some tea."

Charlie's mind was still off in that remote place where bad things could happen and his reply came out more abrupt than he had intended. "Ye best get inside. I've work to do." He regretted the hurt look on Karyn's face as he directed the carriage down to the barn.

Ciara and Michael wore identical expressions of confusion, which only grew more intense with Karyn's entrance. In quick succession Patricia and Karyn had come in the house without a word and retreated to their chambers. "Well, the supper promises to be interesting," Ciara commented as she headed toward the back hall to help the children out of their coats and boots. "Aye, that it does," Michael agreed warily, suspecting that matters of the heart were to blame.

Chapter Thirteen

The Nolan household became a difficult place to be for the men of the family. While the children were pleasantly oblivious to the turmoil created by the unresolved matters of the heart, the men were not so lucky. Alex took the brunt of it. Patricia was still holding a grudge over him chasing Rolland away so quickly the other day. Karyn was also not speaking to him. Alex had made the mistake of asking her if she had had a pleasant visit with the senior Nolans, putting him on the receiving end of a tirade about how pigheaded men were in general, followed by days of silence. Ciara had chastised him for upsetting Karyn. The safest place for him, he decided, was the barn.

Michael was in the uncomfortable position of having to listen to his wife's strong opinions about what could be done to improve things between the two couples currently at odds. It was no easy task to listen and be supportive of Ciara's concerns and totally disagree with her at the same time. Always a slippery slope, that was, especially where her sister was concerned. While Ciara was full of ideas about how they might intervene to encourage either relationship along, Michael was of the opinion that they should not become any more involved with either situation and let those couples resolve matters on their own.

Charlie kept mostly to himself and did not come up to the house save for meal times. He was quiet at the table, finished his meal quickly and returned to his cabin. Karyn struggled to be patient while he worked out things in his mind, but this pattern had been going on for years now (ever since they left the poorhouse) and she was growing tired of the turbulent nature of their relationship. She wanted things settled between them one way or the other.

Finally one evening, after the household had settled and everyone had gone to bed, Karyn exited quietly out the back door and headed down to the cabin. It was cold and dark, a bit too windy for a lamp, even if she didn't have concerns about drawing attention to herself. With eyes fixed on the warm glow coming from the window of the cabin, Karyn proceeded slowly, allowing the cold night air to clear her head as she considered what she might say when she got there. There was no need to knock, Charlie had seen her coming. As he often did when something weighed on his mind, he was staring out the window, watching the quiet settle about the farm as he thought things through. The door opened when she was still a few steps from the cabin and she entered without a word.

With her back turned, Karyn took some time removing her coat, stealing a few more seconds to think about what she would say. Finally she turned and said, "You have been quiet these last few days. Tell me what troubles you." She immediately put her hand up to forestall the explanation of denial that was evident from his expression. "I did not come down here on this cold night to hear less than the truth."

Charlie stared at her for a moment, knowing he owed her an explanation for his behavior, but now that she was here, so close he could touch her, he could not remember why he was so troubled. That always seemed to be the way of it. When he was with her he was enveloped in the sense that all was well. It was when they were parted that his mind wandered down the dark path of *what if?*

Karyn stood by the door, waiting patiently for Charlie to speak, but the bitter cold had followed her into the room and she was anxious to sit by the wood stove. Finally, she took him by the hand and led him over to a bench by the stove. Still holding his hand, she said "I am not troubled by your leg. Surely you know that?"

"I do. I know that," he replied. He continued staring, unwilling or unable to take up the conversation.

Karyn waited a few more minutes until sheer frustration made her speak. "Charlie, we have known each other for many years now. We each have a good life here with the Nolans and I would not be troubled if things were to go on as they have, but I must know if I have been mistaken about what lies between us." He was not expecting such directness and the intensity of her questioning stare caused him to stand immediately and turned away, lest it pull the truth out of him before he had a chance to admit it to himself. She stood as well, pulling him toward her, unwilling to let him hide any more. She asked again, "Was I mistaken about us?"

Her touch seemed to melt whatever reserve he was still holding on to. "No," he said, pulling her into an embrace. All of the confusion and fear evaporated as he kissed her, slowly at first, and then with the passion of a man who had been in love for years and was finally able to really feel it. He ran his hands gently up the sides of her face, then through her hair which he had never seen unbound. He kissed her for a long time. As long as they were touching, all he could think about was her, how she felt, how she tasted. She filled his senses such that there was no room for doubt or anxiety about the future. They parted for just a few seconds, long enough to catch their breath, but it was long enough for fear to reestablish. He stepped back and turned his head. "I'm sorry. I shouldn'a 'ave done that," he said as he sat back down and lowered his head to avoid eye contact.

Karyn felt dizzy from his kisses and all of the emotion they had brought to the surface. In that moment all of the confusion, misunderstanding, and denial was replaced with an emotion so intense it left her breathless. She felt euphoria and a tremendous sense of peace all at the same time. It came on so suddenly and seemed to be dissipating just as quickly. It was as if her senses were impaired. She registered that he had pulled away and that he had spoken, but she had not heard what he said. Karyn wondered briefly if this was how drunk people felt as she struggled through the haze to understand what was happening. He was sitting back on the bench with elbows resting on knees, holding his head in his hands. *No*, he had said. She had not been mistaken about what was between them. Then what was this about? She could feel the warm glow of tranquility and joy slowly begin to fade, but she wasn't willing to give it up so easily. Kneeling on the floor in front of him, she gently removed his hands from in front of his face so she could look into his eyes. "Help me to understand what you want."

"I don't deserve what I want," he said, taking his hands from her and folding them across his chest. It was clear that no further explanation was forthcoming.

Over the years they had spoken little of their lives before the almshouse. Each had lost so much and was not interested in opening old wounds. Now, Karyn suspected that some wounds would have to be reopened in order for them to properly heal. She got up, brushed the dust from the floor off her skirt and returned to her seat next to Charlie. "Tell me about your life before the accident."

He was not expecting this question and just stared at the floor with no expression at all for a minute before he answered. "There's nothin' to tell. I was a groom at the livery on Miller Street. Ye already know that," he answered.

"Surely there is more to tell. You are a handsome man. You must have had many admirers. Was there a fraulein in particular who caught your eye?"

The question caused him to look up from his folded arms with surprise. How could Karyn have known? Charlie had not thought about Ellen McFarlan in years and had never told anyone at the poorhouse about her. They had grown up together in the First Ward. He had lived with her family for a short time after he had lost both of his parents in the cholera epidemic of '32. He started at the livery not long after that.

Charlie had always assumed that he would marry Ellen, but her father would not hear of it after the accident that left him permanently lame. She had come to visit him once when he first came to the almshouse, while he was still healing, but did not resist her father's decision to forbid the marriage. He had not seen her in over six years. He took in a deep breath and slowly exhaled.

"Tell me about her," Karyn asked, gathering from his expression that there had been someone important in his life back then.

Needing a bit more time to collect himself, Charlie got up and reached for his pipe above the wood stove. He took a few moments to carefully pack it with tobacco before he lit up. After a few puffs he began, "There was a family the next door over from us, the McFarlans. Their daughter, Ellen, was about my age. Ma thought I should learn to read and sent me to Mrs. McFarlan after church on Sundays. There were no schools back then, so ma had me go to the McFarlans as I got older to learn arithmetic and the like, although I never did get the way of it. Ellen had a younger brother, and he joined us as he got older." Charlie took a few more puffs from his pipe, blowing the smoke out in a long stream before he continued. "The lad died of the cholera some years later, same as my ma and pa. I stayed on at the McFarlans after that until I started as a stable lad at the livery. I was eighteen then, young and strong. I had hoped that after a while, I could work my way up. I hadn't even been there a year when..." His voice trailed off as the memory of that time became clear once more in his head. While he did not say the words, his expression was clear enough. Charlie had lost more than just his job after the accident.

Karyn sat silently for a while and let him remember the life he once had so much hope for. "Your life has turned out differently than you had expected, as has mine," she finally said.

Charlie said nothing. It seemed as if he had not heard her. He was still remembering the shame of having to seek refuge at the poor farm...how after a while none of his old friends from the First Ward or from the livery came to see him. They seemed to have forgotten he even existed. He hadn't seen or spoken to any of them since a few months after the accident. They all thought he would remain at the poor farm, a pauper, not like them. So did he, if the truth be told. Finally, he spoke so softly, she could barely hear him. "Likely we'd both still be there if it weren't for Miss Ciara and the Doc." It was really just a thought, but it seemed to escape his mind through his mouth, as thoughts sometimes do. Somehow saying it seemed to bring Charlie out of his own contemplation and he repeated the thought louder, although Karyn had heard him the first time.

"Perhaps," she replied. It was Karyn's turn to be pensive for a while. She had not considered what Charlie's accident had truly cost him. With his parents gone, he had no family to help (neither did she, having lost her own parents and been turned away by those of her husband). By entering the poorhouse, he had alienated himself from his friends and the woman he had loved. By the time Karyn met him, Charlie had lost all hope and had given up going out every day to look for work. He truly believed he would have spent the rest of his life as a stable man at the county poor farm. He had given up any prospect for a normal life. As she came to this realization, she also became aware that he was speaking to her.

"...don't ye see? What would become of us if something were to happen to the Doc? Nobody else in the city would hire a gimp. Where would we live? How would I keep food on the table for you and the babbys? I'll not ever go back there. Never! Do ye hear me?"

His hand was shaking as he brought his pipe to his mouth to re-light it. While it was a relief in a way to finally say out loud what he'd worried about for years, it did not ease the frustration of knowing there was no solution to this problem. He went on to tell her that should something happen to Dr. Nolan, it was doubtful that any of them would keep their current positions. On his own, he might be able to leave town and seek work as a stable man elsewhere, or take odd jobs just to keep himself fed. However, he was certain, even if he left Buffalo, that no one would hire him at wages enough to support a wife and two children. He could not in good conscience marry her knowing that he was unable to independently support her and the children.

Karyn considered this revelation for a few moments. From her logical German mind, she realized that he had not thought it through to a reasonable conclusion and she told him so. "It is an uncertain world; I will not deny that. Something could happen to any one of us. Life has already taught us that harsh lesson. But we are a family now, all of us, and we survive this uncertain world as a family." She paused for a moment to let that declaration sink in and then continued. "You are a good man and I do not believe you would leave the rest of us here to starve. If something should happen to Dr. Nolan, *Gott vebiete, God forbid*, you owe it to him - we all owe it to him - to stay here and take care of Ciara and the rest of the family. We would all do whatever has to be done to keep our family safe. Do you not see? The minute you left that poor farm and came to live here with all of us, you had more than just yourself to consider."

Charlie just stared at her as the reality of her words washed over him. She was right. He had not realized it, but he would never leave anyone here in need. Married or not, he would not let anything happen to Karyn and the children, or any of the others, for that matter. Somewhere, deep inside, he knew that all along. It had just been buried under all of the fear and uncertainty that he had felt since he first entered the almshouse. He had never thought he would leave there. He still could not believe his good fortune and had been unwilling to tempt fate by making any changes in his miraculous new life. "Can ye ever forgive me for bein' such a fool?" he asked her.

"You are not a fool, *meine shatz*."

Charlie put down the pipe and cleared his throat. He had learned a few words in German and he wanted to make sure he said them right. "Ich liebe dich."

"I love you, too," she said as she came into his open arms.

"Gott sei Dank," *thank God*, he said and then he was kissing her. He could feel her body press closer to his and her hands moves slowly over his shoulders and back. He was uncertain at first, not about his feelings, or hers. He knew things were finally settled between them. He had thought more than once over the years about what it might be like to hold Karyn and kiss her so deeply that she would lose all of her good German common sense. But now that he held her in his arms, he became aware of how limited his own experiences with women had been. He had kissed a lass or two in his time. After all, he had been a young and healthy lad once, and, although his heart had belonged to Ellen from the time he was ten, there were plenty of other lasses who had taken an interest in him and were creative about getting him alone. Things had never progressed beyond kissing, though, even with Ellen (although that had more to do with her Catholic obsession with chastity than his determined efforts). After the accident, he had been with a few women at the almshouse. He was depressed, frustrated and angry at the world and had taken comfort where comfort had been offered.

Charlie realized that he had never really made love to a woman, a woman with whom he shared affection and respect. Karyn had been married. She had known the tender touch of a man who loved her. He wanted to live up to her expectations, but he was not sure he knew how. His thoughts must have somehow betrayed him because he could feel Karyn pull back. "I am not troubled by the fact that we are not married," she said, thinking that might be the reason for his hesitation.

Charlie was ashamed to admit to himself that the fact that they were unmarried had never crossed his mind. He should have asked her if she was ready for this, if this was what she wanted to do. This oversight only added to his insecurities. Karyn smiled as she read the uncertainty in his eyes. "You have been with a woman before, yes?"

The dim light hid the fact that Charlie's face was turning the color of a tomato. "Not with a woman I loved." He realized that remark made him sound like a scoundrel as soon as it came out of his mouth. He spent the next few minutes stumbling over words trying to explain what he meant. As he was looking down the entire time he was babbling, he did not see the amused look on Karyn's face. When he finally looked up, he was speechless, as she was actually laughing at him. "What are ye laughin' at?" he asked, somewhat annoyed that she found his insecurities funny.

"Meine shatz, you think too much," she said, taking his hands and placing the back around her. "Do what you have done before. I am not shy. I will let you know what pleases me if you will do the same."

They spent the better part of the rest of the night learning what pleased the other. At the first glimmering of dawn they were still entwined on Charlie's cot, which was only suitable to accommodate one person comfortably. There was really no way for either of them to get up without squashing the other, save to roll onto the floor, which Karyn pointed out. Charlie's response was to hold her tighter so that she could not execute her planned exit strategy. "I must get back up to the house before the others awake," Karyn only half-heartedly complained. She was weighing her sense of decency against the sheer luxury of being naked in bed with her lover. As he began to kiss her, this time with the confidence and passion of a man who knew exactly where and how she like to be kissed, she realized that if she did not do something, luxury would definitely win out over decency. Charlie's arms had relaxed as he slowly moved them up her back so that he could run his hands through her thick blond hair. Difficult as it was not to give in, she gave him one last lingering kiss and then rolled onto the floor and out of reach.

"There is work to be done and I must go," she said matter-of-factly as she began to gather her clothes from the floor.

Charlie got up, sat on the edge of the cot, and rubbed his bad leg vigorously. It would take him a while, as it always did, before he could stand. "If ye'll wait a few minutes I'd be glad to come with ye and give ye a hand. It takes a wee while in the cold weather for my bad leg to wake up, is all." Not waiting for a reply, he began to gather his clothes and pull them on as he sat.

Karyn was silent as they dressed, realizing that

Charlie's offer to return to the house with her meant that they were really together, finally. He would not want the others to know about them if he still felt any uncertainty, and they would most certainly know once the couple set foot through the door. After all that had transpired between them the previous night, it would be obvious to anyone who bother to look how things were now between them, and they would all look (the adults, anyway). As they made their way to the door, Karyn gave him one last look. *Are you sure?* It said. *Yes,* was his unspoken reply. He took her hand, and together they walked up to the house.

Part Two

Chapter Fourteen

Ciara awoke to Michael peeking out of the chamber window, trying not to be seen by what or who had attracted his attention. "Whatever are ye doin'?" she asked as she rose to join him.

"Stay back or they'll see ye!" he warned.

"Who?" she asked as she crouched behind her husband to see what was so interesting. However, it was still dark and she could see very little.

Michael turned and moved away from the window before he answered. "Late last night I heard the back door open. I looked out the window to see Karyn walking in the direction of the cabin. She's just now coming back up, and she is not alone."

Ciara pushed her husband out of the way and carefully peered out the window just in time to catch a last glimpse of Charlie and Karyn holding hands as they entered the house. "Oh! Do ye think? Finally?"

"Well, I should think so by the look on both of their faces," he said with a smirk.

"Ach, ye can no' see anything of their faces," she countered.

"Just ye take a good look at the both of them when we go downstairs and that'll answer yer question."

"We can't go down there now. They've only just come in!" Ciara said, shocked to realize they might interrupt something they were not supposed to see. "We don't want them to know we, ye know, *know.*"

Amused by both their conversation and his wife's reaction to it, a wide mischievous grin spread across Michael's face. "Just how long are we to stay up here?" he asked as he took her in his arms and surprised her with a very thorough kiss. "And what are we to do while we are waiting?" Ciara found it hard to focus on his words as gentle fingers caressed the back of her neck and he kissed her again. Somewhere at the edge of her awareness she heard the sounds of the household coming alive, beds creaking as their occupants began to stir, feet padding across the floor.

"Wait! The others are waking. We'd better get downstairs," Ciara exclaimed as she pulled away and reached for her dress.

Michael laughed as he watched her pull the dress hastily over her head. "Ye just said we were not to go down there, now yer pullin' on yer clothes on like the house is a fire. Make up yer mind, lass!"

"We can'na let any of the others down there before us. Karyn would die o' the shame of it if the others knew what she and Charlie had been up to," she replied.

"And how would they know?" Michael asked. "It seems to me if there was any shame in it, they wouldn'a 'ave come up to the house together.

"Just get dressed," she ordered as she pulled on her hose.

A little while later, Michael and Ciara came down to a scene in the kitchen similar to many they had seen before. Charlie sat casually at the table, coffee cup in hand while Karyn went about her usual routine in the kitchen. There was a brief exchange of glances; the hint of a smile in Karyn's eyes as she greeted Ciara, a barely perceptible smirk as Charlie acknowledged Michael, and then things went on as they normally did.

Reaching for one of the many baskets that hung

from the ceiling, Michael asked, "Are we needin' eggs?" At Karyn's nod, he headed out the door. Ciara tied an apron around her waist as she walked in the direction of the pantry for some butter. In another few minutes, the others began to trickle in, the children taking their place at the table as they waited for breakfast and the others helping out where they could. Soon the house was filled with the normal sounds of cooking and several conversations going on at the same time.

Later that evening, Michael, Ciara and Patricia set out for the Farrell house to meet Sean's bride-to-be and her family. As the carriage rolled down West Tupper and turned on to Pearl Street, Ciara was reminded of the first time she had visited the Farrell home. Still an inmate of the almshouse, she had been asked by Colleen to attend a charity ball being held to raise money for the not yet established orphan asylum. It was a controversial move on Colleen's part and had been met with reluctance, to say the least, by many of the other women in the Christian Ladies Charitable Society. Colleen had hoped a firsthand account of the plight of the children at the almshouse by the person charged with their care would help convince the men of the need for an orphanage and loosen their purse strings a bit more. Instead, Ciara left the party disgraced, having been referred to as a liar, a thief and a whore by those members of Buffalo Society who could see an inmate of the almshouse as nothing more. She had been to the Farrell's residence many times since then, as the wife of Dr. Nolan, a member in her own right of the Board of Directresses of the Buffalo Orphan Asylum, the successor of the Christian Ladies Charitable Society, and the managing body of the orphan asylum, and the Keeper of said asylum. Today she was visiting as a cherished family friend, and so the carriage pulled through the massive wrought iron gate and up to the main entrance of the large brick Federal style home, rather than going down the alley that lead to the back of the house and the kitchen door as it once had.

The Nolans were among the last to arrive, and were greeted by the eldest Farrell daughter Evelyn and her husband, John Standish, as Colleen was occupied introducing Anke Metz, the only child of Klara and Dr. Markus Metz, to the who's who of Buffalo Society. Ciara stiffened just a bit as John reached for her hand."Mrs. Nolan, how lovely to see you," barely nodding at Michael, he added, "and you, Dr. Nolan." Turning to take Patricia's hand, his lips lingered for longer than was appropriate for a kiss on the hand. "Miss Sloane, you grow lovelier every time I see you." Feeling both shy and uncomfortable, Patricia made a brief courtesy and mumbled thanks as she strategically moved to stand behind Michael and her sister.

Years ago, it had been John Standish who had assumed Ciara to be a prostitute for hire, attending the charity ball for the entertainment of the young men, rather than to plead the case of the orphaned children. Neither Ciara nor Michael could stand the man and were distressed to learn that Evelyn had planned to marry him anyway, claiming that his behavior was typical of young men of means and that he had promised once they were married to be a loyal and faithful husband. Many times since the marriage, while attending the sick at the almshouse, Michael had seen young Standish heading up the private stairway to enjoy the hospitality of his cousin, William, at the card games that often took place in the Keeper's quarters and so he doubted very much that John had kept his promise to Evelyn.

Ciara embraced their friend Evelyn with enthusiasm. Looking down at her expanding waistline, Ciara asked, "It looks as though ye have news to tell."

"Yes, John and I are in joyful expectation of our first child," she beamed up at her husband, who returned her loving gaze with what could best be described as a condescending smile.

"Oh, that's wonderful news!" Ciara responded, genuinely pleased for her friend. "Yer ma must be thrilled." Their congratulations were interrupted as Colleen, with the Metz' in tow, came walking toward them.

"Ah, I see the Nolans have finally arrive," she said briefly scanning the room, and where are Martha and Johnny?"

"'Tis just the three of us this eve," Michael told her. "Johnny's gone with Pa to Albany. Ma's no feeling so well, so Martha stayed behind to help her while Pa's away."

"Maeve will be disappointed to have missed them. I shall call on Kathleen tomorrow and see what I can do to help. Oh, do forgive my manners. May I present Dr. and Mrs. Metz and their lovely daughter, Anke?"

After all of the pleasantries had been exchanged,

the group splintered off. Michael was pleased to discover that Dr. Metz also donated his time treating sick inmates at the Albany County Almshouse. He and Dr. Metz began an enthusiastic discussion of chronic tinea capitus (ringworm of the scalp) among children, while the women fussed over Anke and the wedding plans.

In terms of Buffalo Society, the Farrell's had been one of the few families who cherished and celebrated their rural Irish heritage when so many other wealthy families had chosen to forget about their poor relations back in the old country. This, many thought, was the fault of Colleen Farrell. Although Cain Farrell had died a rich and powerful man, respected by his peers, his wife had always been somewhat of a problem with her refusal to embrace society. She used her husband's connections to secure herself a seat of the Board of Supervisors for Indoor Poor Relief, and now had managed to become chair of the committee. She disregarded social convention, befriending Dr. Nolan, who had married a pauper and thrown away a lucrative medical career with his continued concern for the health of the city's poor. Beyond all that, the Farrell's were Roman Catholic, which hardly mattered in the early days of Buffalo Society when the Irish were few in numbers and stuck together regardless of religion, but was beginning to matter more and more these days as the wealthy class had expanded rapidly and was predominantly Protestant.

With Cain gone, many of Buffalo's finest families had little to do with her. The Fitzgerald's, the Standish's and the Proctors were among those who avoided her whenever possible, although Rosemary Fitzgerald had served on the Board of Directresses and had helped raise the funds that built the orphanage. They had all come tonight, though, to eat her food and drink her fine wine, and, most importantly, pay their respects to Sean who was, Roman Catholic or not, showing signs that he would take his father's place among the builders of Buffalo. He had chosen his bride wisely, they thought. Anke Metz was the daughter of a prominent Albany physician, rather than some homespun nursemaid from the almshouse. Many thought that if Colleen had her way, Sean would end up with Patricia Sloane, the pauper girl who had, despite of her education, still ended up a nursemaid at the orphan asylum, like her older sister. Sean clearly had gotten his good sense from his father.

"'Tis shameful how that Mrs. Fitzgerald behaves, speaking poorly of Mrs. Farrell in her own home," Patricia said, as she observed the woman making no attempt to hide obviously unpleasant remarks to her sister, and gesturing discreetly in the direction of their hostess, who was fussing over her only son and seemingly oblivious to the insult.

"Pay no mind to the Fitzgerald's," Michael told her. "Mrs. Farrell is no' so thinned skinned and she knows well who her friends are. The others she tolerates for the sake of the work God has given her. The Fitzgerald's don't care a fig for the poor farm or the orphanage, but they'll be the first to donate their cast-offs and a few bolts of calico for all it will look like they do. Appearances are important to the likes o' them, and Colleen knows it well. She'll no' mind a bit of false gossip if it means the children will be well fed and clothed through the winter."

"I'll never understand how some people can be so cruel," Patricia continued.

"Perhaps instead of spyin' on Mrs. Fitzgerald, ye should pay a bit of attention to the nice lad over there in the corner," Ciara suggested. "That's young Michael Malone, is it no?"

"Aye, I believe it is," her husband agreed, "and just ye stay away from young Malone. I don't like the look about him."

"Oh, Michael, he's just a lad, younger than our Patricia if I'm not mistaken," Ciara said.

"He's fifteen, old enough to think the thoughts that men do when they see a pretty lass," Michael warned.

"Just the two of ye stop this instant!" Patricia hissed, terrified that the other guests could hear this mortifying conversation. "I've no interest in Michael Malone, nor any other lad here!" She insisted as she stormed off to look for her friend, Maeve.

"What was that all about?" Michael asked.

"She's still pinin' for Rolland Thomas, I think."

"God save me from the lovesick women in my house," Michael said, looking up toward the heavens.

Chapter Fifteen

Upon their arrival at the orphanage, Ciara and Patricia were immediately greeted by Mrs. Olsen. "Mrs. Nolan, is the doctor still about?" she asked. Michael often accompanied his wife and sister-in-law into the asylum before continuing on to his clinic to check on whomever was ill, injured or otherwise in need of his care.

"Aye, he's just having a word with Miss Annie in the kitchen. He'll be along directly. What's amiss?" Ciara asked.

"Three small lads are just arrived from the First Ward, each with the putrid sore throat I think, and their mother, too," Mrs. Olsen reported.

"What of their father?" Patricia asked.

"I don't know ma'am. It was neighbor who brought them. She came here rather than the almshouse hospital to be sure Dr. Nolan would see them, said they would be orphans soon enough. I daresay she is right. The mother could hardly stand. It took two of us to get her in and settled."

"Where are they now, Mrs. Olsen?" Ciara asked.

"The sick ward, ma'am. They are the only ones in there and I've asked Mrs. Kaiser to watch over them," Mrs. Olsen said as she made a sign of the cross, silently praying there would be no others.

Ciara waited in her office while Michael completed his examination of Margaret O'Shea and her three young boys. All had high fevers and red, raw sore throats. She could tell by the look on his face when he exited the sick ward that Mrs. Olsen had been right in both her diagnosis and in Mrs. O'Shea's prognosis.

"Has she long, then?" Ciara asked.

"A day, maybe," he replied.

Ciara said a silent prayer for the woman and for the boys who would grow up without her. "The lads?"

"They're sick enough to be sure, but they're no' scrawny lads. If they can get through the next few days, I think they'll pull through. Mrs. Kaiser will see that they take their tea and broth and bathe their brows. No need for you to see to them." He knew his last remark would fall on deaf ears. There were three young boys in the sick ward about to lose their mother. He knew Ciara could not ignore that, even if he had expressly forbid it. He had learned early on it was no use to forbid anything, especially when it came to the welfare orphans. Nothing would stand in Ciara's way if a child was in need.

* * *

Patricia heard the familiar clomp of Mr. Thomas (that is what she called him both in front of and away from the children) climbing the stairs as she was handing out the primers to the older students. She had grown comfortable enough working with him when the children were present. However, in those rare instances when they were alone, there was always an awkward silence between them. She still had no idea how such a lovely tea a few weeks ago had ended with such a hasty goodbye. He had lost interest, she assumed. No matter, she tried to convince herself; they got on well enough in the classroom and worked well together. For the sake of the children, Patricia decided that would have to be enough. It was more than generous of Mr. Thomas to give of his free time to teach the children and they loved him. She would not risk making him feel uncomfortable with any overtures that might indicate an interest beyond the children and their lessons.

As she continued around the small room, she noticed Billy Lewis and his younger brother Joey staring glassy-eyed out the window. The Lewis boys, aged six and seven, had entered the orphanage the previous week after having lost their mother and baby sister in childbed. Their father, a canal worker, was gone for weeks at a time, and unable to care for them. Upon closer examination, both boys were flushed and burning up with fever. "There will be no lessons for yon lads today," she said to Mr. Thomas as he entered the room. "I'm off to the sick ward to get them settled."

"Aye, you'll be needin' a hand gettin' them down the stairs," Rolland said as he picked up Joey, who was by now leaning heavily on Patricia, and proceeded toward the door. Turning around to address the rest of the children, he said "Mind the rest of ye turn to page ten and practice your letters." Stunned at how their morning lesson was taking shape, the remaining seven children wordlessly complied.

Patricia and Rolland were met in the sick ward by

Mrs. Kaiser who had seen the other children to their beds and was preparing the room for the new arrivals she knew would be coming."I had a feeling there would be others," she said as she turned down the bed. "The putrid sore throat will claim a few more before day's end I daresay," she continued as Rolland approached with the now quite listless Joey.

Patricia helped Billy into the next bed as she spoke. "Shall I stay and help then, Mrs. Kaiser? Mr. Thomas can handle the lessons for this morning."

"That will not be necessary Miss Patricia," Mrs. Kaiser replied. "I will send one of the kitchen girls to fetch you if need be."

"All right then, I'll come down to check on ye after the lesson." Reluctantly, Patricia left the room with Rolland. About half way up the staircase he turned to her with an understanding smile and said, "Away ye back downstairs. You'll not be able to concentrate for worryin' about the lads."

"Aye, they were fine at breakfast, ate well, the both of them. It seemed to come on them so fast," Patricia said, the worry already evident on her face as well as in her voice. She had seen all too often how a simple cough or a belly ache in one child could turn into a deadly outbreak that would threaten the whole asylum.

"Mrs. Kaiser spoke the truth of it. The putrid sore throat is serious business, so it is," Rolland agreed. Seeing the look of concern growing on Patricia's face, he placed his hand over hers that was resting on the banister. "We've got our Dr. Nolan, though. The Doc will have them right in no time." The smile in his eyes and the warmth of his touch both reassured and confused her. He was right. Michael would see these children through this illness and being reminded of that eased her mind, but the way he looked at her, with concern and compassion…and something else. Without knowing she was doing it, she placed her other hand over his, just to make the moment last a bit longer, but the murmuring in the room above them indicated that the children were no longer content to work quietly. With a quick glance upstairs, Rolland gently lifted her hand. Suddenly embarrassed, Patricia mumbled something about Mrs. Kaiser and hurried down the stairs.

Although the murmurs upstairs were turning into giggles, Rolland watched her go. Reluctant to turn away, he held his place on the stairs even after she was out of his sight. He had thought she was not interested, she seemed so eager to be rid of him that Sunday after tea. Could he have been mistaken? Perhaps it was time to seek some advice on the matter. Mrs. Nolan had always treated him with kindness and would be easier to speak to than the doctor, although, in time, if things worked out, he would have to speak to him as well. Rolland was brought out of his thoughts by a shriek from upstairs, followed by a crash. All thoughts of Patricia were abandoned as he ran up in the direction of the trouble.

Patricia was kept busy over the next few days in the sick ward. Thankfully there were no new patients, and although the five young lads were quite sick, Dr. Nolan was confident in their eventual recovery. Mrs. O'Shea, however, had passed the morning following her arrival. On the way to the kitchen with a tray of empty dishes, Patricia was stopped by the sound of voices in the hall.

"I am sorry sir, but Mrs. Nolan has stepped out on an errand," she heard Mrs. Wilmar explaining to Mr. Proctor. What was he doing at the orphanage? He usually sent a man to fetch Ciara if there was a need to speak to her. Moving quickly back in the direction of the sick ward, Patricia went in search of Michael.

Michael came into the foyer as Proctor grilled poor Mrs. Wilmar about Mrs. Nolan's return. "Mr. Proctor, what business have ye here?" he asked, intentionally skipping over the pleasantries.

"Dr. Nolan, if you must know, I am here to speak with the mistress of this asylum regarding the death of an inmate," he replied.

"You've had a death at the Big House? What's that to do with Mrs. Nolan?" Michael asked.

"No, sir, there's been a death here. One Margaret O'Shea died yesterday, I'm told," (although by whom he did not mention). According to our procedures, which Mrs. Nolan well knows, the death was to be reported, and the body transported to the death house to await claiming for burial," Proctor smugly replied. "The county will be none too pleased to have to pay for her interment, so if you will show me where you have the body stored, I shall have my man take it back and begin the process of contacting the family."

Michael was not surprised that Proctor had news of the woman's death. When it came to the spread of disease, news traveled fast between the orphan asylum and the Big House. He was, however, surprised that the man had come to claim the body himself. The body of Mrs. O'Shea had been carefully wrapped and placed in the back of a small utility shed until such time as she could be removed to the death house. The orphanage was short staffed and had two of the women occupied in the sick ward, so there simply had not been time to send word to the Big House to have someone come to collect the body. Michael said as much to Proctor. "I'll take ye now, have yer man here move the wagon 'round the back to the shed," he continued, anxious to be out of the house before Ciara came back. Anger and frustration over Proctor's suspected theft of unclaimed paupers was still fresh in her mind and Michael could not be certain of her reaction if she were to return and find Proctor here to collect the body of Mrs. O'Shea so soon after her death.

When the body was loaded on to the wagon and the two men were ready to leave, Michael asked, "You'll be lettin' Mrs. Nolan know if she is claimed, then?"

Somewhat irritated, Proctor replied, "Dr. Nolan, I am a busy man and I do not have time to notify the Keeper of the Orphan Asylum every time a dead pauper is claimed for burial."

"Perhaps yer unaware then, Mrs. O'Shea has left behind three lads. Mrs. Nolan will be wantin' to know if there are any family or friends willin' to take them in," the doctor replied. "If I know my wife, she will be looking for the next of kin herself," he continued, searching Proctor's face for some reaction to the news that he would have to search in earnest for the woman's family because Ciara would be following up on his efforts.

Proctor hid his irritation behind a pleasant smile and replied, "You may tell Mrs. Nolan she needn't bother. I will, of course, send word if the woman is claimed."

Later that night as they were about to retire, Michael spent longer than usual brushing his wife's hair. "You spoil me," she said as she leaned into the brush as it caressed her scalp.

"Ach, yer in need of a bit of spoilin'."

They continued on in silence for a few more minutes until she finally said, "Okay, out with it."

"Out with what?"

"Although I am thoroughly enjoyin' your attentions, ye never brush my hair this long unless you've somethin' unpleasant to tell me."

"Oh and yer sure of that are ye? Maybe it's me I'm spoilin' now," he said as he ran his hands through her hair, gently brushing it aside to expose the back of her neck. Her reply was forestalled as lips came around from the back of her neck to meet her own. Encouraged by her response to his kiss, Michael had totally forgotten that he did have something to tell her. It could wait, he decided. It could definitely wait.

After several moments of serious kissing, Ciara pulled away. "I'm no' so easily diverted. Now tell me what you are trying so hard to avoid tellin' me."

Michael took a deep breath and decided to just say what needed saying. "Proctor was by this afternoon and took Mrs. O'Shea." He sat back and waited for her to reply.

"Mr. Proctor? Oh, Michael, the poor woman has been gone less than a day. Why on earth would Himself come and take her away? Do ye think he plans to sell …" so repulsed by that idea, Ciara could not complete her question.

"He made a fuss about the county havin' to pay for the burial if she was to go unclaimed and that he needed to begin the process of finding her family as soon as he returned to the Big House," Michael told her, knowing as he spoke that it was just an excuse Proctor had devised to take the body. Seeing the look of fury on his wife's face, he hastily continued. "Now just ye listen to me for a minute. I've told him that she's left three lads behind and that doubtless you will move heaven and earth to find any family that might take them in. He'd be a fool to try and send her to Geneva knowin' that you'll also be lookin' for her kin."

"Aye, ye can bet I'll do whatever it takes to find her kin, but what if there's nobody? There was no mention of a husband. The woman who brought them in said they'd be orphans soon enough."

"I'll speak to her in the morning," Michael said, "and find out for sure. In the mean time I would ask you not to speak to Proctor directly about this."

"Michael, we cannot let that evil man sell another poor soul to the medical college."

"I know that," he countered, "but 'tis no easy task we've set for ourselves. I will find out tomorrow what I can from the woman who brought them here. Do ye know her?"

"No, but her name and address will be listed in the ledger."

"Right, then, let's see if she's anything to tell us. If there is no kin and nobody willing to pay for a Christian burial, I'll make sure she is laid to rest in the potter's field myself, even if I have to stand over the farmer's shoulder until the last shovel of dirt covers the grave. You can come with me. You've seen many a poor soul to their final place of rest and it will no' seem strange if ye attend the burial. "

"Yer a good man, Michael, and I thank ye," Ciara said, leaning forward to kiss his cheek.

Michael held his wife and assured her that they would put a stop to this nightmare together. "Ciara, I meant what I said before. I do not want you to confront Proctor or to say anything that would make him suspicious. I've asked ye to stay away from the man. Will ye do that for me?"

"Michael, I must continue to do my job, and that means that I must deal with the man as I always have. Not to do so would surely make him wary."

"Aye, your right about that, ye must work with the man as ye have, but please be careful and let me handle this business with Mrs. O'Shea. I need to know that you'll respect my wishes on this matter."

She hesitated for a moment and looked as if she had more yet to say, but in the end simply said, "Aye, I will."

Chapter Sixteen

It was early evening and William Standish Proctor sat in his office very pleased with himself. He had taken the position as Keeper of the Poorhouse to pacify his parents, as the prospect of running the county almshouse certainly did not appeal to him. Uncle Standish had been right, though, the position had its advantages. William had more than a few dollars in his pocket from the elicit sale of goods produced at the almshouse. Bread and coffee were good enough for the likes of those living here. They had no right to expect better, the lazy buggars, although if he were being honest with himself they were far from lazy. The inmates who labored in the fields and tended the livestock worked hard, and the fruits of their labor could be seen in the bushels of cabbages that filled the sheds and the sides of pork that hung in the smokehouse, plenty enough to divert a few bushels for private sale. Funds from the legitimate sale of products, such as milk and butter that were also produced at the poorhouse, should have gone towards medicines for the sick ward, or new mattresses for the dormitories, but they seldom did. Proctor was always hosting card games in the Keepers quarters (in which he did not live, but used nonetheless) and spent the money on liquor and whores.

Proctor was remembering a particularly entertaining evening with twins from Poland (he had tipped generously to make sure they returned again tonight) when he was brought out of his thoughts by a knock on the door.

"Uncle Reg, you're early," William said, still seated, as Dr. Standish entered the office.

"I can see you are hard at work," Dr. Standish gestured at William's legs propped on the empty desk.

"Ah, well, the day is over, is it not? Shall we retire up stairs? The others will be along."

"The new term starts after the Christmas holidays and we are short on cadavers for the anatomical theater." Standish remarked, ignoring his nephew's request.

"Yes, well, that's proven a bit tricky. We seemed to

201

have attracted some unwanted attention."

"Do explain."

"Dr. Nolan's wife has proven to be quite a pest. She's inquired after the last few I've sent you, wanting to place a posy on the grave, or to know what kin had claimed them. She'll follow the farmer out to the field and watched him dig the hole next time, I suspect. We'll have to bury them and then sneak back at night and dig them up. That fool of a farmer is beginning to lose his nerve, says he will need more if he is expected to go creeping about at night robbing graves."

"Don't worry about him. A good piece of meat on his plate and a bottle will keep him agreeable," Dr. Standish advised. "As for Nolan's wife, leave that to me. Perhaps I'll speak to the man."

"Good luck with that, Uncle. The man clearly lost what sense he had when he married a pauper, a fine career ahead of him, thanks to you, and he threw it all away to wipe the noses and arses of bastards and waifs. What's more, the fool clearly has no control of his woman. Thanks to her more than half the goods produced here go to those brats. Not a month goes by that one or the other of them is here demanding more help, more milk, more cheese. It's always something. I'll never understand why they put a woman in charge."

"I did have such high hopes for Nolan," Standish replied. "Still, if I can't get him to control her, perhaps I can get him to distract her."

"And just how do you plan to do that?"

"I'll see to it that Pratt starts putting those brats out to work like he should."

A vicious grin spread across Williams face. "The good doctor and his pauper wife will fight you at every turn."

"I am counting on it, nephew. Now, let's have a drink, shall we."

* * *

The recovery of the Lewis and O'Shea brothers coincided with the first real snow fall. Fat snowflakes had been falling since early morning and into the late afternoon, and the only thing that kept the children focused on their lessons was the promise of playtime outside when they were done. Patricia was still struggling with boots and buttons for the younger ones, when Roland and the older children were ready to go. "Away ye go. We'll be along in just a minute," she told him.

As eager as any of the lads to be out in the snow, Rolland herded the older children out with no argument. By the time Patricia and the small ones followed outside, Rolland and the boys were engaged in a heavy snow ball fight, while Nelly, Sara and Matilde, the three older girls, were well out of their path making a snowman. Patricia led a chain of six little people, aged three to five years old, across the yard toward the girls.

"You're off to a good start," she said surveying the balls of snow rapidly growing in size as they rolled them along, "but it looks as though yer in need of some help. Nelly, why don't you have wee Frania and Mosze help you with the head. There's a good lad, Mosze. Watch how Nelly rolls the snow ball. Erika, you and Tindra help your sister. Matilde, show them how to pack the snow. Now, Sara, you'll have Oskar and Renia to make the base. Now girls, mind the wee ones keep their mittens on. No, Oskar, don't eat the snow. There's a good lad. Renia, love, stay with Sara now. Don't wipe yer nose on yer sleeve. Here's a hanky love."

Patricia watched for a few minutes to be sure the little people would not wander off. When she turned to see what the boys were up to she saw Rolland walking in her direction, while the older boys, now fully recovered from their illness and full of the Devil, continued to pelt each other with snowballs. They had even been able to engage some of the older men who had come from the Big House to help clear the snow in their epic battle. She walked a few yards toward Rolland, but continued to keep an eye on the snowman crew.

"Aye, ye got them sorted, did ye?" he said.

"I'm not sure how long the wee ones will last. 'Tis colder than I expected," Patricia answered. "Still, the fresh air will do them good. They'll be fast asleep shortly after their supper, I expect. And look at ye! Yer covered in snow," she said as she reached to brush off the snow from his shoulders.

"Aye, that Billy Lewis has a strong arm, he does. Got me a twice in the head!"

"'Tis good to see the lads feelin' better." Patricia's comment was cut short by the sight of her sister walking toward them.

"Good day to ye, Mr. Thomas. 'Tis good that yer still here. I wonder, could I impose upon ye to see Patricia home after she has settled the children in for their supper? I've an errand at the Big House before day's end."

Before Rolland had a chance to reply, Patricia asked "What business can't wait until morning?"

"I've had a message from Mr. Pratt. He's made a suggestion to the Board about puttin' some of the children out to work to keep the cost of care down. He says he's had requests from Bowersfeid, the shoemaker on Swan Street, a printer over on Elm Street, and others."

"But they're just wee babes, and surely too young to be put out to work," Patricia argued.

"Aye, I'll speak to Mr. Pratt before he leaves for the day, and get the truth of it. Now, Mr. Rolland, will ye see my sister home?"

"Yes, Mrs. Nolan, it would be my pleasure," he said, trying without success to suppress a grin.

Rolland looked around at the children, still enchanted by the snow and in no hurry to return indoors, and considered how long it would take until the children were properly settled down to their suppers and he could have Patricia all to himself. "We'll be losin' the sunlight in another quarter hour," he commented."Best start rounding them up." It took twenty minutes to convince the boys to give up the snowball fight, and to get the wee ones marching in the direction of the house. It was full dark as they entered through the kitchen. It took another ten minutes (record time, Patricia thought) to strip the children of hats, coats, boots, mufflers and mittens, and yet another ten minutes to see them seated for supper. Patricia wondered if Rolland noticed her hurrying the children through the kitchen and into the dining hall. She had been pleasantly surprised to learn he would be taking her home and she was eager to get going. It would take a while in this weather, but she would enjoy his company on the journey.

It seemed to Rolland that an eternity had passed between when Mrs. Nolan had asked him to take Patricia home and when they walked out the door, though in reality it was less than an hour. By carriage and in this snow, it could take as long as three-quarters of an hour to reach the Nolan's farm. He had thought something passed between them the other day on the stairs. There had been no opportunity to seek Mrs. Nolan's advice, what with the lads being sick, and all. Three-quarters of an hour wasn't much, but it was time enough.

"Are ye warm enough?" he asked as they moved down the drive toward the street.

"Aye. 'Tis kind of ye to do this. I thank ye."

"No thanks are necessary. 'Tis my pleasure."

They rolled on in silence for a while, each unsure of the other's interest. Finally, Rolland became concerned that they might travel the entire route home in silence but before he could speak Patricia began to giggle.

"Ye seemed to be havin' more fun than the lads throwin' snowballs," she teased.

He smiled, relieved to hear the good cheer in her voice. "Aye, I've always loved the snow. I grew up wi' two brothers and we were always throwin' things at one another. 'Twas the snow that hurt the least!"

"Are they here in Buffalo, yer brothers?"

"No, they are both back home in Albany. Matthew, he's the oldest, is a stonemason, and John is a carpenter. I've just had a letter from John and I'm that pleased to tell ye I'll be an uncle again come the spring."

"Have ye many nieces and nephews, then?"

"Aye, Matthew and Jane have three lads but this is the first for John and Susan. They were only just married shortly before I came to Buffalo."

Feeling bold, Patricia asked "Both of yer brothers are married, then, and were there no lasses in Albany who caught yer eye?"

Rolland was not expecting such a question and began to feel the heat creeping up his face. Thankfully, he thought, the cold air could easily be to blame. "No, but there's one here in Buffalo I'd like to get to know better."

"Do I know her?" Patricia asked, genuinely wondering if it was some other lass he fancied.

He did not even try to keep the laughter out of his voice when he answered, "Yes, and quite well I should think!" Now she really was confused and it showed plainly on her face, which made Rolland laugh out loud. "Should ye have an occasion to use the looking glass, she'll be starin' back at ye."

Now it was Patricia's turn to be embarrassed. "Me?"

"Aye, ye!"

"Well then," she smiled, "in that case you'll have to stay for supper."

"I'd be honored." Taking one hand from the reins

and placing it over hers, they traveled the last few minutes in contented silence.

The children were already seated as Karyn and Martha were setting the table. Looking out the window as the carriage pulled up, Karyn said, "Looks like we will need another place at the table. Mr. Thomas has brought your sister home."

Martha went to fetch another plate, unable to suppress a giggle as Johnny made a kissing face. Having caught the exchange between the two, Karyn gave them a stern warning. "Need I remind the two of you that Mr. Thomas is your teacher and you will show him respect while he is a guest in this house?" Their solemn nods quickly became smirks as young Bruns, always eager to emulate Johnny, began to make the kissing face. Barely able to contain her own grin, Karyn mustered up all of her parental authority and said, "There will be no supper for those who cannot behave!"

The giggling had stopped by the time Patricia and Rolland, entered the house. Done with their evening chores, Charlie and Alex were right behind them. After a final brief but stern look at the children, Karin greeted the group. "Good evening, Mr. Thomas. Charlie will take your coat. You will join us for supper, yes?" Not waiting for an answer, she continued speaking, turning her attention toward Patricia, "They are delayed again. What is it this time?" It was not unusual for the Nolans to remain at the orphan asylum if one or more of the children were ill.

"She's off to Mr. Pratt and I daresay she'll likely be in a foul mood when she returns." Patricia answered.

"Michael is with her?" Karyn asked.

"I would imagine he is now. He'll have received word when he came to pick her up. We'd best start without them." Patricia reported.

Dinner passed pleasantly enough and the group was just finishing up as the Nolans arrived home. There was a great deal of shuffling around as the children left the table and plates were filled by Ciara and Michael.

"So, did ye speak to Mr. Pratt?" Rolland asked.

"Aye, she did more than speak," Michael answered. "I could hear her shoutin' as I pulled up to the Big House."

"That man!" The ride home had done nothing to dissipate Ciara's anger. "He insisted some of the lads were old enough to be put out to work. Went on about

211

the cost always rising, and the 'endless stream of waifs who tax the county's resources.' He's had pressure from the county to find a way to reduce the expense at the orphan asylum. They're just children and they do with little enough as it is!

Trying to defuse her anger, Michael interrupted. "Now Ciara, I've told ye not to fret. The lads are no' going to Bowersfeid or anyone else. The board doesn't meet until the first of the year. That should give ye plenty of time to have a talk with Mrs. Farrell and make a plan. Ye know she'll no' allow babes to be put out to work."

Seeing that a change of subject was in order, Charlie spoke up. "Mr. Thomas, I'm pleased to be tellin' ye that there's to be a wedding to mark the New Year. Mrs. Friedlander and I are to be married shortly after Christmas," he said, taking Karyn's hand and pressing it to his lips for a quick kiss.

"Ah, I'm that pleased for ye, Mr. Edwards, Mrs. Friedlander." Rolland said. "As much as I'm enjoin' the pleasant company, I'm afraid I must be off. I'll be locked out of Mrs. Cornish's if I'm no' back by 8 o'clock. Might I have use of a horse, Dr. Nolan? I've no place to keep the carriage for the night."

"Aye, of course, I'll come down to the barn with ye."

"Take yer meal while it's still hot. I can see myself down if ye'll just tell me which horse to take."

"'Tis no bother," Michael replied, getting up from the table. Suspecting Michael wanted a word with the lad, neither Charlie nor Alex offered to accompany Rolland down to the barn.

Patricia stood and made a nervous courtesy. "I thank ye for seeing me home," she said with a shy smile.

"'Twas my pleasure. I shall see ye at week's end."

Michael wasted no time getting to the point on the short walk down to the barn. "I see ye have an interest in our Patricia."

"Aye, I do."

"She was upset when last ye were here. Am I to understand that whatever the trouble, it has been resolved?"

"Yes, sir, I believe it has."

"Good. It'll no' please me if she were to be upset again. Take the mare in the first stall on the right. You'll find her tack just inside the door. I'm back to my supper." Without another word, Michael turned and headed back in the direction of the house.

Rolland watched him go. Smiling, he said to himself, "Well then, that went rather better than I had hoped."

Chapter Seventeen

Ciara sat in her office late one morning awaiting the arrival of Mrs. Farrell. They had missed their monthly meeting in November because the sick children had kept all of the orphanage staff busy around the clock, so there was much to discuss. She heard the carriage pull up to the front of the asylum and soon thereafter the familiar lilt of Colleen's voice as she entered the building. Ciara greeted her in the entrance hall. "Shall I send for some tea? Ye look chilled to the bone," she asked as they passed the kitchens on the way back to her office.

"Thank ye. That would be lovely."

"Were ye well pleased wi' the Metz'?" Ciara asked. "They seemed lovely folks. Anke is a sweet lass."

"Aye, she is at that and Sean is happy, so yes, I am well pleased with the match."

After the tea had arrived, the women got to the

business at hand. Ciara wasted no time raising the issue she was most concerned about. "I've been worried sick since my meeting with Mr. Pratt last week. Surely the Board would not insist that children be put out to work?"

"Well, the county pays for the care of those children transferred from the almshouse, and 'tis true enough that the men are not pleased with the costs associated with their care. It was Dr. Standish who suggested that the children be put out to work to the lowest bidder for their care. To be sure I argued against it, as did a few others, but I daresay if it goes to a vote, I've no idea what the outcome might be."

This was not the news that Ciara wanted to hear. "Most of those who came from the Big House are too young to be put out to work. What are we to do?"

"Well, I am not without allies on the committee, but I suspect it will take the full effort of the Board of Directresses to resolve this, so as a first step, we should meet, and soon."

Ciara knew full well how powerful these women could be when they put their mind to something. They were known to coerce their husbands (many of whom sat on the Board of Supervisors for Indoor Relief, which oversaw the Board of Directresses) however necessary to vote in their favor. It was just such a tactic that had helped Ciara secure her position of Keeper of the Orphan Asylum a few years back. It was also the reason Rosemary Fitzgerald resigned from the group, thinking it bad manners to interfere in the matters of men."Aye, 'tis a place to start, although the number of friends we have among our board members changes as the wind does these days, I daresay."

"Don't worry about the Board of Directresses. We've friends aplenty, you'll see. Sure enough we got more than we bargained for when Rosemary left, what with Kathleen Proctor taking her place. For as much as Kathleen thought herself above the likes of us, she joined fast enough when she thought it would secure her son's position as Keeper of the Poorhouse. If there is anyone serving on our board to worry about, 'tis her. As for Elizabeth Standish, she is nothing like her sister Rosemary. She has a mind independent of her husband's, and a fair amount of influence over him when she has a need to. Oh, and let us not forget my Evelyn. She is a favorite of her father-in-law, and with a grandchild on the way, I suspect Dr. Standish's heart has grown softer still for her. The other ladies will support us as they always have. Yes, we've friends enough, Ciara."

"Aye, yer right." Ciara felt somewhat better knowing Mrs. Abernathy, Mrs. Malone and Mrs. Twitchel could be counted among their allies, even if Mrs. Proctor and Mrs. Standish and some of the others were uncertain. But there was one more thing on her mind as long as Colleen Farrell was sitting in her office. She had given Michael her word that she would leave Proctor to him, but she never promised she would drop the matter entirely.

"Colleen, I've another matter to discuss with ye, should ye have a bit more time."

"What is it, dear? Is it the classroom? How are things going with Mr. Thomas?"

"Oh, aye, very well, but no, that's not it. I've noticed some things…over at the Big House…" she paused, not knowing what exactly to say.

"Ciara, you clearly have something on your mind, so out with it."

Ciara took a deep breath and told of the strange

goings-on with the deaths of Mrs. Lutz, Miss Richter and Mrs. O'Shea. She went on to inform that Michael had done some checking and found that Mrs. O'Shea was a widow and had no family in Buffalo, and that they had accompanied the O'Shea lads to the burial of their mother when she went unclaimed more to insure that she was in fact buried in the pauper cemetery than to allow the lads a proper goodbye. When Ciara had relayed every detail, she sat silently while Colleen processed what had just been said.

"Ciara, are you absolutely sure about this?"

"No, I am not, and I don't know how we'd know for sure."

"Ye say Mrs. O'Shea went unclaimed?"

Ciara nodded, "We saw her buried."

Colleen thought a moment to consider fully what she was about to suggest. Finally, with a nod of certainty, she continued, "Well then, we shall send someone round to claim her."

At this, Ciara looked shocked. "Ye mean dig her up?"

"I daresay 'tis been done many a time when a family member has come along after the time to claim a loved one has passed. With all of the complainin' the Board has done about the cost of burials, they should be glad to have her claimed for all it's the dead of winter. Besides, the ground's not frozen. 'Twould be easier to do it now than in spring. To be sure Mr. Proctor would have some explainin' to do should we find the casket empty."

"Oh, I doubt it would be empty. The farmers had a time of it lowering the poor dear into the ground." Ciara told her.

"Ah well, we'll know for sure when she's claimed," Colleen said.

"Surely ye don't mean to open the casket?" The look of shock returned to Ciara's face.

"I mean to do just that. This is serious business and we must get to the bottom of it. You've asked for my help. Will ye refuse it now?"

"No, I will not, but is that necessary?"

"Ciara, a man who would sink so low as to profit from the sale of those who have passed on would surely not be hindered by a few feet of clay. The only sure way to know if Mrs. O'Shea was buried, and not removed from her tomb the minute you turned your backs, is to have her claimed and to open the casket. There's many who'd have the casket opened to say a final goodbye, or to make sure they've got the right person before they travel the road home. It should not alarm Mr. Proctor or his men, should they have no sins to cover. "

"And who would come to claim her?" Ciara asked.

"We've a new man in the stable, just come from Rochester. I think he and his wife might be persuaded." Colleen replied.

"What's to become of Mrs. O'Shea…should she be…in there," Ciara asked.

"Well, we will certainly give her a decent Christian Burial, make no mistake. She deserves as much, poor soul."

Ciara was certainly relieved that Colleen had taken her suspicions seriously and was willing to investigate the matter further; however, the idea of digging up Mrs. O'Shea, and her boys still at the orphan asylum, just didn't sit well with her. "I've no reason to believe she's not there, and us disturbin' her eternal rest with her lads still livin' here. How will we explain it when yer stable man takes their ma, but leaves them here?"

"Ciara, the lads need know nothing of this. The

couple who comes to claim her will be unable to take the lads and will say so, if the issue is raised. To be sure that's happened more times than we would like, and the children are none the wiser. This will be no different."

Seeing the uncertainty still in Ciara's eyes, Colleen added, "If you are right, and poor Mrs. O'Shea lies in that grave the county will be spared the expense of her burial, which should please Mr. Proctor and she will be given a decent Christian burial. If the poor soul is not there, I should think him unlikely to attempt such atrocities for a while, and that will buy us some time to devise a proper plan."

Ciara took another few minutes to consider the plan. At least they were doing something, she thought. It seemed a safe enough plan and if it put a stop Proctor's horrific business venture, then it was worth it. "Aye, yer right," she finally said, making the sign of the cross as she spoke. "Sure enough Michael will no' be pleased about it, though."

Later that night, when all the house had retired and they sat watching the last of the smoldering coals in the sitting room next to the kitchen, Ciara was surprised to learn that her husband was not unreceptive to the plan that Colleen Farrell had devised. "I agree 'tis time we do something. Before the winter's through there will be more than a few poor souls claimed by exposure. The death house already has three who've gone unclaimed and are awaitin' burial. To be sure, Proctor would not pass up the opportunity to send one or two off to Geneva, and who would be the wiser?"

"I must say, I was expectin' a bit of a stern word fer sharin' my concerns with Mrs. Farrell. Yer not cross with me?" Ciara asked.

"Darlin', you've kept yer word and stayed away from Proctor and I'm no' fool enough to think that ye'll let the concerns ye have go unanswered. As long as this plan of Colleen's in no way involves ye and doesn't place the stable man and his wife in any danger, I'd agree 'tis a start, at least."

"I shall be none the wiser until all is said and done. Mr. and Mrs. Dote have been told to go to the poor farm and introduce themselves as second cousins, only recently arrived from Ireland, to find their cousin had passed. 'Tis true enough, but for the part about findin' their cousin dead."

"Aye, and what about the lads?" Michael asked.

223

"I doubt Mr. Proctor will even remember the O'Shea lads, but should he mention it, they'll say they are unable to take them in, but they would like to provide their cousin with a decent Christian burial, and could they lay eyes on her so that they may say a proper goodbye."

"Aye, and will Mr. and Mrs. Dote, newly hired in the Farrell's employ, be wonderin' why they have been asked to do such a thing?" Michael asked.

"Colleen will tell them that Mrs. O'Shea had worked in the Farrell house before she was married, and that she would like to provide the woman a decent burial. I doubt they'll question the rest. They both have good positions and should be only too glad to do as they are asked by such a kind and generous employer."

"She's thought of everything, and no surprise. Sure enough Dote and his wife will have themselves a good fright if the casket turns up empty."

"Sure enough, and let us hope that it does not."

Michael turned to his wife and took her hands into his own. "Ciara, are ye prepared to go where this road takes us? I've said it before, but it bears sayin' once more: the Board of Supervisors may very well turn a blind eye to Proctor's activities, however horrific they are. They'll likely see it as a grand solution to a persistent problem. To them, sendin' the poor departed souls to Geneva saves the county money and provides valuable goods to the medical school in the bargain." Seeing her face grow dark, he quickly added, "Ye know well I don't see it that way, but they very likely will. If our worst fears are confirmed by Mrs. Farrell's plan, it may not turn out as we hope."

"Oh, Michael, what kind of world do we live in here where good people have no other choice but to live and die in places like the poor farm, and then not even the hope of eternal peace once they've passed from their wretched lives?" Moving her hands slightly, so that she now grasped his, her grip hard to emphasize her resolve. "We have to stop this Michael."

"Aye, I know. I've been thinkin' that the solution might rather be with the Board of Directresses rather than the Board of Supervisors. If word got out, and it most certainly would if the other women on the Board of Directresses found out the unclaimed dead being sold to the medical college, there's many who'd be outraged to be sure. The Board of Supervisors would have a hard time ignoring public sentiment. Now, mind, we need proof of our suspicions, to be sure, and Colleen's plan is a start. Let us see what happens with the Dotes, and then we'll have another word with the formidable Mrs. Farrell, but for now, it is time for bed."

Chapter Eighteen

Ciara and Michael were constantly amazed at what Colleen Farrell could accomplish with the sheer power of her will. How she managed to convince her newly hired stable man and his wife to go the almshouse and claim the body of Mrs. O'Shea, they did not know. They each spent the day in tense anticipation of any word from Mrs. Farrell on the outcome of her bold plan. However, it was not until two days later that Mrs. Farrell came to the orphan asylum with news from the adventure of Mr. and Mrs. Dote.

Ciara saw Mrs. Farrell's carriage approaching the orphan asylum. She exited her office into the long hallway just as Mrs. Olsen was opening the front door. Seeing the look of anticipation on Ciara's face, Colleen said "Mrs. Nolan," (it was always Mrs. Nolan and Mrs. Farrell in front of the staff) "I must speak with you immediately. There is influenza up at the Big House and we must be sure to keep the children and staff away from there."

As she was speaking, the two women were already walking in the direction of Ciara's office. Once the door was closed Ciara asked, "Influenza?"

"Aye, 'tis true enough, better your people think that the reason for my visit." Colleen removed her coat and immediately launched into the telling of her tale. "It appears that you were right. There is trouble afoot at the Big House. Mr. Dote and his wife arrived around mid-morning to claim Mrs. O'Shea." Colleen went on to provide the details about how Mrs. Rowan had told the couple that Mr. Proctor was busy and they would have to come back tomorrow, and how creative the Dotes were, insisting they had to claim the body today. If it could not be today, they said, they would have to leave her there and could Mrs. Rowan kindly fetch Mr. Pratt if Mr. Proctor was unavailable (who would be only be too happy to allow them to claim the body and have the county re-reimbursed for the cost of the coffin). She went on to discuss how agitated Mr. Proctor was when he finally did meet with the Dotes (and no, Colleen, continued, there was no discussion of the children or whether the couple would be taking them as well). It seemed to take forever to fetch the farmers, Mr. Mulligan and what was the other man's name? Oh, yes, Mr. Buxton... Ciara thought she would burst with anticipation waiting to hear if the coffin was empty or not.

Finally, seeing Ciara on the edge of her seat, Colleen got to the details she had been waiting hear. "Well, you can just imagine Mr. Proctor's reaction when our man Dote asked to open the casket 'just so as to be sure 'tis our dear Margaret before we start on the long road home to Batavia'! There was a great deal of pointing at the grave number in the ledger and the number on the stake, proof enough they had the right person, Proctor told them. I shall have to give the Dotes a bit extra in their wages at week's end for their superb performance for they did convince Mr. Proctor to have his men open the casket after going on for a time about the hard journey, the loss of two full days work and the money it would cost to bury her."

Finally, Ciara could wait no longer, "And? Was it empty or no," the impatience evident in her voice.

"No, dear, 'twas not empty, but neither did it contain Margaret O'Shea. 'Twas a log in the coffin, a large one, to make the weight of a woman."

Ciara was not aware that she had stood up until she fell back into her chair. "A log? That would mean…oh no!" Tears filled her eyes as she realized that the log filled casket could only mean that Mrs. O'Shea had been sold to the medical college. "That man is truly the Devil himself!"

"Aye, you're right about that," Colleen agreed. "Sure enough he feigned shock when they lifted the lid, as did the farmers. He sent the poor Dotes on their way with sincere assurances that he would get to the bottom of this, didn't give them the chance to even ask how such a thing could happen or where their dear Margaret had gone, and him not a few minutes earlier pointing to the ledger and insisting the poor soul was in that casket. Sure enough, he is the Devil."

"Mr. and Mrs. Dote, they just left?"

"Well, there wasn't much else to be done. 'Twas clear that Mr. Proctor and his men would offer no explanation of the matter. Sure enough, the Dotes were not told any of why they were really there and 'twas quite a shock when they saw the casket was empty. I should imagine they were only too glad to leave. In fact, they were quite confused when they came back to give me their report. To be sure, I gave quite the performance of my own when I feigned surprise at their news. I told them not to fret over the matter and that I would handle the situation myself."

"And just how do you intend to handle the situation?" Ciara asked, surprised that, for the first time, Colleen didn't have a plan.

"We must proceed carefully," her mentor replied. "Consider what I've just told ye. Tell yer husband and hear his thoughts on the matter. We'll talk again soon."

Later that night, during their usual evening ritual, Ciara relayed the highlights of the Dotes' experience at the almshouse to Michael. He continued to brush her hair in silence for a while when she had finished, realizing that they were likely correct in their suspicions and what the implications of that realization might be. "Well, we still have no real proof of what Proctor is up to," he finally said. "'Tis true enough something's amiss, but it could just as easily be explained by the incompetence of the farmers."

"And what about the log?" Ciara countered, growing agitated and moving away from the brush as he raised it to her head again. "Just how will they explain burying a log instead of a person, Michael?"

With just a moment's thought, he said "Well, they could say as they had placed the log in the casket to test its strength, and through some mishap or other, it was buried by accident, and Mrs. O'Shea likely buried elsewhere in the potter's field."

Ciara turned, astonished, to face her husband, "Michael, you don't really believe that to be the case?"

"'Tis a likely explanation, and believable, given the characters of those two farmers."

Ciara was angry now."Michael Nolan do ye mean to tell me that you believe Mrs. O'Shea is lyin' in peaceful slumber somewhere in that field and not on a wagon headed for Geneva?"

"No, I don't believe that," he tried to resume brushing her hair, as much to gather his thoughts as to calm her down, but she would have none of it. There would be no sleep tonight until they had discussed the matter and formulated a plan, but he had to choose his words carefully or risk upsetting her further, although that was an inevitable conclusion, he knew. "Ciara, ye know full well that it doesn't matter what you or I believe and, for what it's worth, I do believe that blackguard Proctor is up to no good and that poor Mrs. O'Shea is, indeed, headed for Geneva." Holding his hand up to forestall her argument, he continued. "I agree that we can't let this continue, but we've got to go canny from here. The Board, even the Directresses, are likely to believe any explanation the wee demon puts forth. However, they, especially the women, will likely be outraged at such incompetence. However he chooses to explain the presence of a log and the absence of Mrs. O'Shea, he will have to admit to the incompetence of the farmers and the poor recordkeeping at the very least. A formal reprimand from the Board of Supervisors will require regular inspections for a few weeks at least. That should slow him down a bit until we can figure out a better plan. For now, we need to consider how to bring this to the Board's attention without letting on that we know what happened yesterday with the Dotes."

"Aye, well, it won't surprise ye to find out Colleen's already got that end sorted. She had the Dotes stop at the Eagle House on their way out of town, as it were. By the time they left the whole tavern was abuzz over what had happened at the poor farm, likely nobody even noticed the Dote's wagon heading back in the direction of the city."

"Colleen Farrell is a corker, so she is!" Michael said with admiration. "Who else would send the stable man and his wife out on command to fetch a corpse, and them playin' the parts of the bereaved cousins to perfection without any explanation as to why their mistress has sent them on such an unusual errand! If the situation were not so dire, I'd find the whole thing a lark." He quickly re-arranged his features, seeing his wife did not find the slightest bit of humor in the situation.

"'Tis not funny, Michael," she scolded.

"No, 'tis not, and I'm that sorry. It appears as though Mrs. Farrell has matters well in hand."

"That's just it. I don't think she does. We're to meet again in a few days, after we've had a chance to think on the matter. Michael, 'tis not like her to be uncertain about anythin'."

"Now just ye listen to me, in a day or two, the news will have gone through the whole city. Tattle of that nature usually does. It may be that the matter will come before the Board without any of us havin' to intervene. Try and put this out of yer mind for a time and sleep." He knew as he said that there would be little sleep this night. They would each go over and over the events in their mind, feeling that it was the least they could do to honor the souls whose eternal rest had been disturbed in such a horrific way.

Chapter Nineteen

January 3, 1841
The Board of Directresses met yesterday. Needless to say the ladies were outraged at the news of matters of burial at the poorhouse, which had been reported in the Buffalo Sentinel, the Daily Sun and the Gazette. Mrs. Farrell assured us that she would take the matter directly to the Board of Supervisors. She has promised us that there will be a full inquiry…

Ciara was reluctant to write anything about Mrs. Farrell's prior knowledge of the events at the poorhouse, although she did a fine job of feigning shock when Ciara announced the purpose of the meeting she had been invited to attend. She put down her pen, a gift from her husband at Christmas, and closed the journal. There were happier events to focus on today.

Patricia looked out the kitchen window in the direction of the bunk house, which after the ceremony this morning had become the home of Mr. and Mrs. Charles Edwards. It wasn't much of a day for a wedding. The wind blew furiously, and the falling snow swirled such that she could not see if it actually touched the ground. Still, they all managed to get to the church on time and a short time later Karyn and Charlie were man and wife. Surely Rolland would not make the trip to the Nolan farm on horseback in this weather to attend the wedding supper? A knot began to grow in the pit of Patricia's stomach as she began to think of what might transpire should Rolland decide to stay at Mrs. Cornish's Boarding House instead. *She* was also staying at Mrs. Cornish's, Martha and Johnny had told her that. *She* being one Lucinda Shaw, a new teacher brought in as a temporary replacement for Mr. Lawrence who had broken his leg after his carriage hit an icy rut in the road and he was thrown onto the street. Patricia was unaware of the scowl on her face as she thought of Rolland and Miss Shaw in the sitting room by the fire chatting companionably about the next day's lesson until her thoughts were interrupted by the sound of her older sister's voice. "Whatever has got you in such a foul state?" Ciara asked.

"I don't know what you mean. I'm no' in a foul state," Patricia countered, walking toward the pantry to retrieve more onions.

"That sour puss yer wearin's no' just from choppin' the onions," Martha chimed in, and Ellie giggled as Patricia's expression darkened and she continued to huff and sputter that she was indeed in a perfectly fine mood.

"Just ye mind yer business," Ciara scolded the younger girls, who by now were both laughing out loud.

As the girls laughter wound down to stifled chuckles, Karyn placed a lid on a pan of simmering sauerkraut (finding nothing unusual in helping to prepare her own wedding supper, despite the protests of her friends) and said "Do not fret, he will come."

"Who will come?" Patricia asked, pretending she had no idea who Karyn was talking about.

"Why, Mr. Thomas, of course!" Martha announced as she and Ellie once again succumbed to giggling fits.

Before Ciara could chastise the girls again, Karyn said simply "Perhaps it was a mistake to include die kinder in our preparations." The two young girls wanted desperately to be included in this special gathering of women as they prepared the wedding supper, so they quickly adjusted their behavior and began refolding the fine linen napkins that had been a gift from Colleen Farrell to Ciara on her wedding day.

After a stern look at the two girls for good measure, Ciara confirmed Karyn's prediction. "Aye, he'll come."

With a sigh of resignation, there was no point in denying her fears, Patricia said "I'm no' so sure. 'Tis a long ride on such a frightful day. Would not a wise man stay in on such a day?"

"A wise man, perhaps, but not a man in love," explained Karyn. "A man in love would travel twice the distance under conditions far worse than these to see his woman."

"A man in love might not have to leave the parlor on a day such as today if the woman he loved lived right under his nose," Patricia said matter-of-factly.

Karyn and Ciara both looked confused as Patricia turned and looked out the window again, hoping the snow had let up a bit. It had. Before either of the older women could ask what on earth she had meant, Martha spoke to clear things up. "She means Miss Shaw, the new teacher. She fancies Mr. Thomas. They both are staying at Mrs. Cornish's and so walk to school together each day."

Ciara, who placed to loaves of bread into the oven for baking, noted the look of devastation on her middle sister's face. Placing a hand gently on Patricia's shoulder, Ciara said, "Just because she fancies him doesn't mean he fancies her. Just a week ago, he told Michael 'twas you he wanted and agreed to attend the wedding supper of two people he barely knows to be with you. He said he'd come and he will, you'll see."

"I'm going to marry Johnny when I'm older," Martha declared to no one in particular.

"Are ye now?" It was Patricia's turn to giggle."And just when did ye decide that?" she asked.

"He asked me when we were still livin' at the Big House, when I was just a wee lass." (Now ten years old, she was barely five when they were living in the Children's Ward at the Erie County Poorhouse.) "He asked me would I marry him when I was grown, and I told him yes." Without further comment, she helped Ellie, who also thought nothing more on the matter needed saying, placing the newly refolded napkins into a neat pile.

Ciara and Karyn were shocked into silence until the sound of hoof beats, muffled by the snow, were heard coming up the drive. Looking out the window, Ciara said "Aye, I told ye he would come, and Ma and Pa Nolan right behind him. Now you lasses hurry. We've a wedding supper to put on!"

Patricia helped the young girls make final preparations to the table with a lighter heart as she heard Michael open the front door to receive their guests. *He came*, she thought and smiled.

Seeing the look on Patricia's face Karyn said to Ciara, "She reminds me of you when the doctor was trying to get your attention, always getting in her own way." Ciara had been uncertain about Michael's intentions when they were working side by side at the poorhouse seeing the children through everything from food poisoning to scarlet fever. When she did finally realize how he felt about her, she was reluctant to give in to her own feelings for fear that, as his wife, she would be taking away his chances for advancement. Certainly he would be shunned by decent society for marrying a pauper. However, with a little help from the Mrs. Farrell, the two were finally married and continued to work side by side to protect the orphaned children of Buffalo.

Taking her friend by the hand Ciara said, "Sometimes I wondered if we would ever leave that place…if we ever could leave that place, knowing what the children would face without us. I would have never been able to leave without your help. You showed me that we could have a life outside of there. You have kept my home and helped raise my sisters. I could not do any of this without you. Thank you." By the time she had finished speaking, both women had tears streaming down their faces.

"No, mein freund, it is I who should thank you. You took me in, took us in, and gave us a home and a purpose. All that I have, I have because of you, meine schwester, my sister." True to her practical German self, rather than hug her friend, she patted her hand and said, "No more of this weinin. We have guests to serve."

An outsider looking in would not have known it for a wedding supper, as the meal was plain and served at the kitchen table without ceremony. They all shared a supper of sausages smothered in onions and sauerkraut, ham, boiled potatoes and turnips. Father Mertz had been unable to join them, but the addition of Rolland Thomas and the senior Nolans made things a bit cramped at the table. Nobody seemed to mind and several conversations were going on at once as dishes were passed and glasses of beer refilled. Charlie and Karyn behaved not like newlyweds, shy and nervously focused on their wedding night. Rather they looked like they had been together for years. There was no awkwardness between the couple who had lived in the same household for nearly five years and, for the last few months of that time, as covertly as could be managed, shared a bed. There was no nervousness, only relief that there was no reason to pretend otherwise now. Karyn would share the cabin with Charlie and in the spring they would make the additions necessary to enlarge the single room into a home for Bruns and Ellie to join them.

Rolland, normally not one to shy away from a delicious meal, had hardly touched the food on his plate. Instead, he made great efforts to engage Patricia in conversation, which at first were received with what could best be described as reserve on her part. Out of shyness or something else, Rolland was not sure. He was unwilling to risk offending her again and so he decided to focus their conversation around the children from the orphan asylum, encouraging her to share her thoughts and opinions on how they might make the best use of their classroom time as cabin fever had set in during the cold winter months. Patricia began to relax and participate more actively in the conversation and Rolland remembered he had news that was sure to please her. "Ye might have heard we've a new teacher at the school to fill in while Mr. Lawrence is on the mend."

Patricia managed to affix a smile on her face, a smile that men typically did not recognize, but women did. It is an insincere expression, meant to hide the wearer's true emotion. It was recognized as frozen and unflinching, often with eyes opened slightly more than was natural, and repetitive nodding (the intent to show enthusiastic interest in whatever the other individual is saying). Through her frozen smile, Patricia said "Aye, Martha's told me about her."

Misunderstanding that smile and its accompanying gestures as most men do, Rolland proceeded to deliver his good news. "I've told her all about ye and the children at the orphan asylum and she's keen to help. She's willing to help me with the older children so that you can spend more time with the wee ones." The enthusiastic smile on his face was quickly replaced with confusion as the smile frozen on Patricia's face began to melt.

Patricia's smile was quickly replaced with a look of confusion and betrayal. "She's keen to help you?" Her voice trailed off and her lower lip began to tremble. She stood and made a general announcement about not feeling well and made a hasty exit, fearing she would burst into tears before she had made it safely to her chamber. Rolland looked after her, wondering, again, how such a delightful visit had gone so very wrong.

Seeing Michael's expression darken, Ciara gave him the "let me handle this" look and then addressed the group. "'Tis been a long day for us all. Children, clear the dishes. Martha see Bruns and Ellie to bed when yer through. Shall we take some tea in the parlor? Rolland, if ye'd be so kind as to help me set the tray."

The children reluctantly went about their chore and Michael's parents took their leave. With Ciara and Rolland in the kitchen, the party had dwindled to Alex,

Michael and the Edwards. Making no effort to hide it, Alex let out a jaw-cracking yawn. "Well, I'm off to me bed. I've a feeling there will be no help with the morning chores." With a pointed look at Charlie, he rose from his chair and went to his chamber. There was a bit of awkward silence, and silly grinning before Michael looked at the newlyweds and said, "Ach, away wi' ye and let me bank the fire for the night."

Ciara waited until the others had dispersed before she spoke to Rolland. "Would ye mind tellin' me what that was about?"

"I've no idea," he said defensively. "We were talkin' pleasantly enough about the children and our plans for the classroom, when it occurred to me as I had good news to share. The new teacher, Miss Shaw, has been kind enough to offer to help me with the older students so that Patricia can spend more time wi' the babes. She's been feelin' as though they could use more of her time, but it takes the two of us to keep the older ones settled and focused. I thought she would be delighted." With a sigh, Rolland leaned against the counter, forgetting all about the tea. "It appears I've offended her again. I swear, Mrs. Nolan, I don't mean to."

Ciara suppressed an understanding smile. She was tempted to feel sorry for the bewildered lad, but she was determined to get to the bottom of his relationship with Miss Shaw. "Tell me about this new teacher and in her interest in the orphan asylum." As Rolland began to explain it became apparent to Ciara that Miss Shaw was more interested in him than the orphans, but that interest was not returned. During their walks to and from school, Rolland talked mostly of Patricia and their work together educating the children. Ciara was unable to contain her smile as Rolland, as clueless a man as ever there was, could not be redirected from his favorite topic of conversation. Try as the new teacher did to divert him, all conversation threads led back to Patricia. Miss Shaw's interest in the orphanage was clearly a way to spend more time with Rolland, and at the same time separate him from Patricia. Miss Shaw was a determined young woman.

Before Ciara could offer some words of understanding and advice, Michael sauntered through the kitchen door. Eyeing Rolland dispassionately he asked, "What's amiss, then?"

"'Tis just a wee misunderstanding," Ciara explained.

Looking sternly back at Rolland, Michael said, "This had better be the last of these misunderstandings of yours."

"Yes, sir, I hope so too, sir." Seeing Michael's expression grow sterner yet, Rolland added, "I'll make sure of it, sir."

"See that ye do." Handing the younger man his coat, Michael continued, "I've brought yer horse 'round. Best ye get home while there's a break in the snowfall."

"Yes, sir, and thank ye again for a lovely visit. I'm that sorry to have caused ye trouble, again. Please give my regards to the happy couple."

As he made his way out the door, Ciara stopped him, placing her hand on his arm. "I'll speak to her. I'm sure this will sort itself out."

With profound gratitude, he replied, "I thank ye, ma'am."

After Rolland had left Ciara turned to her husband. "Michael Nolan, ye should be ashamed of yerself. Ye were that rude to the lad!"

"Ach, I told him there'd be hell to pay if he upset her again. By that reckoning, he got off easy."

"Did I not tell ye I would handle it? There's much ye don't know about."

"Aye well, then it's business as usual, so it is. What is it that I don't know about now?"

"Well," she began, "Patricia's woes are the least of it. There's a new teacher at the school with her eye on our Mr. Thomas, although he seems entirely unaware of it and is hopelessly in love with our Patricia." Seeing the questions begin to form in his mind, she continued, "Ye needn't concern yerself with Rolland. He'll sort things will Patricia soon enough. 'Tis wee Martha ye need to be thinkin' about. She announced today she plans to marry Johnny when she's old enough."

"What?"

"Aye, when they were but wee babes, he asked her to marry him when she'd grown and she said yes. Evidently, she plans to stay true to her word."

"She can't be serious! She's still but a wee babe," Michael argued.

"She'll be a woman soon enough and he's nearly a man. He's but one year of school left and then he'll be off to work wi' yer da," Ciara pointed out.

Michael had always had a special place in his heart for wee Martha. She had a keen interest in medicine, which, now that he thought of it, may have started when she had helped to take care of Johnny back in the Children's Ward at the poorhouse. At barely five years old she would bathe his head with a wet washcloth to help with fever just after the horrific procedure that saved his life and his leg. Later, as he was healing, she helped him to sit up, and stretch his bad leg. She made sure that he ate his meals and sat with him when the pain was too much to bear. As she got older, she accompanied Michael to the orphan asylum when she could to help with the sick children there. It was Michael's hope that her interest in medicine would stay with her when she became a woman. "She's too young to be thinkin' about marriage. She has school to finish and then, well, I hope she will consider continuing her education before she marries. Ye heard Thomas: she's a bright lass."

"Aye, she is that," Ciara agreed. "But ye can't deny there's somethin' special between those two. They've been protectin' each other since they were but babes."

"Ciara, they've lived as brother and sister all these years. Of course they'll protect each other, and Bruns and Ellie too, for that matter. In a few years they'll go their separate ways and we can only hope they'll come home and visit when we're old."

That thought made Ciara sad. "It grieves me to think that eventually they will leave us. Patricia will be gone one way or another before ye know it. If she doesn't marry Rolland, she'll find someone else soon enough and Johnny will likely move in with your parents next year when he starts to work for them full time. Oh Michael, what will we do when they all leave?"

Taking her in his arms, he kissed her forehead. "Well, we'll just have to make some more to take their places." He was aware that it was a risk to make such a suggestion. They had spoken only a few times about their inability to have children and each time he remained hopeful that one day they would bring a child of their own into the world.

She looked into his eyes, ever hopeful that they would tell her what she desperately wanted to hear. "Oh Michael, do ye think we can?"

"Well, I am a doctor, and I can say that engaging in

certain activities would greatly improve our chances." He bent to kiss her, and with that kiss transmitted the hope that he so fiercely held on to. She kissed him back, feeling his optimism and praying silently that he was right. He broke the kiss a bit breathless, but managed to say, "As a doctor, I would suggest that certain activities can be carried out to greater effect in the bed chamber," and he lead her in the direction of the stairs.

Chapter Twenty

Early the next morning, just as objects were starting to distinguish themselves against the darkness, Charlie Edwards lay naked in his bed, his bride still sleeping peacefully in his arms. For the first time in his adult life he felt that he was truly a man, not because of what he had done, what they had done, last night (although, the man in him was quite pleased with himself and with her). No, this morning he felt he was truly a man because he would, from this day forward, live his life as a man should: with a job to do every day, a woman to come home to, and children to protect. He and Karyn and the children would live as a family, and, God willing, give Bruns and Ellie a few brothers and sisters. So pleased was he at this prospect, he was tempted to wake Karyn so they could continue what they had only ceased the night before when their lovemaking had left each of them utterly and completely exhausted. *Will it always be like this?* He thought. Had he said the words out loud? He thought not and was surprised when Karyn answered him.

"No, some days will be better, and others a chore to endure, but we will face each one together, meine shatz," she said as she turned to face him, just able to make out his profile as the sun was beginning to rise.

"And just how did ye know what I was thinkin'?" he asked, turning slightly, so that they were each lying on their sides, facing each other.

"Because my thoughts were the same. I was married before, as you know, and without the approval of my husband's family. We were in love, yes, but there was always a shadow hanging over us. For him, it was the guilt of going against the wishes of his father, and for me it was shame for being selfish enough to let him do it. I am not sure how things would have remained been between us had he lived."

"And now?" he asked, pulling her close so that their foreheads were touching.

"There is just you and me, with no burden of disapproval from anyone else. Together we will greet each day and see what happens next. For now, there is work to do," she said, making a half-hearted attempt to extract herself from his embrace and rise from their small bed. Reluctant to let her go, Charlie held on and kissed her thoroughly, and she soon gave up her feeble attempt to leave.

Later they stood at the door of their home and kissed again for a long time before she headed in the direction of the house and he toward the barn. After all, it was just another day and there were chores to be done. They parted with a smile and the knowledge that at the end of this day and every day forward, they would meet back at the door to their home, have their meal with the children, read by the fire, and return to their bed to pass the night as lovers do.

* * *

Patricia and Ciara were already in the kitchen, assuming the preparation of the breakfast would be their responsibility that morning. Patricia sighed as she watched Karyn reluctantly turn from her husband and walk up to the house, a silly grin spreading across her face as she approached the door. Seeing the wistful look on her sister's face, Ciara cleared her throat. "Now just ye get away from the window. She'll think you've been spyin' on her, for all ye have been!"

Turning away from the blissful bride, Patricia sighed again. "She looks so happy."

"Aye, and ye if give that poor lad a chance you could be happy as well," her sister said.

"Who, Rolland, all he can talk about is Miss Shaw, the new teacher. Did ye hear him telling' me as she's willing' to help him teach?" The look of indignation on her face matched the tone in her voice as she continued. "Can ye imagine? He's all but put me out of my own job!"

Finding it difficult to suppress a smile at her sister's misplaced outrage, Ciara came over and put a hand on Patricia's shoulder. "Now just ye calm down. He's no puttin' ye out of yer job. You've got it all wrong." Adopting her husband's gesture, Ciara put a hand up to forestall another outburst. "Now just ye listen. Miss Shaw has her eye on yer Rolland, and no mistake, but all he can talk about when he's with her is ye. 'Tis true enough she would work at the orphan home to be closer to him, and ye occupied with the babes in the bargain, but Rolland has no clue she fancies him. He told ye about her offer because he sincerely thought ye'd be pleased to have more time with yer wee ones."

"Oh," was Patricia's reply, cut short by the arrival of Karyn who had come through the kitchen door bringing a blast of cold morning air with her.

"Good morning, meine schwestern, my sisters," she said as she closed the door and removed her cloak.

"Good morning to ye, *Mrs. Edwards*. I must say I'm that surprised to see ye up so early this mornin'," Ciara teased.

Ignoring this remark, Karyn turned to Patricia and said, "You fret needlessly over Herr Thomas," again demonstrating her uncanny ability to read minds. "He cares not for that girl. However, if you continue to behave like a, how do you say, a school girl, he will tire of you and turn his attentions elsewhere. You will speak to him and settle this nonsense, yes?"

Knowing there was no point in further discussion, for once Karyn had given her matter-of-fact German opinion on a matter, there was seldom anything left to say, Patricia nodded, "Yes," and turned her attention to the oats as they began to simmer.

* * *

Colleen Farrell had a peculiar habit of taking the

carriage out herself from time to time, much to the dismay of her children. Her father had taught her to drive back in Ireland, and she rather enjoyed it, taking great pleasure in the look of shock on the faces of people as she drove by. The stable lads had strict instructions from Sean not to let her go out anywhere alone, so she waited for the completion of the morning chores and snuck down to the stable while the lads were having their breakfast. In no time her favorite mare, Aine (whose name meant radiance in Gaelic) was hitched up and she was driving out the gate into the alleyway between the houses. So pleased with herself, she didn't see the man step out on the road and she was jarred out of her personal celebration as the carriage came to an abrupt halt and the mare reared up at the intruder.

"Aye, and where's a fine lady like yerself goin' without a driver on this fine mornin'?" The stranger staggered a bit, drunk or perhaps just cold, for his coat was no protection against the chilly January morning. It was of poor quality, badly worn at the elbows and his hat just a bit too big. The man himself was gaunt and filthy. She could smell him from where she sat.

Colleen was startled, but not frightened, and took

A Whisper of Bones

control of the horse before she spoke. "May I help you, sir?" she asked with all the authority she could manage as the horse continued to prance nervously around the stranger. The man took a hold of the harness and began to stroke the mare's nose, which only increased her anxiety as she shook her head and attempted to back away. "Unhand her before you get run over and state your business, sir!"

He released the horse, who would have backed up all the way to the barn if Colleen hadn't kept her in check. "Aye, just so, mi' lady, just so. I've business with a man called Dote. Do ye know him?"

"I do not, so kindly leave and I will be on my way, sir."

"No' just yet, mi'lady. Ye see, this man Dote and his wife went to the poor farm and tried to claim my dear wife, sayin' as she was kin and they wanted to give her a decent Christian burial. I find meself wonderin' why he should want to claim a stranger as kin."

The look of confusion on her face was genuine but the emotion behind it remained hidden as she tried to work out who this man was and how he learned that the Dotes worked for her. If he had come from the almshouse, how would they have known to send him here? "I am certain I do not know what you are talking about, so kindly leave!"

He began walking slowly toward the horse, deliberately agitating her. "I think ye do, mi'lady. I think that ye sent Dote and his wife to the poor farm, ye and that nursemaid from the orphan home, and I've been sent to tell the two o' ye to mind yer business or ye'll be sorry ye didn't." He then charged at the mare, again causing her to rear up, then turned abruptly up the alley toward Pearl Street. Colleen struggled to get control of the horse, and in a maneuver that would have made her father proud, backed the carriage down the alley and into her yard.

She climbed down from the carriage, shaking, tied the horse and headed for the kitchen door. She stopped just outside, took a deep breath, exhaled and then entered the house. The heads of all three grooms, the kitchen maid and the cook all looked up from their boiled oats, shocked to see their mistress come in from outside. "Mr. Hannigan, when you've eaten your breakfast I'll need you to drive me to Dr. Nolan's farm. Mr. and Mrs. Dote, I shall need you to take Maeve to Batavia to stay with Evelyn."(Colleen's oldest daughter had gone to Batavia before the new year to stay with her husband's aunt, who had recently been widowed.) "Please leave immediately. I shall send word when I wish you to return. She left the kitchen, but returned within minutes with a sealed envelope in her hand. Handing it to Mrs. Dote, she said "Give this to Eve and tell her I will write soon. Now, Mr. Hannigan, let us be off. Aine is already hitched up and ready for us. Without even a questioning glance at each other, Hannigan and the Dotes rose from the table and went about complying with Mrs. Farrell's demands.

* * *

There was the usual organized chaos in the Nolan kitchen as plates were emptied, cloaks were gathered as the children went off to school and the adults went off to work. However, the commotion ceased when they heard the familiar sounds of hooves and wheels on frozen earth as a carriage approached the house. "It's Mrs. Farrell," Bruns announced.

Ciara looked at Michael, who returned her questioning stare with one of his own. "Right, then, off ye go or ye'll be late for school." He opened the door to shoo the children out and waved as Colleen walked toward the house. "Mrs. Farrell, 'tis a pleasant surprise. All is well I hope?" he asked as he ushered her inside.

Smiling in acknowledgement as the children left, she returned the greeting. "Good morning to ye, Dr. Nolan, Ciara. I'm that sorry to be barging' in as ye are about to leave for the day, but I must have a quick word."

"Of course, just ye come in the parlor and Patricia will fix us some tea," Ciara said as she reached out to take Colleen's cloak.

The three were barely in the room and the door shut before Colleen spoke. "Something terrible has happened. I was on my way out this morning when I came upon a dreadful man in the alley. He scared Aine out of her mind, poor thing. He was looking for Mr. Dote and claimed to be the husband of our Mrs. O'Shea, although I very much doubt the veracity of his claim." She paused and let the Nolans absorb what she had said.

"What was he doing in your alley? Was anyone with ye? How did he know where to find Mr. Dote," Michael asked.

"He was looking for Mr. Dote, just as he said, I expect. I was alone and I don't know how he knew to come to my home. I told him I had no idea what he was talking about, but he had none of it. He knew well enough that the Dotes were no kin of Mrs. O'Shea and accused us," nodding toward Ciara, "of sending them to claim her."

"How in God's name did he know all of that," Ciara asked?

"I've no idea. Servant's gossip, I guess. That is the usual path of illicit information. He told me we were to mind our business or we would be sorry if we didn't. Then he charged my carriage and sent my mare into a fit. She reared up and almost put the carriage over. I had a time getting her back to the barn."

"Dear God, were ye hurt?" Ciara asked.

"No, dear, I'm just fine, mad as a bag of spiders, though. I'm that certain the drunkard was sent by William Proctor."

"Aye, I expect yer right about that," Michaela greed. "Mr. Pratt was none too pleased to find out that Mrs. O'Shea could not be found and to have the Board involved to boot. He's asked for a full accounting of all of the patients in the hospital and wants us to inform him personally of any deaths. There's only a few of us who keep good records on the patients we see, but that will change now."

"He threatened you? I mean, us? What of the Dotes? Do ye think they are in any danger?" Ciara asked.

"I've sent them away with Maeve to stay with Eve in Batavia. They will be safe enough there, I should hope."

"Aye, they'll be safe enough; 'tis you two I'm worried about," Michael said. "Colleen, ye must go nowhere without an escort, do ye understand? Ciara, the same goes for ye." The stern expression he wore was enough to forestall any false assurances that they would comply with his wishes. "Now just the two of ye listen to me. This man means to cause ye harm, do ye understand? Ye must do as I ask. Ye must!"

"Aye, yer right. I will. I will do as ye ask," Ciara promised.

"As will I," Colleen agreed.

Chapter Twenty-One

Michael seldom took the time during his day to have lunch at the American Hotel on Main Street, as was the usual practice of other well-to-do physicians and business men in Buffalo. He had never had an interest in society and when he was not occupied with the patients in his medical practice, his time was better spent at the poorhouse or the orphan asylum, he thought. While other prominent physicians also gave generously of their time, if not their resources, the number of inmates requiring regular medical care due to injury or illness always outnumbered the physicians present at any time. However, a few days after Mrs. Farrell's encounter with the man in the alley, Michael received an invitation from Sean Farrell to join him there for lunch. The two men had become good friends over the years and Michael valued Sean's counsel. It was time, he thought, to share a few secrets with another member of the Farrell family.

Affluence and privilege filled his senses as he entered the hotel lobby. A delicate cloud of expensive pipe tobacco with notes of port and brandy followed him as he first peeked in the bar to see if Sean had already arrived. There were plenty of men in expensive suits sitting in the bar, but his friend was not among them. The clink of silver on fine china could be heard above the hum of conversation as the founding fathers of Buffalo strengthened alliances among friends, and planned the demise of their enemies. Important things happened at the American Hotel, things that would have an impact on the entire country, so important was the city of Buffalo becoming. Michael's eye caught the maître d' trying to get his attention as he began to scan what he could see of the main dining room. The man spoke as Michael approached. "Welcome to the American Hotel, Dr. Nolan. Mr. Farrell has asked that we seat you at his usual table. He will be along shortly."

It was only a matter of minutes after Michael was seated at a table in the far corner of the dining room that his friend arrived. Sean had taken the table that had been regularly used by his late father as his "usual" table. Cain Farrell had preferred a more private space, where confidences could be exchanged and not overheard, a pearl of wisdom he had passed on to his son. Michael stood and greeted Sean.

"Thanks for joining me on such short notice. I've only just arrived back in town." Sean told him.

""Tis no bother. And how is your lovely fiancée and her people?"

"All are well. I trust the same to be true with the Nolan clan?"

"Aye, we're all well, thank the good Lord."

"I'm glad of it. Please pass on my good wishes to the Edwards. I was that pleased to hear they'd married."

"Aye, I'll do just that. Ye've spoken with yer ma, then?"

"Aye, a bit, about the man in the alley. What on earth was she about sendin' the stable man to the poorhouse, and what's this business about logs in the coffin? What the Devil is she up to now?" Since Cain's death, Sean had become solely responsible for the welfare of his mother and two sisters in addition to running the

Farrell Flower and Seed Company. With Evelyn married and Maeve betrothed, it was his mother who seemed to cause him the most worry. She had always been strong willed and opinionated, but his father had seemed able to keep her in check. Sean was not so skilled at managing his rather determined mother. He had a lodge meeting this evening (like his father, Sean was a Freemason) and he was hoping that Michael could bring him up to speed on Colleen's latest trespasses, as they were bound to be discussed by one or more of the other lodge members.

Michael looked around. He could see William Proctor across the room with his uncle. Confident their conversation could not be overheard, he leaned forward and began to speak. "I won't lie to ye. 'Tis serious business, and no mistake."

Sean's face grew dark as Michael explained that their suspicions had all but been confirmed when the body of Mrs. O'Shea could not be found when Colleen had sent the Dotes to claim her. "Dear God, I'll be after a new stable man, sure enough! Poor old Dote must be thinkin' her mad. They're safe though, the Dotes and Maeve?"

"For now 'tis Ciara and yer ma I'm worried about. Between Pratt trying to save a few dollars by sending the young lads out to work and Proctor misplacing the dead, the Board has been paying closer attention to the poorhouse and its Keepers. I imagine neither man is well pleased about it."

"Ye don't think Pratt sent that blackguard into my alley, do ye?" Sean asked.

"No, I don't, and if Proctor is selling the unclaimed dead to the medical college, I doubt Pratt knows about it. He may have no regard for the people under his care, but he's not a criminal. Now Proctor, he is capable of this and much worse, I fear."

Sean leaned back as the waiter approached the table. Before the lad could even speak, Sean said "Two whiskeys, and bring the bottle." He waited for the waiter to return and pour out two healthy drams before he spoke of the matter again. "What's to be done about all this," he asked.

"For now, nothing, I think," Michael answered. "I should think the Board's directive for better record-keeping and their scrutiny of the day-to-day activity at the poorhouse should be enough for now. Proctor would be a fool to try and continue taking bodies from the death house now."

"And what of yer Ciara and Ma?"

"I've asked them not to confront Proctor and not to go anywhere unescorted. But ye know well they'll do as they see fit."

"Aye, I know that well enough. I'll be in Buffalo for the rest of the winter, and what needs doin' at work can be done from home this time of year, so I'll be able to keep a closer eye on Ma and at least see that she doesn't leave the house without a driver."

Michael raised his class and, with a somewhat suppressed smirk, said "Aye, best of luck to ye!"

On the other side of the room, Reginald Standish sat quietly at his table, plate of food untouched, and watched the exchange between Dr. Nolan and Sean Farrell. It was obvious from the way their heads were bent toward each other that they were discussing something confidential. With his mouth still full of roast venison, William continued to argue his point.

"Shut up, you fool!" his uncle chastised. "What were you thinking sending that drunk over to the Farrell's? You've taken a difficult situation and made it worse. I told you to behave yourself for now and give that damned Board a chance to lose interest. If Sean Farrell believes what Nolan is telling him, and he most certainly will, he'll see to it that the Board's involvement in the management of the poorhouse continues through the winter." As he was speaking he noticed that that both Farrell and Nolan were looking right at him. They held eye contact for longer than what was normal for brief acknowledgement, so Standish raised his glass and smiled briefly in their direction. Turning back to his nephew, he continued, "and you better hope that does not happen or you will have no extra money to spend on your whores!"

William looked briefly over at Sean Farrell's table, unable to keep the arrogant scowl from his face. "Uncle, surely you are not afraid of that an old busy body and a pauper nursemaid? The Farrell's are Catholic, for God's sake. Nobody takes them seriously any more, and Dr. Nolan long ago lost the respect of decent society when he gave up a respectable medical practice in favor of treating vagrants and lunatics. They are fools, the lot of them and they pose no worry for us."

"You'd better hope not."

* * *

It was a cold day, typical of late winter when the white fluffy snow turns to hard-packed grey ice as the Nolan's carriage made its way up the drive to the orphan asylum. Before the carriage could come to a complete stop, the back door flew open and Rolland Thomas came running out. Michael pulled the horse up sharp and still almost ran over the young teacher. Recovering his balance, Rolland stood in front of Michael, heaving as he tried to speak.

More than a little annoyed at this near collision, Michael spoke with an edge to his voice. "Now just ye take a deep breath and tell me what you're on about."

"'Tis Mrs. Kaiser. She's taken a fall down the stairs…" Rolland did not get a chance to finish his sentence because Michael hastily threw the reins at him and jumped down from the carriage with Ciara and Patricia close behind. Just inside the back hall was a stairway leading to the boy's dormitory. Mrs. Kaiser, looking somewhat dazed, was at the bottom landing, with a basket of clean homespun trousers scattered about her and Mrs. Olsen holding her shaking hand. Other than a large and angry bruise taking shape on the right side of her face, he could see no outward sign of injury.

"When did this happen?" Michael asked, taking in the scene of the old woman on the landing, arm clutching the banister, legs sprawled out in front of her. It looked more like she had tried to break her fall, rather than an actual tumble down the stairs. *Thank God*, he thought.

"I wish I could say, and me just arrivin' minutes before ye. I found her, just as ye see her. To be sure I yelled for some help; then I heard the carriage and the good Lord had sent ye just in time," Rolland reported.

Helping Mrs. Olsen up and out of the way, Michael spoke in a gentle voice so as not to startle the disoriented Mrs. Kaiser. "Mrs. Kaiser, you've had a fall, do ye hurt anywhere?" When he received no response to his question, he gently lifted her chin, realizing that she must have hit her head when she fell. After a quick appraisal of head and limbs indicated only the severe bruising on her face, he turned to Mrs. Olsen, hoping for more information. "Had she mentioned as she was feeling unwell this morning?"

"Yes, Doctor, she was telling me she had a fearful

headache not an hour ago. She was going to her chamber to rest after she had seen that the older boys were settled in the dining hall. She could not have been long here because we left the laundry together just a short time ago, only I went up the front to the nursery."

Ciara approached her husband from behind and asked, "What's happened, Michael?"

Turning toward her and at the same time moving her away from the rest of the group, he answered in hushed tones, "An apoplexy, I expect, but I'll need to examine her to be sure." Giving her arm a squeeze and a look that indicated that he could spare no time in conversation until he had examined his patient thoroughly (a look Ciara had seen many times before and knew not to question), he directed his next comments to Rolland, who was still standing by the door with Patricia. "Help me get her up to her chamber." Turning back to Mrs. Kaiser, he said "Let's get ye upstairs for a wee bit o' rest, shall we?"

Rolland was not aware that he was holding Patricia's hand until he had to let it go to help Michael. Giving her hand a squeeze, he told her, "I'm just going to help the doc and then I'd like a word before I leave."

He waited for her nod of agreement and then turned toward Michael. Together they carefully shifted Mrs. Kaiser so that Michael was able to gently lift and carry her up the stairs.

Addressing Mrs. Olsen, Ciara asked "How is it that she was carryin' a basket up the stairs when any one of those lads could 'ave done it for her?"

"It is very important to Mrs. Kaiser that she do her job and do it well. She has said often that it is a blessing for her to be here to take care of the children. She never had any of her own you see, and I think that she is afraid she will be sent back to the Big House if she cannot carry out all of the daily chores."

Ciara looked briefly up, unable to do anything but say a silent prayer for the poor old woman who had believed her one joy in life threatened by her aging body. "Aye, well, she's in the Lord's hands now."

"And Michael's," Patricia added.

"Aye, and Michael's, and there's none who will take better care of her than the two o' them. Now there's work to be done. Patricia ye'd best see what the lads are up to since they've come up from breakfast," she said motioning the two women toward the stairs.

As Ciara headed to her office and Patricia continued up the stairs. She was surprised when she reached the boys dormitory to see Rolland open the door and exit into the hall.

"I thought I'd check to make sure the lads are about their mornin' chores," he told her.

"I thank ye for helping Michael, but will ye not be late for all you've been here a while?" Patricia asked.

"'Tis no bother. I explained to Miss Shaw that I had business to attend to before school that could'na wait, and could she start the morning lesson. She can manage until I arrive."

Patricia stiffened at the mention of Miss Shaw and pressed her lips firmly together, which did not go unnoticed by Rolland. "'Tis lucky for ye to have Miss Shaw to help ye see to yer business."

"Indeed it is, for if she were not able to do the lesson for the mornin', I'd not have been able to come here and see ye." His smile faded, as he realized, yet again, he had managed to say the wrong thing.

"Hmph," Patricia made a noise that indicated that she had not meant the school when she referred to his "business". "And what was so important that ye must leave the children wi' Miss Shaw?" She asked with a slight edge to her voice.

Sensing the conversation might take a turn for the worse, Rolland took both of her hands in his and pulled her away from the door of the dormitory. On an impulse, he kissed her. It was a sweet and gentle kiss, his first as well as hers. While a bit startled, Patricia did not pull away. She felt her lips touch his and relaxed into the kiss. She was secretly relieved that her lips seemed to know what to do, having wondered about that when she had thought about kissing Rolland. When they parted, Patricia, a bit flustered, smiled and said, "So this is the business ye were on about, kissin' young lasses and keepin' them from their work?"

"Not just any young lass, one very special lass," he smiled and kissed her again, longer this time, pulling her closer so he could wrap his arms around her and feel her body melt into his. Her mouth was warm and soft; he wanted to spend the rest of his life right there, in front of the boy's dormitory, kissing her beautiful, warm, soft mouth. His fantasy was rudely interrupted as Patricia abruptly broke the kiss and pushed him away. In a split second, surprise and hurt gave way to understanding and acknowledgement as he, too, heard the squeak of the door and one of the lads on the other side slowly and quietly trying to open it. Nudging Rolland out of the way, Patricia grabbed the handle and jerked the door open from her own side. She gave the boys a fright and struggled to keep the stern look on her face as they all scattered back from the door. "Just what do ye lads think yer doin'? Now just ye clean up this mess, the lot o' ye, and be quick about it while I have a word wi' Mr. Thomas." With a glare that could have turned them to stone, and a slam of the door for good measure, she turned to Rolland, "I'd best get in there or they'll be out the window!"

"Aye, 'tis a long way down from the second floor. Wait just a minute." He took her hand again and lifted her chin with his other so that he could look her in the eyes. "Miss Shaw is a colleague, and a fine one at that, but ye are the lass I can'na stop thinkin' about, and no mistake. I've already asked the Doctor's permission to court ye, but now I'll ask for yours. Patricia Sloane, will ye allow me the honor of courtin' ye? "

"Aye, I will," she answered as a shy smile crept across her face.

"I'm glad of it. Now I'm off to the schoolhouse, but I'll be back for the afternoon lesson and I'll take ye home at day's end." He kissed her one final time and, with a smile, turned to continue down the stairs.

* * *

It had taken Michael about an hour to examine his patient. Still disoriented, the old woman had become agitated over all of the fuss and was still plagued by a severe headache. After he had seen her settled in her room he went to update Ciara and give her instructions for Mrs. Kaiser's care. He opened her office door without knocking, closed the door and took the seat opposite her desk before speaking. "It seems she's suffered an apoplexy," he told her.

"'Tis to do with her brain, aye," Ciara had heard him use the term before.

"Aye, she's lost control of the left side of her body. Ye'll notice her eye and mouth droopin' a bit on that side. She can't use her arm or support her weight with her leg on that side, either," he informed.

"Dear God! What's to be done for her?"

"For now she must rest. She's confused, to be sure, and in pain, I expect. She's a few broken bones on the right side of her face from the fall. There's not much else to be done. If she's to recover any of the use of her body, or her mind, it will be in the next few days, but it could be that she stays this way. For now, keep her comfortable and see that she takes her meals. I'll examine her again when I come to get ye."

"Oh, Michael, that poor, dear woman, I'll see to her myself."

"I expected ye would."

Ciara looked at her husband and realized that an apoplexy was likely something from which Mrs. Kaiser would not recover. "Will she die of this, do ye think?"

"Not right away, but 'tis unlikely she will be able to continue her duties here," he told her.

Ciara's expression changed, as it sometimes did when concern for one thing gave way to concern for something else entirely different. "Michael, ye must have a word wi' Mrs. Olsen and the others and tell them that they are not speak of this outside this asylum. Mrs. Kaiser is technically a ward of the poorhouse, and if Mr. Pratt or, worse yet, Mr. Proctor gets wind she's ill, they'll likely send her back there to convalesce. Michael, that would surely kill her, I know it would. I'll not have her spending her last days in that place!"

Michael rose from his chair and came around behind her desk. Taking her hands, he pulled her up into an embrace. "Now don't ye fret, I'll have a word wi' the women before I leave. Go about yer business and check in on her when ye can. Tomorrow we'll have a better idea of how she'll fare. Ye know well if it comes to it, I'll not let Proctor take herto the Big House, aye?"

"Aye, of course ye won't," Ciara agreed. "Is she in need of anything just now?"

"She's sleeping. If she wakes still with a headache, give her some willow bark tea, but take care, she may have difficulty swallowing it. I'll be back as soon as I'm able." Michael kissed his wife on the forehead and exited the office. He was thinking as the carriage rolled down the drive toward York Street that Ciara was quite right about keeping Mrs. Kaiser at the orphan asylum. He was certain any number of his colleagues who gave of their time at the poorhouse would bleed her freely, or employ cupping (the application of suction cups to enhance the flow of blood, in this case to the brain) or worse yet blistering of the head (the application of caustic agents to the skin to create blisters, which could then be drained and thereby remove any offending toxin). None of these, Michael was certain, would do any good. He had read recently in the Boston Medical and Surgical Journal that apoplexy resulted from a disruption of blood flow to the brain, rather than an imbalance of humors. Indeed, he had seen a few patients treated with these traditional practices die within just a few days. He feared that, in fact, very little could be done and that Mrs. Kaiser would continue to decline until she, too, died. How quickly that might occur, he did not know. The few cases he had seen in his medical practice varied in their symptoms and in their outcomes. One fell into a coma shortly after the incident, never to wake up, another had difficulty swallowing, among other symptoms, and ultimately choked to death; yet another made almost a full recovery, suffering only slight sagging on the left side of the face. The horse seemed to know to turn left on Sixth Street and Michael was so absorbed in Mrs. Kaiser's prospects that he wasn't even aware he had been traveling down that road until he passed the intersection of Sixth and Pennsylvania Streets. He pushed Mrs. Kaiser out of his mind, lest he miss the turn on to Virginia, and pass right by his first house call, for which he was already late.

Chapter Twenty-Two

Mrs. Kaiser saw only minor improvement by day's end. While she still couldn't speak, she had been able to swallow enough to take some tea and broth, and her headache seemed to subside. She and Mrs. Olsen and Mrs. Wilmar were the only three members of the staff who resided at the orphanage. The daytime staff left after supper was served and the children had been put to bed. Four women, all widows, were paid a small wage to come in at night to assist the other three women in the event the children needed anything during the night. The absence of Mrs. Kaiser had left them short staffed in the dining hall, and Rolland had been kind enough to stay and help Patricia while the children had their supper. He had promised Ciara and Michael that he would see Patricia home despite her arguments that she should stay the night to look in on Mrs. Kaiser and help the other women. "I've already asked Annie from the kitchen to stay the night and she's agreed, so remind my sister of that when she tells ye to go on without her. We'll keep a plate warm for ye, so don't let her dawdle," Ciara told him as she prepared to leave for the day.

It took some persuading, but Rolland got Patricia to leave just as the children were being sent off to bed. It had been a busy day and she had not had much time to think about what had transpired between her and Rolland earlier that morning and she was a bit nervous as he took her hand and helped her into the carriage. He was sitting so close and she wondered if he would kiss her again before they arrived home. Now that she had a moment to consider it, she realized that she very much liked kissing him. She enjoyed how his soft lips felt against hers and the way his strong arms felt around her. They passed the ride home in casual conversation. The Lewis boys would be leaving soon, as their aunt had come to keep house for their father. That was a relief, because the Board still hadn't voted on whether they would lower the age that the children could be put out to work. Still, they would both miss the boys terribly when they left. Try as they might, most of the staff almost always became attached to the children who came to live at the orphan asylum, and although they wanted to see them settled with family, or in homes where they would be loved, it was hard to see them leave.

As they chatted, Rolland became aware of how close Patricia was sitting to him. He wanted so badly to put an arm around her and draw her closer still, but he wasn't sure. It seemed so long ago that they had kissed in the hall outside of the lad's dormitory. Her thoughts were still with the orphanage and the people who needed her there. He did not feel that it was right to indulge his own selfish needs. At one point, when they had nearly reached their destination, she was telling him how wee Oskar had given her such a big hug for no reason at all and the smile on her face took his breath away. Rolland stopped the carriage just before turning on to the drive that lead to the Nolan's house. "Ye might think me a scoundrel given all that's happened today, but I find I cannot stop thinkin' about ye and when I might have the chance to kiss ye again."

Patricia smiled, "I don't think ye a scoundrel."

"Would ye mind then if I kissed ye again?"

"I think I'd like that very much."

Dropping the reins and removing his gloves, Rolland held her face in his warm hands. "Ye are truly the most beautiful lass ever I've seen." She smiled as he tilted his head and kissed her gently on the lips. As he pulled away, he could see just a flicker of disappointment in her eyes. She had hoped it would last longer. So he kissed her again, longer this time, sliding his fingers back into her hair and pulling her closer. It was a revelation for both of them that a kiss could have such an effect on their physical bodies, dizziness, racing heart, and other feelings they were just beginning to understand. They parted only when the need to breath required them to, both too overwhelmed to speak. For a while they just held each other, paying no mind to the cold winter night that was settling around them and tried to make sense of what they were feeling. Finally Rolland spoke, quietly at first, testing the words, but then loud enough for her to hear, "I'm that sure I'm in love with ye, Patricia Sloane. I think I've loved ye since the first day I saw yer sweet face, and I'm wonderin' if there's a chance, down the road, that ye might love me back?"

Patricia pulled back so she could look at him. Warm tears stung her cold face as she reached to take his hands in hers. "I think I do love ye back, right now."

"Dear God, can it be true?" Rolland, tears streaming down his own face, kissed her wet cheek.

From the house, Michael could just see the carriage at the top of the drive, although it was too dark to see what its occupants were doing. "What are they still doin' out there?" he asked Ciara who had sent Karyn down to the cabin for the night, insisting that she would clean up the kitchen after Rolland and Patricia had eaten.

"And just what do ye think they're doin'?"

Michael made for the door as he realized the implications of his wife's answer. "Now, just ye stay put," Ciara said, placing a hand on his arm. "Rolland is a good lad, and I'm sure he would do nothin' to compromise Patricia's good name, and it's freezin' out, so let's given them a wee bit o' privacy." Reluctantly, Michael moved away from the door, but was relieved to hear the carriage rolling towards the barn. "Good lad or no, if she follows him into the barn, I'm goin' out there."

"Oh, Michael, can ye not see how in love they are? If they've finally settled matters between them, would ye begrudge them a wee kiss in the barn? After all, the first time ye kissed me was in a barn."

"Aye, I remember it well," he reminisced, with a devilish grin creeping across his face, "and it was all I could do not to take ye right there on the bench, wi' that foolish brute of a horse droolin' down our backs! Ye best hope yer sister doesn't kiss as well as ye do or it will take the both of us to beat Mr. Thomas away!"

"Just ye be nice to the lad and there will be plenty of kisses for ye later," she said as she leaned in to give him a preview of what he might expect should he be on his best behavior while Rolland was there. As it turned out there was no need for either of them to go rushing down to the barn to protect Patricia's virtue. Charlie, having also seen the two parked at the top of the drive, had met them at the barn door and assumed care of the horse and carriage.

Ciara and Michael, still enjoying a playful kiss, parted suddenly when the door opened and Patricia entered with Rolland just behind. The silly grins on both of their faces as they shed cloaks, hats and gloves, left no doubt how things stood between them. Michael stiffened just a bit to see how familiar they were with each other as Rolland helped Patricia off with her cloak, but relaxed his posture and adopted a silly grin of his own when his wife winked and blew him a kiss.

"How was Mrs. Kaiser when ye left?" he asked Patricia.

"Sleeping, poor dear. The women had things well in hand with the children when we left, but I daresay it will not be easy managin' without her."

"Aye, I was thinkin' about how we've a few less children than we did in the fall, for all we're still burstin' at the seams, so Mr. Proctor may wonder about a request for more help, and him thinkin' Mrs. Kaiser is still able to work," Ciara mentioned.

Before Patricia could even speak, Michael gave her a stern look and said, "Just ye save yer breath. We'll no' have ye livin' at the orphan asylum!"

"But Michael, did ye not just hear yer wife? There'll be no help from the Big House and there's no money to hire another girl at night," Patricia protested.

"Now Patricia, don't ye fret," Ciara said. "Mrs.

Kaiser had charge of the older lads during the night and ye know well that it's usually quiet up there. 'Tis only when the sick ward is occupied that we'd be in need of help. We'll manage for now as we are and not risk asking for more help unless we are in desperate need."

"I could help," Rolland offered. His words struck them silent and all eyes were on him. "I'm there most days anyway, and 'twould be no trouble to see the children to their supper then to bed. The orphan asylum is closer to the school than Mrs. Cornish's is, so were I to spend the night when need be, I'd be that much closer to work."

Patricia turned to him, eyes glistening with tears. "You would do that for them?"

"Aye, I'd do it for them, and for ye," he said taking her hand. "The Doc is quite right about ye not livin' there. Ye must be home with yer family at day's end." The expression of joy on her face was enough to make him want to kiss her again, but he just held her hand and returned her smile with one of his own.

Michael cleared his throat to break the spell that seemed to be cast between Rolland and Patricia. "That is a most kind offer, Mr. Thomas, but one we can't take ye up on. 'Tis one thing usin' yer time to help teach the lads and lasses, but 'tis quite another to ask ye to take on their full time care."

"Aye, Michael's right," Ciara added. "Yer that kind to help us the way ye do. We can ask no more of ye, Mr. Thomas."

Rolland paused a minute and considered what he was about to say. Taking Patricia's hand again, he said. "As yer likely to be seein' quite a bit o' me in the future, I'd like it fine if ye'd call me Rolland. As for helpin' out more at the orphanage, I'm glad to do it, and as I see it, ye've no other choice in the matter. Mrs. Nolan, ye said as ye'd have Mr. Proctor wonderin' why ye needed more help when ye have fewer children. Ye also said as ye could manage most nights unless some of the children take sick. So, we are only talkin' about a few extra hours after lessons to help with the supper and putting the young ones to their beds. I might also add that should I stay those extra few hours, I'd be that happy to see that Miss Patricia comes home at a decent hour."

Ciara looked at her husband, who nodded and said, "I thank ye, Rolland, and we'd be that pleased if ye'd call us Ciara and Michael."

A Whisper of Bones

* * *

The door to the bunk house opened and Charlie came in, bringing the cold winter night with him. He quickly shut it and quietly tiptoed over Bruns and Ellie, who were sleeping on a pallet on the floor until the cabin could be enlarged in the spring. Karen was sitting at the small table (another thing that would have to be made larger come spring) watching her children sleep peacefully in their new home. She often thought, and was glad when she did, that they would have no memory of their brief time at the poorhouse. They were both born there, and had it not been for the graciousness of the Nolans, the two might have spent a good portion of their childhood there.

So much had happened during that first year of their lives. It would have been unlikely that they would have even survived their own births but for the fact that Dr. Nolan had delivered both of them. More than half of the infants born before Dr. Nolan came were not so lucky. As it was, Ellie's birth mother died in childbed. Just a few months into their short lives, they had survived a deadly outbreak of scarlet fever that had claimed the other four infants in the nursery. They narrowly missed exposure to influenza, which had struck the poorhouse inmates the very day they left that place for good.

Life outside the poorhouse was not without risks. Children still died of diseases like scarlet fever and influenza, but with the Nolans they had regular and healthy meals and the undivided attention not only of their mother, but of the other adults as well. They were safe and protected here, and above all else, they had the unconditional love of a large family. That was something Karyn feared they would never have. Hearing the door open, she lit a candle to accompany the pot of tea that was waiting for her husband's return from his virtuous errand. "You could have allowed Herr Thomas to put away the horse," she said as she poured tea.

"Aye, well sure enough the Doc will thank me in the mornin'. He should be also be thankin' the good Lord that he didn't see what Herr Thomas was doin' wi' our Patricia up at the top o' the drive, or he'd 'ave been wi' his rifle to greet them."

"Ah, you did not seem to mind when the doctor and Ciara lingered in the barn before they were married. She was not much older than Patricia is now. You know they will be married, I do not see the problem with a little kiss in the barn."

Looking at his wife with a fiendish smirk that appeared more dangerous in the shadows of the candlelight, he said "There's no such thing as a little kiss in that barn! For all they've been married for years now, the Doc and Miss Ciara still spend too much time in the barn. Ye know full well what that young lad would 'ave been about in that barn, and Patricia still an innocent young lass!"

Karyn smiled. "Meine shatz, she is no longer a young lass. She is a young woman. No doubt they will have their time in that barn, as we all have. You cannot stop them from growing up. Patricia has always been wise beyond her years and she has chosen well. Herr Thomas would not be with her just to please himself. He loves her and he will marry her."

"Well, we'd best build a bigger barn, aye!" Charlie said and then he kissed his wife such that the talking portion of the evening was over.

Chapter Twenty-Three

March 3, 1841

In an otherwise busy day, I have permitted myself a few moments to consider the events that lead to the current status at the orphan asylum. It has been many weeks since Mrs. Kaiser's fall down the stairs and very little has changed in her condition. She can swallow broth and tea, but still cannot chew, or speak. The poor dear can only whimper or grunt should she even try and speak. She stays to her bed and most of the time confined within her own mind. I can only imagine what's in her thoughts. Twice in the last two days I have brought one of the babes from the nursery to visit. Although Mrs. Kaiser could not hold them, she seemed comforted by their presence and was at peace, if only for a short time.

Sitting in this chair, I realize that it has been some time since I have actually sat in my own office. The bookwork is done at home these days as there is not a moment to be spared during the day for such activities. Patricia and Rolland (God love them both) are kept busy seeing the older children through their lessons, their chores and their meals, which leaves me to help with the washing and such. Surprisingly, the entire staff has remained silent and Mr. Proctor remains unaware of Mrs. Kaiser's accident or her convalescence here. This is nothing short of a miracle, given the speed at which news like this usually travels, and is either a testament to the staff's loyalty or to their dislike of William Proctor. I suspect 'tis a bit of both.

William Proctor was in a foul mood as his driver turned up the long road that led to the poorhouse. Plans to visit the family hunting lodge in Clarence were thwarted by a heavy snowfall and he had lost at cards for the third night in a row the previous evening. He was short on funds these days, as the usual sources that supplemented his meager income had apparently run dry. He had been unable to divert anymore of the poorhouse's winter stores for sale to the taverns in the Canal District. It was always easier in summer when produce from the farm was plentiful, but that damned doctor and his wife seemed to be aware of every head of cabbage, ounce of cheese and dried beef that stocked the pantry shelves. Also, there hadn't been a death in weeks, not that it would have been easy to accommodate the desperate need of his uncle's anatomical theater with the poorhouse physicians reporting directly to Pratt. Proctor's mood did not improve when he saw that Mr. Pratt's carriage was parked near the barn. *What the hell does he want?* Proctor thought, as the carriage pulled up to the front door. Exiting without a word to the driver, for he had no respect for servants and spoke to them only when necessary, he approached the building. Mr. Pratt was waiting in his old office, now William's, not in the chair reserved for guests, but in the one behind the desk. He had the death book open and was writing something in it when William entered.

"Have you taken your old job back?" William asked casually as he removed his coat and casually glanced down at the ledger.

"I had come to see you on another matter, but was just informed by Dr. Ferris that one of the men has died." Looking at the note next to the ledger, he continued, "One of the stable men, name's Buchman, Owen Buchman. Was dropping hay and had a heart attack, poor fool. I was just entering him into the ledger. There were Buchmans in the First Ward a few years back. I seem to recall one of grandfather's grooms with that name, so hopefully someone will claim him. See to it first thing tomorrow."

William's face betrayed no interest in what his superior had just told him, but his mind immediately began to consider the possibilities. The man had had a heart attack. That would do just fine. He would worry about the details later. Feigning indifference, which he had perfected over a lifetime, he asked, "What was the other matter you were here for?"

"I daresay, you will not be pleased, but the Board met yesterday specifically to discuss the age limit at which children could be bound out. Of course, Mrs. Farrell saw to it that Dr. Nolan was there to speak on the children's behalf and he was successful in convincing the rest of the board not to lower the age despite my detailed explanation of the costs associated with the orphan asylum."

Truthfully, Proctor couldn't care less how much it cost to run the orphan asylum or the poor farm, for that matter, but he knew better than to reveal his true thoughts on the matter. "We should have known better than to expect otherwise. The Nolans care not for the cost involved in providing for the poor. Mrs. Nolan is constantly over here demanding more milk, more cheese. The sale of these products helps to defray our costs, but she keeps insisting the children need more. The Board should have never placed a woman in charge at the orphanage or as their Chair. They know nothing of financial matters." Proctor chose his words carefully. Keeping Pratt's attention focused on the costs of the orphan asylum rather than on the death at the poorhouse was important to the success of his plan to divert the recently deceased inmate to the medical college. He needed the Superintendent out of his hair.

"Well, I am glad that you have finally decided to take your position seriously. We have lost this argument for the time being, but we must devise some cost cutting measures at the orphan asylum. I would like to replace the night nurses with inmates. There are enough able-bodied women here, and their duties at the orphanage would be at night, so they would not interfere with any tasks that need doing here during the day."

"Shall I send for Mrs. Nolan this afternoon?" Proctor asked. After several surreptitious glances at the ledger, he had noticed that Pratt had only written the date of Buchman's death thus far in the death book. If he could keep him distracted, the man might just leave without completing the entry. "I can speak to Mrs. Rowan immediately and have four women over there by this evening."

Rising from behind the desk, the entry in the death book all but forgotten, Pratt agreed that it was best to replace the paid widows with poorhouse inmates as soon as possible. "Send word for Mrs. Nolan to come straight away." Just before he exited the room, Pratt turned for one final statement. "Make this work, Mr. Proctor. We've had enough interference from the Board. A favorable review at year's end is in both of our best interests."

William smiled, pleased with himself for having manipulated the situation to further his interests. "I will handle Mrs. Nolan." After Pratt left the office, William went to his desk and read the ledger to be sure nothing other than the date of Mr. Buchman's death had been entered. Seeing only a date, he closed the book and tossed the death notice into the coal stove.

Proctor stayed in his office for the next hour, not wanting to arouse any suspicion by visiting the death house too soon after Pratt's departure. He began to contemplate the problem of Mrs. Nolan. The body would have to be moved soon, before Mulligan or Buxton realized there was a body in the death house. The two men, who were currently helping in the snow removal outside, had lost their nerve after the incident with Margaret O'Shea and could no longer be relied upon to act discreetly on Proctor's behalf. Moving the body during the day was risky, particularly today, when there would be foot traffic between the orphan asylum and the Big House. The last thing he needed was for Mrs. Nolan to become aware of his activities.

Perhaps this recent turn of events with the night nurses would be enough of a distraction to keep her out of his business for a while. He doubted it and annoyance was again gaining favor as he realized that he would have to pay a call on the orphanage himself. He could not risk her coming here and learning of Buchman's death, although he had doubts that she would even come if he sent for her. The woman simply did not know her place. His mood continued to sour as he dwelled on what a thorn in his side she had become, and now he was all but broke because of her. He needed to get rid of Ciara Nolan. Nothing too drastic. He didn't have the stomach for violence. He just needed her to stay out of the affairs of the poorhouse. William Proctor was not a violent man, but he knew someone who was. A smile spread slowly across the face of The Keeper as he realized a way to make sure Ciara Nolan would not set foot near the poorhouse for the foreseeable future.

The men were still clearing snow from the path between the Big House and the orphan asylum, and he knew the person he was looking for most certainly would not be among them. Patting the pocket on the inside of his coat to make sure that the flask was still there, he headed down to the barn. He would have a brief word with a particular inmate before he set out.

Ciara was just coming up from the laundry, a basket of clean clouts in her arms, when Proctor entered the asylum using the back door, which was the closest to the path between the two institutions. As the man was never at work this early and had never before used the back door, Ciara greeted him warily. "Mr. Proctor, whatever are ye doin' here at this hour?"

"I have just had a discussion with Mr. Pratt, who is growing even more concerned with the costs associated with your facility." Taking in her appearance (she had been wearing less formal clothes to work since she was, once again, sharing in the daily chores) and the basket in her arms he commented, "I came hoping to have a word, but you appear to be otherwise engaged."

"Just ye take a seat in my office and I'll run these up to the nursery."

"Mrs. Nolan, I believe I sent over several inmates to help with these chores. I do not have time to wait while you do their work for them. Put down that basket and accompany me to your office where I can state my business and be on my way! We don't tolerate such behavior at the poor farm and you should not either. I can have a word with the women and remind them of the consequences of shirking their duties if you are unable to control them."

The look of panic turned so quickly to anger that Ciara doubted Proctor even saw the expression on her face change. She placed the basket on the stairs and turned toward the keeper. "Mr. Proctor, ye may run the poorhouse as ye see fit, and I'll do the same here. Now, if ye are in such a hurry, state yer business here, as I, too, have little time to be waitin' around."

"So be it. As I said, Mr. Pratt is concerned with the growing costs of this asylum. Since you are unwilling to put the younger waifs out to work, costs have to be cut elsewhere. As of this evening, your night nurses will be replaced by inmates. No sense in paying wages when we have able-bodied women." When he finished talking, he took a half step back, anticipating her wrath. He was surprised when it did not come.

"Aye, well, if it keeps the children here until we can find suitable home for them, 'tis worth the sacrifice, I suppose." She did not mention her concern for the widows and how they would continue to survive without their income because she was as anxious for him to leave as he was and she knew he did not care. "I'll send word 'round this afternoon. Be warned: ye'll have Mrs. Farrell in yer office tomorrow if ye send over anyone fond o' the drink."

He was too surprised with her willingness to accept his news to reply with disdain or indifference. He simply said, "I shall see that they come over early this evening to receive whatever instruction you deem necessary. Good day, Mrs. Nolan."

As Mr. Proctor left, Patricia was coming down

stairs in search of the basket of clean clouts desperately needed up in the nursery. "Was that Mr. Proctor?"

Ciara let out a sigh of relief and answered, "Aye, and no. He knows nothing of Mrs. Kaiser, thank God."

"What brought him here," Patricia asked?

"Mr. Pratt wants to replace the night nurses with women from the Big House. I assumed there would be some price to pay for the board's decision about the children, and I don't think Mr. Pratt was deliberately trying to be cruel…still, I worry about how the widows will get by."

"I'm that sorry for ye havin' to tell them tonight. To be sure none will be pleased about the change," Patricia remarked.

"They won't be needed tonight, Mr. Proctor is sendin' over four women this afternoon, so I'll have to go and tell them straight away. The poor dears, I can only hope they find some other way to make ends meet. 'Twas not much they earned, but it put food on the table."

"Will he not give us some time to give these new women some proper trainin'?" Patricia asked.

"Oh, to be sure he's sendin' them over early so as

to receive any instruction we deem necessary!" Ciara rolled her eyes as she repeated William's statement. "Ye know well that he thinks just about any woman would be suited to carin' for children and therefore little instruction would be necessary. Just the same, I shall keep Mrs. Mc Claverly on for just a few more days until I am sure that the children are comfortable with the new women. They love her as much as they love ye." Ciara's expression became sad as she realized what an adjustment this would be for the children.

"Ciara, I would like to stay too. Ye know that wee Oskar has been havin' nightmares, and Molly and Sean are newly arrived and still scared to sleep at night, poor wee things, and someone's got to remember to wake up wee Mosze to use the chamber pot," Patricia argued.

"Now sister, I'll not have this conversation with ye one more time. Not one more time, ye hear? Just ye write down all of the children and their special needs and when the new women arrive, ye'll tell them the whole of it. Now, I've got to go across town to Cherry Street and call on Mrs. Schneider and then to Rogues Hollow for the rest. Mrs. Dorsey and Mrs. Clark live near one another, so if I take the carriage, I should be back by midday. Can ye spare me until then?"

"We've no choice about it, do we? Just ye go now. We'll be fine until ye get back."

Ciara started out on foot towards Michael's clinic on Niagara Street, where she could pick up the carriage and continue on her journey across the city of Buffalo. Michael would be none too pleased at her driving unescorted to Rogues Hollow, but William Proctor had left her no other option. She would not let these poor widows make their way through the snow to the orphanage only to be told that they were no longer needed.

Owing to the remote location of the poorhouse and orphan asylum with respect to the center of the city, the walk to Michael's clinic on Niagara Street would be a solitary one, as there was seldom any traffic and but a few farmsteads on the outer rim of the city. As Ciara walked along, her thoughts focused on how she would break the news of their termination to each of the widows. She hadn't noticed that a man crossed the public square running between York and Connecticut Streets. Walking briskly, he caught up to her as she was about to turn on to Niagara Street."Ah, Miss Sloane, beggin' yer pardon, Mrs. Nolan, imagine meetin' ye here on this chilly day."

Ciara froze, she recognized the voice immediately, and suddenly, even before she turned around, her other senses filled with memories of him: the smell of cheap whiskey and rotting teeth on his breath, the shabby clothing and grime beneath his fingernails, the thud of metal hitting bone (so hard did she hit him over the head with a shovel, she again felt the searing pain travel up her arms). Panic had begun to take root, but she quickly pushed it aside. It would do her no good, here on an empty road with Angus McLean. Taking a deep breath, she steeled her nerves to face the man who had attacked and nearly raped her at the poorhouse, the man whose brutality she believed had left her barren. Anger replaced fear as she turned toward him. "I should have let them kill ye in the barn that day!" she spat.

"Now, now, Mrs. Nolan, can ye no' spare a kind word for an old friend?" He made no attempt to hide his appraisal or his approval and she felt as if something was slithering down her neck as his eyes fell below her cold stare. "Ye've improved yer prospects to be sure. Bein' the wife of a doctor suits ye."

"Mr. McLean, ye are a blackguard and certainly no friend of mine. I've no business with ye, so be on yer way."

"Oh, I'll be on my way in just a bit, but yer wrong, Mrs. Nolan." His voice dropped just a bit, no longer playfully taunting her, and his expression became more serious, almost menacing. "We've business to discuss, ye and I."

"I've nothing to say to ye!" She turned to walk away, but he grabbed her arm. She stiffened, realizing she had no means of defending herself. "Let go of me!"

"Aye, I let go of ye once, I'll no' be so quick to do it again, for all ye damned near killed me last time. To be sure yer still a feisty wee bitch, so ye are, but 'tis just ye and me, and no stable men about to come to yer aid, and I've a thing or two to say to them as well."

"Let go of me!" Ciara tried again to jerk her arm away, but only succeeded in losing her balance. The terror of that day in the barn came flooding back as McLean dragged her by the arm to her feet. She began to kick him as hard as she could, not even knowing what part of his body she was hitting, and was only spared the back of his hand across her face when

McLean ducked to avoid being hit by a flying object.

"Just ye get away from her!" Rolland was galloping down Niagara Street and pulled up abruptly in front of them, both he and the horse heaving and nearly obscured by the steam their collective breath made as it hit the cold air. He swung down from the horse, grabbed the wooden paddle that had narrowly missed its intended target and advanced on McLean. "Get back, I say!"

Wary from past experience and weakened from years of living in the streets, McLean had no interest in a physical confrontation with the younger and stronger man, even if his only weapon was a wooden paddle. "Now, just ye calm down sir. Mrs. Nolan and I were just havin' a friendly word."

"It didn't look friendly to me. Be on yer way, sir," Rolland demanded.

McLean held up his hands in a gesture of surrender. "I'll be on my way back to the poor farm," he said, catching Ciara's eye as he turned and walked away.

"And just ye stay there, and if I should find out you've darkened this woman's path again, ye won't be welcome there either!" Turning to Ciara, he did a quick visual inspection and could find no evidence of injury.

"Are ye hurt?"

"No, frightened is all. I knew that man before, years ago."

The expression on her face told him that whatever had happened years ago still left scars today and he did not press her for details. "Let's get ye home. Yer freezin'." Rolland tried to steer her in the direction of his horse, but she resisted.

"I was on my way to Michael to get the carriage, and then I'm afraid I must find each of the night nurses and tell them they've been relieved of their duties."

"What? Why?"

"Mr. Pratt has decided to save a few dollars by replacing the night nurses with women from the Big House. Mr. Proctor is sending them over this afternoon. I'm tryin' to spare the poor widows the trip in only to find out their not needed anymore. If ye could just take me to Michael's, I'll get the carriage and be on my way."

"You'll do no such thing; yer as white as the snow. I'm takin' ye home, and no argument. I'll see to the widows and ye tell me where each of them lives."

Suddenly feeling her stomach lurch, Ciara turned

and was sick right where she stood. When she was finished, she was even paler (if that was possible) and she began to shake uncontrollably. Rolland took her in his arms "Now, ye've had a good fright, but we'll just get ye home and a good hot cup o' tea and you'll be that much better for it."

Ciara stood in his arms until she got control of herself. When she felt she could, she pulled away. "He was cruel to me back then, very cruel." She was about to say more, but her expression became curious and she asked instead, "Whatever were ye doin' out here at this hour, and yer supposed to be at school?"

"Well, I daresay, I scarce believed it myself until I saw ye in the road and that man about to whack ye. I was goin' about the mornin's lesson, and wee Martha screamed and looked as if she'd seen a ghost. She insisted that ye were in trouble and that I should ride out here straight away. She carried on so, I'd no choice but to ride out. I just happened to grab this on my way out the door." Rolland held up the paddle still in his hand. It hung on the door of the schoolhouse and was meant for disciplinary action when the kids misbehaved. Its mere presence kept the children in line and Rolland had always been grateful that he had never had to use it until now.

With Ciara astride, he walked the horse the long distance to the Nolan farm. He left her in Karyn's capable hands and had a quick word with Charlie and then both men left the farm. Rolland set out in the direction of Rogues Hollow while Charlie went down Niagara Street to inform Michael.

"Now just ye stop fussin' over me, I'm fine," Ciara protested as Karyn laid out her dressing gown and lit the fire in her chamber. "'Tis not even noon yet and I've no intention of spendin' the day in bed. I'll just have a cup of tea and Alex can take me back to the children. Patricia will be wonderin' where I've gone off to. "

"You will stay where you are. Charlie will stop and have a word with Patricia after he has spoken to your husband."

"I've already told ye, I'm fine. There's no need to be botherin' Michael. He's likely already left to do house calls by now."

"Ciara, you have just told me that Angus McLean has come back. I know what that man did to you. Surely you do not expect me to let you go back to the orphan asylum with him just over at the Big House."

"What on earth is he doin' back here?" Ciara asked, taking the hot cup of tea into her cold hands.

"Why would he not go back? The man knows nothing of hard work, only drink. He has grown tired of living on the street."

Ciara shivered, although the chamber was warm. Karyn took the cup from her and handed her the dressing gown. "Here, get into bed and I'll bring you something to eat."

"No, don't leave!" The reality of Angus McLean living back at the poorhouse, a stone's throw from the orphan asylum, left Ciara feeling frightened and insecure. "Could ye maybe just sit with me for a bit?"

Chapter Twenty-Four

Alex walked out of the barn at the sound of hoofs galloping up the drive. Michael dismounted a horse Alex had never seen before, borrowed in haste no doubt. "Is she hurt?" he asked as he handed his friend the reins.

"She's had a good fright to be sure, but she's seems well enough."

"I'll be the judge of that," Michael stated as he began to walk in the direction of the house.

"Doc, 'twas Angus McLean who she met on the road."

"What? When the Devil did he come back?"

Alex had no answer to that question and Michael was torn between checking to make sure his wife was unharmed and going to the poorhouse and beating McLean to within an inch of his life. Alex could see the war going on in his mind. "Now, just ye go and see te yer wife. As soon as Charlie gets back, he and I will go after McLean."

"No, don't do that. I will go and see Proctor tomorrow. If McLean is there, we'll tell the Keeper and insist that the man is sent away." Alex was not pleased to receive this directive. He and Charlie had sent McLean on his way once already with a few broken bones and several missing teeth and they were willing to do it again for anguish he was causing Ciara. However, he would respect the doctor's wishes, for now.

Michael took the stairs two at a time and reached his chamber on the second floor before he had removed his coat. He opened the door without knocking and stood in the entry for a minute, a sigh of relief audible. She had no outward signs of injury, unlike the last time, when her faced was bruised almost beyond recognition. He went to her and pulled his wife into his arms. "Dear God, did he hurt ye?"

"No, I've just been tellin' Karyn that I'm fine and I'll need to be getting' back to the children." Karyn got up from her chair, announcing the need for more tea as she left the room. The minute she did, Michael took Ciara's face in his hands and looked into her eyes. "Tell me." Ciara let loose the panic and fear she had been holding back since the moment she recognized the voice of Angus McLean. Her lips began to quiver and tears streamed down her face, within seconds she was sobbing.

Michael held her for a long while and did not say a word as she worked her way through the fear, the heartbreak and then the anger. When she had calmed down, still holding her, he asked, "Are ye able to tell me what happened?"

Ciara reached under her pillow for a handkerchief, wiped her eyes and her nose before speaking. "I was on my way to you to fetch the carriage. Mr. Pratt had replaced the night nurses with women from the Big House and I didn't want the widows making their way over to the orphanage in the snow only to be told they were no longer needed. I was distracted in my thoughts and didn't hear him come up behind me."

"Did he grab ye?"

Nodding she said, "Only when I tried to get away. I started kicking him and then Rolland was there and threw a paddle at him."

"Thank God for Rolland and his paddle."

"Actually, we should thank Martha. She had some kind of fit at school and insisted that I was in trouble. She just kept carryin' on until he rode out to find me."

"How on earth did she know that?"

"To be sure I've no idea. We'll have to ask her when she comes home."

"'Tis not the first time wee Martha has seen danger before it's happened, now that I think on the matter. She told me to check my horse carefully before I set out for the Abernathy's lodge a few weeks past. Sure enough the mare had a stone lodged in her hoof."

"Do ye know, she told me just the other day that the babes will have itchy eyes. I asked whatever did she mean by that, and she told me she saw three newborn babes with red, puffy eyes that felt itchy. I asked when she had been to the orphan home, and she said she hadn't been, but the babes would come. I thought she was tellin' tales. Do ye think we've a seer in the family?" Ciara asked, unsure herself if she was asking seriously or not.

"Well, I guess we'll know soon enough!" Michael answered.

* * *

William Proctor had returned to his office, waiting for Angus McLean to report back. What a stroke of good luck that the man should return to the poorhouse now. Although he was older and worse for wear, Mrs. Rowan had recognized him right away. She had an annoying habit of bending the Keeper's ear with tales of recidivist inmates and their habits. Her discussion of Angus McLean began like all the others, with comments on his laziness and fondness for whiskey, but Proctor became interested when she told him about how McLean had attacked Mrs. Nolan, then Miss Sloane, in the barn. She went on, sparing no detail, about the brutal beating and the extent of Ciara's injuries. "She nearly died, so she did," the matron had told him. Proctor had sent McLean out to find Ciara as she walked the long road to Niagara Street. He had been clear; she wasn't to be harmed, just scared sufficiently to stay away from the poorhouse for a while.

Proctor had no tendency toward violence, but he was more than angry at Mrs. Nolan's interference with his activities. Furthermore, he had run out of money. If McLean accomplished his task, Proctor would trust him with the rest of the plan. With Buxton and Mulligan no longer available to do his bidding, he would need someone who wasn't afraid to do what needed to be done. He was brought out of his thoughts by a knock on the door. McLean did not wait for a response before he walked in the Keeper's office.

"Did you find her," Pratt asked.

"Aye."

"Mr. McLean, I don't have all day to hear the details. Tell me what happened."

"Aye, I followed her out as ye asked. We were just gettin' to our business when some young lad came galloping up and chased me away. But don't ye fret, Mr. Proctor, she knows I'm here and I daresay she'll no' be comin' here any time soon."

Proctor smiled, he had found his man. "Mr. McLean, you appear to be a man I can rely on to help with some of the more difficult tasks. I believe I can make it worth your while if you should be willing to assist me with a transportation issue."

"I'm listenin'."

Proctor passed the next half hour filling McLean in on his relationship with the Department of Anatomy at the Geneva Medical College and the specifics of how the bodies were transported. "We've got to move the body tonight. I'm sure after your little reunion with Mrs. Nolan the good doctor will be in my office first thing in the morning to demand I put you out. He could be a bigger problem than his wife if he starts poking around the sick ward."

"No, don't ye fret, sir. Ye've put yer faith in the right man. I'll see to poor old Buchman and anyone else who comes along, so long as ye stick te yer end of the bargain."

Since Proctor only used the Keepers quarters for card games, he had no problem consenting to its occasional use by McLean for "entertaining." As long as he cleared the whores and the whiskey bottles out when Proctor needed the place, it made no difference to him."I'll see that you have a key," the Keeper assured him.

"Well then, enjoy yer card game tonight and leave the rest to me. And if ye'd be so kind as to leave me a bottle when yer done for the night, I'll be needin' something to warm me bones when I get back from my long journey."

* * *

Knowing that Ciara's absence from the orphan asylum would place a heavier burden on the other women, Rolland made a quick stop at the school on his way back from the first Ward to tell Miss Shaw that he would not be returning. He arrived at the orphanage just as Charlie was leaving and he assured the man that he would see Patricia home safely.

"Now just ye listen, lad. This McLean is trouble and no mistake. Ye know as well as I do that with Mrs. Nolan not here and four new women coming from the Big House that Miss Patricia won't leave. I know the Doc would be that grateful if ye took a pallet here in the kitchen for the night, and ye keep Patricia safe. He's a cruel man, is Angus McLean."

Rolland had been running all over the city completing Ciara's errand and was only now beginning to understand the threat that Angus McLean posed. There was no way he would allow Patricia to stay there unprotected. "Aye, I'll stay."

"And ye'll *stay* on a pallet in the kitchen or ye'll have me to answer to if the Doc doesn't kill ye!"

The rest of the day passed in a blur. The remaining staff worked together seamlessly to cover for the absence of Ciara and Mrs. Kaiser. Rolland helped where he could, keeping the older children busy so that the women could see to the regular daily chores. They each took turns looking in on Mrs. Kaiser. There wasn't much time to talk until late afternoon, just before the arrival of the new night nurses. Rolland quietly opened the door of the nursery, being careful not to wake the babes who slept peacefully, oblivious to the flurry of activity that was going on around them. Raising his hand, he motioned for Patricia to join him in the hall.

"The women will be over from the Big House within the hour, I expect," he told her. "What are we to do about Mrs. Kaiser?"

"Oh dear, with all that's happened today, I never even gave it any thought." She had been preoccupied all day with worry over her sister and concern about how the children would take to the new nurses. She had not realized that the new night nurses might threaten their secret.

"Aye, I hadn't either, until Mrs. Olsen asked me," Rolland told her. "She suggested we tell the women that Mrs. Kaiser has a touch of the ague and has been confined to her bed by Doctor Nolan."

Patricia looked worried. They had all been very careful not to speak of Mrs. Kaiser's little improved condition inside or outside of the orphanage. Without knowing who Mr. Proctor would send over to help, they could not be sure if any of the women would betray their trust. "Aye, I think that will do for now," she agreed, although she was still unsure."Oh, Rolland, what will we do if they find out about poor old Mrs. Kaiser?"

Rolland took her hand and tried to give her a reassuring smile. "I don't think they will, at least not tonight anyway. They'll be busy meeting the children and learning the way of it here, so there won't be much time for anything else. They'll be gone tomorrow first thing, so 'tis only these next few hours we need be concerned."

"I'll stay, just in case Mrs. Kaiser or one of the children needs me," Patricia declared, "and I'll hear no argument from ye about it."

"I wouldn't dream of it," he assured her. "I'll be right down in the kitchen if I'm needed during the night."

Patricia smiled. "Yer a good man, Rolland Thomas and I love ye for it."

"Aye, I'm glad of it, now away ye downstairs. With yer sister gone it's on to you to meet the new nurses and show them around. I'll send Mrs. Olsen up to sit with the babes. I should think she'd be grateful for a wee sit down." Pulling her in for a reassuring kiss, he noticed that she looked tired and a bit pale. "Is there somethin' else on yer mind?" he asked.

"I'm that worried for Ciara. I can't stop thinking about the last time she met Angus McLean. He nearly beat her to death. Charlie and Alex threatened to kill him if he came back here, and they meant it. He left here in nearly as bad a shape as my sister. I can't stop myself from wonderin' what would have happened if ye hadn't ridden out to find her. He is an evil man, Rolland, and he frightens me."

Rolland pulled her closer again, holding her as he spoke. "But I did find her and she was unharmed. Don't ye fret about the McLean. He's no match for the lot o' us. If he crosses paths with ye or yer sister it will be more than just Alex and Charlie he'll have to deal with." He pulled away so that she could see the certainty in his eyes. "Yer mine now, Patricia Sloane, and I'll see to it that yer safe, always." He kissed the palm of her

A Whisper of Bones

hand and then held it to his heart.

* * *

The early part of the evening passed in a similar fashion as the rest of the day had. The four women had come over just before supper and only had time for a brief introduction to the rest of the staff and a quick tour before they met the children and commenced their duties. It was during supper that Patricia and the other staff members got to know a bit more about each of them. Jane Loderick was born of German parents, but had lived all of her 35 years in Buffalo. She was a kind woman who had lost her husband to typhoid fever over the winter. Barbara Whaler had recently arrived from Ireland with her husband. They had been in and out of the poorhouse all winter owing to her husband's failing health - intermittent fever, the doctor had told her. Emily Munroe, a young Scottish woman, had lost her baby and nearly died of childbed fever a few months back. Only recently recovered, she seemed happy to be out of the poorhouse, if only for the night. Susan McManus was reluctant to share her story, and was content to just listen as everyone became acquainted each other.

All things considered, Patricia could find no fault in any of the women that Proctor had sent over, and although many of the children were shy around the newcomers, none seemed frightened of them. They all accepted the explanation of Mrs. Kaiser's absence without question, much to the relief of the rest of the staff. Patricia lay in her cot late in the evening, having given up any possibility of sleep hours before, and listened to the sounds of the house settling around her. Having spent most of her young life caring for children, she had learned the knack of sleeping with an ear for crying or otherwise distressed children. Concerned that the new nurses might sleep through the night, oblivious to the sound of small feet padding across the floor or the chamber pot sliding out from underneath the bed, she lay on her cot still fully clothed, ready if any of the children needed her.

Too tired at the end of the day to make a proper pallet, Rolland laid his coat on the scrubbed floorboards of the kitchen and rolled up his scarf for a pillow. He marveled at how so few women could accomplish so much in a single day, and was even more impressed that they were able to continue their pace day in and day out. This wasn't the ideal place for a child to live, but the women here did their very best to provide a clean and nurturing place for the growing number of children who had no parents to call their own. His thoughts were interrupted by the unmistakable sound of wagon wheels traveling fast over the frozen road. He lay still, straining to hear if his ears had betrayed him. They had not; someone was leaving the poorhouse. *Where would anyone be going at this hour?* he thought.

Getting up to look out the kitchen window, the full moon shining down on the snow covered road allowed for visibility all the way over to the Big House. He could see the wagon. What was it hauling? Was that a casket? Who would be leaving the poorhouse with a casket in the middle of the night? Rolland's eyes tracked the wagon as it made its way along the access road that passed behind both the poorhouse and the orphan asylum. Within a few minutes it was close enough as it continued toward the main road that Rolland could see the driver. Although his face was obscured by the darkness, he recognized, even in the moonlight, the oversized, threadbare coat with holes at the elbows as one belonging to Angus McLean.

"What the devil is he doing?" Rolland thought as he watched the wagon fade into the darkness of the night.

The next day nobody was surprised when Ciara insisted on going to work. However, when she and Michael exited the house, they were not expecting Charlie to be at reins ready to drive them in. "I recall as ye mentioned the other day the pump handle on the well was stickin'. To be sure it will be weeks before Proctor sends a man from the Big House to take a look, and ye havin' to walk over there to fetch yer water. Alex can handle to things here for today so as I can see to it for ye."

Michael knew the man's willingness to accompany them to the orphanage had little to do with a tricky pump handle and everything to do with the fact that Angus McLean was back at the poor farm. He had a few patients with chronic problems who needed to be seen and would not be able to stay with his wife and keep an eye on things, not that she would let him anyway. Although Ciara was afraid, she was too stubborn to admit it. He did manage to get her to promise not to go over to the Big House for any reason until they were

A Whisper of Bones

certain her attacker was gone. He helped his wife into the carriage and gave Charlie an approving nod. "I'd be that grateful to ye. I've been meanin' to take a look at that myself."

As the group pulled on to the access road between the two asylums, Michael was surprised to see William Proctor's carriage making its way up the drive toward the poorhouse. "I'll just go and have a quick word," he told them as Charlie pulled up to the back door of the orphanage. Setting off at a brisk trot, he managed to pull up in front of the Big House just as the Keeper did. "Mr. Proctor, I'm that surprised to see ye here so early," he said by way of a greeting.

The doctor's lack of cordial formality was not lost on William and he returned the greeting with the same. "I know why you are here Doctor Nolan. News travels fast between these two asylums." Proctor had arrived uncharacteristically early in the hopes of catching Doctor Nolan upon his arrival, assuring him of McLean's eviction and sending him on his way before he could enter the building. He couldn't risk the doctor making a quick trip through the sick ward, as was his usual habit, and learning of the death of Owen Buchman. "I can assure you that Mr. McLean was sent on his way early yesterday. Mrs. Rowan was quick to inform me of his habits and the vicious attack on your wife. I have no need of trouble here. He was told not to return."

Michael was unprepared for the Keeper's cooperation, let alone the news that McLean had already been sent on his way. "I thank ye, sir. Do ye happen to know upon which direction he traveled?"

"As he was heading in the direction of the city on foot when he happened upon your wife, I should guess he was heading there in the hopes of finding work. Mrs. Nolan should have no business in the areas frequented by the likes of him. I would imagine that she is safe enough, providing she does not wander off. Now if you will excuse me, I have work to do." William turned and walked toward the door, again deliberately leaving out a formal farewell.

Michael met Rolland Thomas on his way out as he returned to the orphanage. "Ye stayed the night, did ye?" His tone was neutral as he had not yet decided whether he was grateful or annoyed.

"Aye, Mr. Edwards thought it a good idea, what with that blackguard McLean so nearby." Rolland would make no apologies for assuring Patricia's safety.

"Well, he'll be well out of our way by now. I've just been over to see Proctor. He turned McLean away yesterday mornin'. 'Twas just bad luck Ciara had set out when she did."

Rolland looked both confused and alarmed. "Are ye sure? Do ye know where he was headed?"

"I don't, why do ye ask?" Michael asked wary of both Rolland's expression and his tone.

"Late last night I heard the sound of someone travelin' fast by wagon over the access road. I can't be sure, mind, but the driver was wearin' the same coat I saw on McLean yesterday mornin'. It looked as if he was haulin' a casket."

"Did ye by chance mention that to my wife?" Michael asked.

"No, she seemed fearful enough of the man I couldn't see any reason to add to her worries."

Michel surprised the younger man by grabbing his shoulder with a squeeze of approval. "Aye, ye were wise to keep it from her. I'd be that grateful if ye'd keep it to yerself for just a bit longer."

"I can, for a while, but I find myself wonderin'

what a man like that is doin' makin' off in the middle of the night with a casket. If there's somethin' amiss that puts Patricia in harm's way, I should like to know about it soon enough."

"Fair enough, lad, fair enough. I've a few things to consider and some questions to ask before I can tell ye what I'm thinkin'. For now, if McLean is where I think he is the women are in no danger. Can ye give me the day to work it out?"

"Aye, I can. Ye say that ye think ye know where he's gone. Is he likely to return?"

Michael nodded grimly. "Aye, I'm afraid so. I need to see Ciara before I'm off. See Patricia home for supper and I'll have more to tell ye then." At Rolland's nod, Michael once again clasped his shoulder, then entered through the back door. He spared only a moment to acknowledge, finally, his approval of Patricia's young man, before he considered what on earth he would tell his wife.

Chapter Twenty-Five

Michael found himself, once again, walking through the front doors of the American Hotel. He was hoping to run into Dr. Ferris, whom he knew stopped in for a pint every day around lunchtime. Ferris was one of the doctors in the city who also gave of his time to help the city's poor. If there was a death within the last few days at the poorhouse, he would likely know about it. Michael was pleased to find the man seated at a table by himself in the bar. "Dr. Ferris, good day to ye, sir. May I join ye for a pint?"

"Ah, Dr. Nolan, good day to you, please join me." Ferris motioned for the barkeep to bring two more as Michael took a seat.

"*Slainte!*" Michael held up his pint to drink to his colleague's good health.

"*Slainte*! I trust you and yours are well," Ferris asked.

"We are, and I thank ye for asking. I understand ye are recently wed. Please extend my warmest wishes to yer new bride."

"I will and thank you, sir."

Michael took a sip of his stout and then took a moment to enjoy the robust, almost charred flavor, with just a hint of sweetness. He seldom had time to stop for a pint during the day, but it was a habit he could get used to. Ferris seemed to read his thoughts. "The orphans keeping you busy, are they?"

"Aye, but no complaints, to be sure. I am blessed with good health for me and my family. I can't deny the same to those poor wee souls. I daresay they've been blessed with good health both at the orphan asylum and the poorhouse this winter. The death house stands empty these days."

Ferris nodded in agreement. "There have been more than a few cases of recurrent ophthalmia in the women's dormitory, but they've managed to keep fever out of the poorhouse for the most part this winter. There was a death just the other day. One of the stable men had a heart attack…still, an isolated case. We have been lucky this year."

"I understand all deaths now must be reported directly to the Superintendent?" Michael asked.

"Yes, and it's about time they became stricter on the recordkeeping procedures. That fool of a Keeper cares nothing for what goes on in the sick ward."

"Mr. Pratt is seldom there. How does he mean to keep track of things?"

"We'll have a case book in the sick ward, although I will still keep my own records, as you had suggested to me when I started seeing patients there. The specifics of each illness will be detailed in the casebook, including death, which will then be transcribed to the death book. I assume Mr. Pratt will come in regularly to inspect the ledgers."

"*Will be* recorded in the casebook? Do I take that to mean that as yet there is no casebook?" Michael asked.

"You know how things work around there. It will be weeks before we have a proper book. As it happened, Mr. Pratt was at the poorhouse when the man died. I made a note of the death so that he or Proctor could add it to the death book. I must say that I am pleased to have some record of treatment on site. It is nearly impossible to manage the treatment of chronic cases when they are seen by different doctors, and speaking of chronic cases, I've had a mind to consult with you on an unusual case I observed there recently."

Michael drained his pint. He had been about to take his leave, but his professional ethics would keep him where he was to hear the details of this patient. Also, he was curious. Ferris was a very competent, if relatively new, physician, and very capable of treating the typical illnesses and injuries that occurred at the poorhouse. If he needed Michael's help, it must be something interesting. "Aye, of course, what 'ave ye got?"

"About a week past a woman came to the hospital with a most unusual case of chorea. Of course, Mr. Proctor wanted to admit her to the lunatic asylum, and likely would have, but luckily I was there to intervene."

Now Michael was curious. There had been documented cases of chorea, also called St. Vitus Dance because of the jerky, convulsive movements that were typical of the condition, for centuries, but it was still very poorly understood. "I dare say just about all cases of chorea are unusual. What's troubling ye about this one?"

"Well, after an extensive interview with the woman who brought her in, I learned that the patient had recently lost nearly all of her relatives from her mother's side of the family to the disease. She lost three of her own five children, her mother, grandmother, aunt, and three of her nieces."

That was very unusual and did not agree at all with the current understanding of the condition. Michael had read about chorea in medical school and it was typically seen in families, but not this many individuals within the same family and it usually occurred in the third or fourth decade of life. Also, it was typically not immediately fatal unless a patient seriously injured himself during the fits that accompany the condition. People could go on for years with the affliction, and sometimes lived out their lives in lunatic asylums. For so many individuals, especially children, to have been afflicted and died defied everything the medical community currently knew about chorea.

Michael looked at his pocket watch and realized he would be late for his clinic appointments if he lingered any longer. "Aye, that's highly unusual. I should like to look at yer notes and examine the woman myself. Can ye meet me at the poor farm first thing tomorrow morning? I can go straight over after I drop my wife at the orphan asylum."

"Of course, I'd be grateful for your assistance in the matter."

Michael rose from his chair and made a quick bow. "I'm afraid I must be off. I'll be seein' ye tomorrow first thing. Good day to ye, sir."

"And to you, sir," Ferris replied, and motioned the barkeep for another pint.

Michael hurried out of the hotel as he had one more stop to make on his way to the clinic. The Farrell residence was a quick ride by carriage, and he would speak to its mistress even if it did put him behind schedule.

About fifteen minutes later he was seated in the Farrell's parlor with a steaming cup of tea in his hands, informing Sean and his mother of the return of Angus McLean. "And so I'm wonderin', could it have been himself in the alley that morning?"

Colleen had seen Angus McLean only once many years ago during an altercation in the dining hall at the poorhouse and took a moment to see if she could recall his face. "I'd have to see him again to be sure, but I daresay it could have been. He's much the worse for wear if it was him, he was skin and bone and his coat hung loose about him. It was worn thin at the elbows."

Michael informed them that her description of the man's coat matched the one Rolland had observed both on the man whom he had seen on the road threatening Ciara and the man leaving the poorhouse late last night, the man Ciara had identified as Angus McLean. He went on to tell of the death of the stable man and of the casket Rolland had seen in the back of the wagon McLean was driving.

"It seems as though Mr. Proctor has found a new man to do his dirty work," Sean observed.

"Aye, and I think it is safe to assume that Proctor intentionally sent him after both yer ma and my wife."

"Mr. Thomas' observations last night all but confirm what we have suspected of William Proctor. We shall have to proceed very carefully from here if we are to put a stop to his diabolical activities," Colleen stated.

"Now just ye listen, Colleen," Michael seldom referred to the woman by her first name, but he wanted her full attention. "This is serious business we've discovered. I'll not have my wife or ye involved anymore."

"Michael has the right of it, ma. I'll not have ye involved in this anymore," Sean told her.

"Gentleman, I appreciate your concern, but I am the chairwoman of the Board of Directors on Indoor Poor Relief. I have a duty to expose this and put a stop to it."

"Do ye recall what that man did to my wife?" Michael's voice was raised in frustration. "He nearly beat her to death and now Proctor's got him sneakin' up on the both of ye in alleys and lonely roads. Ye must think of yer own safety. Ye can't do anything to stop the man if yer dead!"

"Michael, kindly lower your voice. If Mrs. Donavan thinks I'm being harmed she'll come running in with the meat cleaver. I have already given Sean my word that I won't go anywhere unescorted and I'll give my word to you as well. More importantly, I'll trust you if you have a plan."

Michael was relieved to hear her words, but an overwhelming sense of dread began to take root deep in the pit of his stomach. He had no idea what to do now. "Aye, well, I'll need to consider a few things before I can decide how to proceed. Sadly, there's naught we can do for poor Mr. Buchman, may God have mercy on his soul, and with the canal still frozen it will take a few days, at least, for McLean to complete his errand over land. Even if there is a death at the poorhouse that goes unclaimed, it will be a while before Proctor can attempt to transport it to Geneva. Aye, we've some time to consider the situation and maybe ask for some help."

"Know this, man," Sean told his friend, "whatever ye decide to do, ye have the Farrell name behind ye."

"Aye, I thank ye, friend."

Later that evening, after supper had been served and the younger children were put to bed the adults of the Nolan household were gathered in the parlor. It took some convincing, but Rolland had been able to persuade Patricia to leave the orphanage and they now joined the others, unsure of what was about to happen.

It was time to trust the rest of the family with this secret, Michael had decided, and ask for some assistance. Besides, he thought it would be easier for Ciara to hear about McLean's involvement in Proctor's nefarious activities with others around her to provide strength and comfort. Well, maybe it would be easier for him to tell her with the others present. He began in a strong and confident voice and, from their earliest suspicions to the most recent events that had confirmed their worst fears, he told them everything. When he was done, they were all speechless. Karyn had made the sign of the cross and Patricia had tears rolling down her face, but it was Ciara who spoke first.

"So 'tis true, what he's been doin', and now he's got that devil McLean to help him." Surprisingly, there was little emotion to her voice. "Michael, they must be stopped."

"Aye, I know. That's why I've asked ye all here this evenin'. Truth be told, I've no idea what to do." It was a testament to how much he loved and trusted these people that he could admit that.

"To be sure these men must be stopped," Rolland began, "and if it's help yer askin' for, ye can count on me, whatever the task, but right now we've the women to be concerned with. Ye say that Proctor sent McLean after Mrs. Nolan and Mrs. Farrell and he's livin' at the poor farm, a stone's throw from where Patricia spends her days. What's to stop him from sneakin' 'round there, should he have a mind to?"

"I'll be there," Charlie spoke up. "Spring is just around the corner and there's much to be done around the orphan asylum, and ye know well any request for a handy man will fall on deaf ears. I can find a reason to be over there for a good while, and Alex here in case the bastard gets the idea to pay a call." Charlie glanced at Alex, who nodded in agreement.

"Aye, I think that is a good idea, and I thank ye both. Rolland and I will be also there throughout the day, so I think the women will be safe enough." Looking at Ciara, Patricia and Karyn, he continued, "Provided ye don't go off anywhere on yer own." Each of the women agreed not to go out unescorted.

"That settled, there's still Proctor to deal with," Alex remarked. "How are we to know when he's likely to… ye know…" Alex had been horrified to learn what the Keeper of the Poor was up to and couldn't bring himself to speak aloud of it.

"He's sure to know if ye start pokin' around the sick ward, and ye putting most of yer time in at the orphan asylum," Charlie warned Michael. "We don't want to give him a reason to send McLean after ye. For all he's only frightened the women, I'm no' thinkin' he'd be so gentle wi' ye." Charlie's expression betrayed what he really thought. While Proctor was not a violent man, McLean was. If Michael became a threat to their scheme, he had no doubt that McLean was capable of killing him.

The true meaning of Charlie's remark was not lost on anyone in the room. Ciara began to speak, her voice at the same time revealing her anger, confusion and fear. "Michael, the situation has become dire with Angus McLean in the mix. 'Tis the worst kind of evil what these men are doin' and it frightens me that they are willing to use violence to continue it. Could it be time to report all of what we know to the constable and let him deal with the matter from here?"

"Aye, I'd be lyin' if I said I wasn't a bit frightened myself, but I'm not so sure the constable will be of help to us. We've only Rolland who saw McLean leave with a coffin, and that was in the dark of night. 'Twould be easy enough for Proctor to say the body had been claimed, should the constable ask. No, if we bring in the constable now, we'll only anger Proctor, and we don't want to do that. We need to catch them at it,"

Surrounded by the people he trusted, Michael's thoughts, previously clouded, shifted sharply into focus. "Aye, if we know when he's likely to try again, we can call the constable then, and at put a stop to it once and for all."

"But how are we to know when he's likely to try it again," Alex asked again?

Michael had now formed a plan in his mind. "As it happens, I've reason to be at the poorhouse regularly for a while, at least. Dr. Ferris has asked for help with a patient there. 'Tis a complicated case and it will give me reason to pay a call there several days each week. Mr. Pratt has been directed by the Board to keep a record of all patients and their treatment. I'll know who is there and if they likely have anyone to claim them should they pass. That alone might just solve the problem for us."

"Aye, but what about poor Mrs. O'Shea and them findin' logs in her coffin," Ciara asked.

"I'll be makin' more than a few trips over to the work shed for tools and such," Charlie mentioned. "I'll keep an eye on the death house, and whether there's anyone in there waitin' to be claimed."

Until now, Karyn had remained silent, listening to the others and considering their words. "I was there and saw with my own eyes what that man did to you, meine schwester," turning to from Ciara to Charlie, "and to you, mein shatz. Angus McLean is a brutal man and I hope, Michael, mein bruder, that you would not ask my husband to face him unarmed. Now if you will all excuse me, I must return to my children."

Karyn's words hung heavy in the air. This was dangerous business and she wanted to be sure they would consider the possibility that they would, themselves, have to do violence against McLean. He had found himself a way to survive in a world that had been very cruel to him, and he would not give it up easily.

"I'm afraid Karyn's right," Michael said looking at Charlie and Alex, who were seated near each other. "I think it wise if ye both keep a rifle close to hand." Michael had grown up in a very different Buffalo where many folks still hunted for their meals, and it was not unusual to see people carrying an assortment of weapons. Although he seldom had the time to hunt, he still had two rifles at the house.

The men were nodding in agreement when Patricia

spoke up. "I saw him too."

Taking her hand, Rolland asked, "What did ye see?"

"I saw him, too, Angus McLean. I heard the sound of the wagon and I looked out the window to see who would be about at such a late hour. I saw the man with the tattered coat sleeves in a wagon wi' a big long box, although I didn't know at the time it was McLean or that he was carryin' a coffin." Patricia's voice gained more conviction as she continued on. "Surely the constable would believe us if the two of us saw it. Mr. Proctor's a right devil for sendin' that man out to terrorize Mrs. Farrell and my sister, and now yer talkin' about usin' rifles to defend against the man. I think maybe this is too much for us to handle on our own."

"To be sure we're in over our heads, but if we go canny from here, I think we can avoid any violence," Michael told her, continuing on to address the rest of the group, he said "It'll be days, possibly even a week before McLean returns from Geneva, so we're safe enough for now. I think all we can do now is wait. I'll know if anyone passes who is unlikely to be claimed by kin for burial. If that happens, McLean will need to transport the body under cover of night, as he just did. That gives us time to call the constable and lay in wait until he comes to fetch the body."

They all agreed that was the safest way to proceed. Ciara and Patricia excused themselves to the kitchen, the tea pot having gone cold. Michael waited for the parlor door to close before he spoke to the other three men. "I've got some business to settle with McLean, and no mistake."

Nodding in agreement, Alex said, "Aye, we should have killed him back when we had the chance."

Rolland spoke up, surprising the others with what he had to say. "Now to be sure, I've not the history with this man that the rest of ye have, and God knows he'd meet a violent end at my hands should he try harm Patricia or the others, but if we're to put a stop to this nightmare. We must not provoke confrontation with Angus McLean. He's a desperate man, and no mistake. If he thinks we pose a threat to his plan it could be dangerous for all of us."

"As much as I'd like to see the man wi' a dagger in his chest, the lad is right," Alex admitted. "The three of ye best stay clear of Angus McLean. The man is desperate and greedy;, he'll make a mistake soon enough."

Charlie took a moment to light his pipe before he spoke. He took a long drag, billows of smoke surrounding him as he exhaled. Speaking in a soft but menacing voice, he said, "Aye, but if he comes 'round looking fer trouble, he'll find more than he bargained for."

Chapter Twenty-Six

Michael sat in his office the next afternoon, head down, pouring over the notes Dr. Ferris had given him on his patient Lucinda Gefroren. Michael had met her earlier that morning and found her to be soft spoken and withdrawn. The woman who had brought her to the almshouse had told the doctor about her fits and of all of the family members who had died from the same condition, but when Dr. Ferris tried to speak with Lucinda, she would not speak. One of the reasons he had wanted Michael's help with the case was his colleague's bedside manner. Patients seemed to trust Michael right from the beginning, and Lucinda was no exception.

Dr. Nolan's initial questions met with nods of the head or one word answers. "Do ye recall as a lass yer ma or da, or maybe yer Gran havin' the St. Vitus Dance?" was answered with a shake of the head to indicate "no." "What about yer auntie?" Another shake of the head. "How old are ye?" "38." "Where is Herr Gefroren?" "Gone." "What were the ages of yer babes when they passed?" The last question upset her so that her lower lip began to tremble and her eyes welled up with tears. "Now, don't ye fret, we'll take a wee break and talk again later."

He had managed a cursory medical examination and could find no outward signs of ill health. She was painfully thin, but that was not unusual for individuals who sought care at the poorhouse. He had read Dr. Ferris' brief notes several times already and was reconciling them with what little information his interview yielded. She had come dressed in decent clothing, nothing fancy, but relatively clean (he had seen people admitted in the filthiest of rags, but her dress only reflected daily wear) and in no need of mending. Her age, 38, was within the range that had typically been observed for the onset of chorea, but none of her older family members suffered from the disease before now. No husband, although whether "gone" meant he was dead or that he had simply left, Michael did not know. Perhaps, with no husband, she was living with her mother's kin. Had they all taken sick? From what? Fever? Fits were often associated with high fevers, and could easily been taken for chorea. He needed to speak with someone who could give him some answers. He knew better than to speak with the Keeper or Mrs. Rowan. They did not care what circumstances brought people to their door and likely would remember nothing of what the woman who brought Mrs. Gefroren in had told them. They would have a record of her admission, though. Although the recordkeeping in the hospital was sloppy at best, the intake ledgers for the poorhouse were always complete so that an accurate accounting of expenditures per person could be reported to the county. The intake record would tell him where Mrs. Gerfroren lived. He made a note to find out where she had lived so that he could, hopefully, pay a call on the woman who surrendered her.

March 6, 1841

I fear Mrs. Kaiser won't be with us much longer. She hasn't touched a bit of food in two days and this morning I couldn't rouse her to take some tea. Michael says she's in God's hands now as there is naught he can do for her. I pray that she finds peace.

Mrs. Rowan climbed the stairs to the woman's dormitory, grumbling as she went. She had tried to tell Mr. Proctor that she could spare no able-bodied women for the orphan asylum, but he assured her that they would be back in the morning to do their chores at the Big House. Yet, here she was with a kitchen full of dishes to be washed and one woman short in the laundry this morning. She opened the door without knocking.

"Yer needed in the kitchen," she growled to Mrs. Loderick, "and there's laundry to be done," this remark directed at Emily Munroe. "Everyone works 'round here. There's no time for layin' abed. If ye were in yer beds at night like respectable women, ye'd 'ave no trouble risin' in the mornin' to do yer chores," she lectured.

Emily grudgingly began to climb out of her cot,

but Mrs. Loderick had a few words for the matron before she would get up. "Mrs. Rowan, you know full well we were both at the orphanage last night. As they are short of help in the infant's nursery and several of the babes were bothered by teething, we were up most of the night. I am sure that the dishes and the laundry can wait just a bit longer."

Ordinarily, Mrs. Rowan would not suffer such insolence from an inmate, but she had a nose that could smell trouble and she was prepared to let the indiscretion pass in order to learn why they were short of help in the nursery. "There's three others of ye livin' there, do ye mean to tell me they are shirkin' their duties? For if they are, they'll be dragged back here straight away!"

Jane Loderick was a kind woman and had no wish to cause any of the other women difficulty and did not see the harm in telling the matron that one of the women was sick. "...confined to her bed, they seem to be worried about her, truth be known." This last comment was made in the hopes of gaining some sympathy from the matron.

"Aye, well then, get ye out of yer beds and get to work!" Mrs. Rowan exited the dormitory deep in thought. Something was definitely up. Sick inmates were not allowed to stay at the orphan asylum, that much she knew, and yet Dr. Nolan had not transferred her back to the Big House. A greedy smile slowly spread across the matron's face. *I wonder,* she thought as she descended the stairs, *how dear is this secret they are keepin', and how much is my silence worth.*

Ciara was finishing up some of the work in her office that could not be brought home and was long overdue in its completion when she caught sight of Mrs. Rowan heading in the her direction. The snow had melted as fast as it had fallen, typical of weather in Buffalo during that time of year. The temperature could drop again without any warning and they could have snow again by nightfall. Mrs. Rowan looked not to be bothered by the sloppy mud, which almost certainly had seeped into her well-worn boots. In all of the years that the orphan asylum had been just up the path from the Big House, the matron had never set foot through its doors. Ciara knew immediately that she had found out about Mrs. Kaiser.

They had all worried that one of the new women would let it slip eventually. They had only casually mentioned Mrs. Kaiser's illness so as not to draw attention to her. Ciara's thoughts were interrupted by a rapid knock on her door. Patricia had also seen the matron walking up the path, and had come to warn her sister.

"Surely she knows," Patricia exclaimed. "What other reason could she possibly have to come here?"

"Aye she knows, but Mr. Proctor surely doesn't, or it would be him comin' and not her. She wants somethin', and no mistake."

"What will we do? We've nothing to give her."

"Aye, to be sure, and we'll tell her as much." Ciara would not have bartered anything for Mrs. Rowan's silence, nor anyone else's, for that matter, even if she had something to trade."Let's just see what she has to say if we expose one of her secrets."

Patricia had no idea what her sister meant by that and there was no time to ask as they both heard the front door open and the matron demand to be taken to the Keeper's office straight away. "Do ye want me to stay?" she asked.

"Aye, stay if ye like."

Mrs. Rowan entered the office without knocking, with Mrs. Wilmar behind her making apologies for the rude intrusion. The matron of the poorhouse removed her cloak, handed it to Mrs. Wilmar and shooed her out the door. "You too, deary," she said to Patricia, trying to push her in the direction of the exit. Patricia shook her off and took a seat, her expression daring the matron to object.

"Whatever ye have to say, ye'll say it in front of my sister," Ciara said.

"Aye, I should 'ave known she'd be in on it," Mrs. Rowan accused.

"In on what? Whatever are ye on about?" Ciara asked.

"Now look here, ye've already taken three of my inmates, leavin' the rest o' them to divide the work that needs doin' and now ye've got four more, and them too tired from doin' the work for the first three to be of any use when they come back!"

"Mrs. Rowan, it was not my idea to replace the night nurses with women from the Big House, it was Mr. Pratt's. Go and speak to him if yer troubled by it." Ciara explained, her tolerance for the greedy matron already wearing thin.

"I know one of the women 'as taken sick to her

bed. If Mr. Proctor hears of this she will be sent back to the Big House where she belongs," the matron threatened.

"Well, as none here intend to tell him, he would only find out from ye, and if ye've come over here hopin' to make a bargain for yer silence on the matter, I'd think carefully before ye threaten me!" Ciara had grown tired of being in the middle of a situation that was too dangerous for her to do anything about. She may be frightened of Angus McLean, but she was fully capable of dealing with Mrs. Rowan.

"Now just ye listen here," growled Mrs. Rowan, "'tis not me breakin' the rules here. These women were sent here to work, and ye let them lounge abed. If the woman is too sick to do the tasks she was sent here for, she should be sent straight to the sick ward," she argued, pointing in the direction of the poorhouse. "Don't cross me, Mrs. Nolan, ye'll be sorry if ye do!"

"No, ye listen to me! What little time that poor old woman has will be spent here, among people who care about her, and when she passes I'll make sure of it myself that she has a decent Christian burial. Ye think I don't know Mr. Proctor pays ye handsomely to let him know who among the folks there have no kin, and to look the other way when the poor souls are taken from the sick ward and loaded on a wagon? Just ye go back to the Big House and keep yer mouth shut about what's goin' on over here or I'll tell the constable what ye've been up to!"

Mrs. Rowan's face betrayed no surprise at Ciara's threat. Instead her expression grew dark and menacing. "Ye've been trouble since the day ye set foot through the door. Just ye watch yer step from here, deary. 'Tis a dangerous path yer on, so it is, and ye get in the way of Mr. Proctor and his *man.*" She placed special emphasis on the word man and looked her directly in the eye, so Ciara would know to whom she was referring.

"Leave, now!" Ciara growled. Mrs. Rowan held her stare for just a few seconds longer before she turned and walked out the door.

Patricia waited until she was sure the matron had left before she spoke. "How on earth did ye know that Mrs. Rowan was mixed up in all of this?"

"I didn't really. I was up half the night again thinkin' things over and I realized that Mr. Proctor isn't around enough to know who has died and whether they have kin or friends who might claim them. To be sure the farmer wouldn't know such things. It made sense that Mrs. Rowan would be involved somehow. At the very least, he'd have had to pay dearly for her silence for well ye know nothin' goes on 'round there that she doesn't know about. But the more I considered it, the more I realized she would be of use to him."

"Do ye think it wise to have threatened her, and ye promisin' Michael ye'd let him handle the matter?" Patricia asked?

"What was I to do, sister? Michael's not here. Should I let them take poor Mrs. Kaiser back there, for she doesn't have much time left?"

"She's a cruel woman, is Mrs. Rowan, and ye've made her angry, and no mistake. If she sends Angus McLean after ye, ye won't be able to tell the constable anythin'." Patricia had been worried before when she had first learned of what was going on at the poorhouse, but the men had assured her that they would be safe if they stayed out of the matter. Now Ciara had both exposed Mrs. Rowan's involvement and threatened to turn her into the constable. Patricia was frightened of what the matron might do.

"Aye, and it's a risk I'd no choice but to take. Could ye live with yerself if they sold off her body to be cut up on a table for all to see?" Patricia had not really stopped to consider the horrors a body would endure should it end up in the anatomical theater. Like Ciara, she had no real understanding of what was learned in medical school. Only wee Martha had been interested enough to talk to Michael about the particulars of his profession. The look of shock on her face made Ciara realize that she had said too much. "I'm that sorry, Patricia, but I've not told ye a lie. The poor souls taken by Mr. Proctor are abused in such a way so that the doctors can learn how the body works."

"Did…did Michael do that? I mean did he cut people up?" Patricia asked, stunned.

"Ye know well my husband is a good man and the finest doctor around. What he did, he did to help living people, and to be sure he wouldn't have if he'd known they were stolen from their place of eternal rest in the dead of night."

Patricia looked unsure. She could think of no reason to do such a thing to any departed soul. Seeing the uncertainty in her sister's face, Ciara continued to speak in defense of her husband. "Would ye judge the man so harshly who took ye in and gave ye a home? Would ye think poorly of the kind and gentle man who endured the very things that horrify ye so that he could save lives?"

In her heart, Patricia loved Michael and could not hold against him things she did not truly understand no matter how much they frightened her. "No, of course not. Michael is a good man and a fine doctor, as ye say. What are we to do now?"

"Wait, I suppose. Michael says Mrs. Kaiser could pass any day now. We owe it to her to keep her comfortable and allow her to pass in peace. Besides, I think we've got some time."

As it happens, they did not have much time. The following afternoon Michael had come to check on his patient and announced that she would not likely last the night. Although they all knew this day would come soon, Ciara and Patricia were still grief-stricken by the news. They held each other and cried for the woman who had become their friend.

"I'll stay with her," Patricia announced, her expression resolute.

"Aye, me too," Ciara agreed.

Both Michael and Rolland had been prepared to argue with the two women, but seeing how devastated they were, neither could bring themselves to say a word in protest. "Aye, I'll be back later then, I'll not have ye stayin' here by yerselves," Michael told them.

"I'll stay as well," Rolland agreed.

Ciara, Patricia and Mrs. Olsen were with Frederika Kaiser when she took her last breath in this world. Each took time to say goodbye before they went down to the kitchen to inform the others. Michael held his wife while she grieved the loss of a dear friend she had known only a short time. She had seen many friends pass since coming to America, and to this place where only the desperate sought refuge, but felt the loss of Frederika Kaiser much deeper than the others. She had suspected the woman had not, at least in her adult life, had a loving family to call her own. After a while they were joined in the kitchen by Patricia and Rolland who had done their grieving in the hall. At first there was silence, each person lost in his own thoughts. "What will we do now?" Ciara finally asked.

"Well, as she died here and we've kept her condition from the Keeper, we'll be in a bit o' trouble with the Board when we report her death." Michael was thinking out loud rather than answering his wife's question directly.

"We can hardly keep her death a secret," Ciara pointed out. "The whole asylum will know come mornin'. Mr. Proctor is sure to find out. Mrs. Rowan has already discovered she's been ill, so he may well be over here come mornin' demandin' her return to the Big House."

"If we don't report it, there's no record of her death," Rolland added. "If he were to find out she died and there's no record…"

"Oh no, we can't let him take her!" Patricia had followed Rolland's reasoning to its logical conclusion.

"No, we won't let him take her," Michael assured her, "but I agree 'tis a good idea to report her death and transfer her to the death house come mornin'."

"No, I won't risk her like that," Ciara argued. "I want her buried tonight, if I have to drag those two fools out of bed to do it."

"What's to stop Proctor diggin' her up once we've seen her buried?" Patricia asked her sister. Her question was followed by silence as nobody seemed to have an answer. They couldn't risk the possibility that McLean could slip in unnoticed and steal her off into the night.

"Logs," Rolland said, "we'll use logs same as they did."

"I don't follow ye," Michael told him.

"Mrs. Nolan has the right of it. We need to bury Mrs. Kaiser now, while none but us know of her death. We need to bury her where she won't be noticed should anyone go lookin'. Tomorrow, Mrs. Nolan can go rouse the farmers to come and dig a second grave in the proper numbered spot and they can bury a casket of logs. Report it to Proctor once she's safely buried, tellin' him as ye knew she had no kin to claim her, so there was no need for a waitin' period. If Proctor does make McLean go back and dig her up, she'll still be safely hidden away."

"To be sure when Proctor finds out, he'll have the casket out of the ground and on the way to Geneva by nightfall," Michael was thinking out loud again. As if just noticing that the others had heard him, he continued speaking. "Aye, let's you and me see her to her final resting place now. I know a spot just behind the tree at the far side of the yard. We'll have to dig through the roots, but if we get started, we can be done with our business by first light."

As Rolland and Michael exited out the back door, they saw a small flicker of light just inside the shed. Neither was surprised to discover that the flicker belonged to Charlie's pipe. Without knowing when she would die, or what would be done when she did, he was there, ever watchful, if he was needed. "She's gone?" he asked.

"Aye," Michael answered.

"The women will be safe enough while yer about yer business. I'll see to it," Charlie assured them as he blew billows of smoke into the night.

Part Three

Chapter Twenty-Seven

Per her husband's request, Maude had taken a few weeks off from burial number 116. It took some arguing, but she managed to get Don to agree to let her finish cleaning the other partial skeletons to which she had already committed herself, although he managed to find excuses to be around when she was working with the burials, just in case. As it turned out, the remaining three burials were incomplete, with mostly long bone and skull fragments, and were quickly finished. To Don's relief, none had healed traumas and the cleaning process was concluded without any supernatural incidents.

This particular Monday, Maude was about her usual morning routine in the shop, applying Casey Lee's latest payment to the treasures she had on layaway (a courtesy they allowed only a few very special customers, like Casey)when her eyes drifted over to the armoire.

She knew the skull of burial 116 still needed to be cleaned and photographed, and had been feeling guilty for leaving the skeleton unfinished for so long. It would take her the better part of an afternoon to clean an intact skull, with all of protuberances, fissures and foveas on its underside. The boys both had sleepovers Saturday night and would be gone all the next day. She wondered if she could convince her husband to spend a few hours in the lab on Sunday (she knew he would not let her clean the skull of number116 without him present). He had recently finished a few projects he had been pushing to the back burner and had some free time, so she didn't think it would take too much convincing. Hockey season was over so there would be some time to talk with Don after supper that evening.

"No! I have been thinking about it since you finished the others and I really want you to ask someone else to finish cleaning it," Don told her when she brought up the subject just before bed. "Truth be told, I am really not comfortable with you continuing on with the lab work on this project. We have no way of knowing if this will happen again if you encounter any individuals with trauma, or worse yet, some kind of disease. You have no idea what's going on here, Maude, and I don't like it."

Maude was not prepared for such an extreme reaction to her suggestion that she finish up the skeleton on Sunday. She needed a moment to process what Don had just said. He was uneasy about her connection to this burial and concerned that her visions could become a pattern as she continued on with the project. (However, Maude felt confident, although she could not say why, that this was the only burial to which she had a supernatural connection). He was letting his reservations interfere with his objectivity. If she pointed that out, the discussion would turn into an argument that would solve nothing. It was time to negotiate. "Okay, I understand that you'd rather me not continue to work in the lab. So, although I think there is no danger in my working with the other skeletons, I will let Jean know that it would be easier for me to just work in the archives. However, I am not leaving burial number116 to be finished by anyone else. I'll wear gloves the entire time, even when the bones are dry and I am packing them up."

Don couldn't argue this, knowing how much she

was giving up by redirecting her efforts away from the skeletal analysis and toward the documentary evidence, so he reluctantly agreed. "Let's make a few things clear before we settle on this plan. First, if anything happens to you while you are working and I feel that you are in danger, your time with this particular skeleton is over, finished or not, agreed?" Maude took only a moment to think before she agreed. "Second, when this skeleton is finished and you pack it up, I would like you to be done with it. In other words, I don't want you going back to examine this burial after you are finished with it."

That request took his wife longer to process. She knew she had an extraordinary connection to this individual. However, she was not sure if this special relationship was exclusive. If there was a possibility any of the other researchers would have similar experiences, she would have to warn them. Every inch of this skeleton would be observed, measured and analyzed by the team of researchers. She would not want any of them hurt during that process. But just how do you tell a group of scientists that they might get psychic visions when they touched the skeleton? Don's second stipulation would not be easy to agree with. "Don, I can't agree with that right now. I think this woman is trying to tell me something and I may not know what it is until I have finished cleaning her bones. I don't even know if this unusual connection with her is unique to me. If it isn't, I can't let a team of graduate students work with this burial without knowing what I have experienced. Please just let me do this and I promise we will discuss my continued work on the project again after I am done."

Don was growing more uneasy with the situation. He could see that his wife was determined to see this through to the end, come what may, and he knew well that when she was this resolute, there was usually no stopping her. "Do something for me first?"

"What?"

"You were likely going to do this anyway, but please, before we go in there on Sunday try and find out whatever you can about this person. Maybe you can figure out why she has chosen to communicate with you."

"Don, that's much easier said than done. The inmates of the Erie County Poorhouse were, for all intents and purposes, buried in unmarked graves. They had a numbered stake that linked their burial location to an entry in a mortality ledger, but the stakes were pulled up and reused each year. It is virtually impossible for me to find out this person's name. The only clues we have to her life are housed within her bones…and from the look of them, she had a pretty miserable life."

"Maude, you're a researcher; it's what you do. I've seen you travel to every museum, library and moldy basement in the state of New York to ferret out more information based on a single entry in a ledger that just happened to pique your interest. Please try to find out what you can about this woman before Sunday."

"To think all these years you were actually paying attention!" Maude's attempt at humor did nothing to redirect her husband's focus. "Okay, I will try, but the chances are slim to none that I will find anything."

Maude was up half the night trying to inventory the archival records at her disposal that might help to provide an identity to number 116. The municipal records only contained year-end reports of inventories, expenditures and the like, rather than any information about specific inmates. Without knowing the woman's name, none of the records kept by the poorhouse keepers would be of any help either. As she continued to think, Maude remembered that she had received an e-mail from Brian Jameson, the archaeologist in charge of the cemetery excavation, about work on a map of the excavated burials. At least from that, she would be able to determine where the woman had been buried. Content that she had something tangible to follow up on the next day, she made a mental note to call Brian and drifted off to sleep.

The next morning Maude rose at seven to see the boys off on their last day of school for the year...well, what she considered their last day. In order to have as many official school days as the public schools, the last week of school in the parochial schools was a bizarre shuffle of half days and movie days that were nothing but an inconvenience for the parents and boring for the children. Several years ago, Maude and Don had decided to make their busy lives much easier by calling the last full day of classes the end of the year and ignoring the rest of it. Nobody seemed to notice or mind, so it became a yearly thing.

As she hit the "on" switch for the coffee pot and distributed cereal bowls on the table, Maude thought about how, unlike Billy and Glen, the university students and faculty were already well into summer. Realizing that Brian might already be in the field if she waited until she got into work to call him, she reached for her cell phone. She paused for a minute and considered which number to dial. Brian was the only person in the twenty-first century who did not own a cell phone, so looking at her watch she thought it likely that he would not be in the office just yet, so she decided to try his home number first. He picked up after two rings. "Hi Brian. It's Maude. Am I catching you on your way out the door?"

"Hey Maude, no, I'm working at home this morning. What's up?"

"I have a question about one of the burials from the poorhouse cemetery, but you're going to need to take a look at the map. Do you have a few minutes?"

"Sure, tell me what you need while I get into my office and turn on my laptop."

"I've been working on burial number 116 for a little over a month. I am really surprised at how complete and intact it is compared to some of the others I have cleaned. I was wondering if you could tell me anything about her burial location."

"Wow, funny you should mention number 116. We have been wondering about burials 97-120 because they were all interred with just shrouds, whereas the rest of the locations had coffins. I'm wondering if those two rows represent some sort of temporal boundary, with the shrouded burials from an earlier period than the cemetery's later use than the coffins."

"Interesting," Maude replied, "I read an account in the Keepers report for 1851, the year the poorhouse moved from the Black Rock location to what is now the South Campus. The inmates moved 120 burials from the poor house on York Street to the new location on Main Street. I wonder if you have excavated some of the Black Rock burials."

"That's possible," Brian agreed. "Those graves are shallower than most of the others. That makes sense in this context if the inmates had to dig a large number of graves all at one time."

"Was there anything else unusual about number 116 specifically?" Maude asked.

"Not that I recall. I was in the field the days that both rows of shrouded burials came out of the ground.

There were a few grave goods other than the shrouds, but I'd have to look into my notes to see if any of the items found were associated with number 116."

"Do you still have the items?" Maude asked.

"Yes, everything catalogued and numbered so that each can be reinterred with its rightful owner. We weren't so lucky with the coffins. What nature and time didn't destroy was damaged during the excavation and the removal of the skeletons. Are you thinking of coming to take a look at them?"

Maude wanted desperately to examine the burial shroud of the woman whose sad life she had been seeing in short clips. Perhaps if she held the fragile cloth in her hands she might get a glimpse of how she died? Tempted though she was, she felt that would definitely betray her promise to Don not pursue any supernatural connection to this individual. "I'd like to, but I doubt I'll have the time now that the boys are on summer vacation. Thanks, Brian. I'll send you the account for the 1851 Keeper's Report."

"Great, talk to you soon. Take care, Maude."

"You, too."Maude hung up the phone, putting thoughts of the poorhouse on the back burner so that she could give her full attention to getting two amped up tweens out the door and on the school bus. As they both shot down the driveway, she said a silent prayer for the bus driver. It would be a rough week for him.

With the kids off, Maude began to consider her conversation with Brian. Could burial number 116 have been an inmate of the original poorhouse? That would mean that she had died sometime between 1829, when the institution opened and 1851, when the poorhouse moved to Main Street, what was then called Buffalo Plains. The transcribed inmate records from her dissertation research were still saved on her computer, and she reconsidered taking a look at the records from the Black Rock period to see if anything looked interesting. Looking at her watch, it was just after 8, not enough time to give the digital files a thorough examination before she had to open the shop, but enough time to load the files on her laptop to take along for later.

As it turned out, "later" would be several days after Maude downloaded the inmate records on to her laptop. The shop was experiencing a flurry of morning activity that was typical of that time of year. Summer in Buffalo was a time for restoring, renovation and remodeling which meant that Maude had a steady stream of customers, old and new, who were either looking to furnish their restored antique homes or looking to sell old luminary treasures in favor of more modern accessories. The city also offered only four days each year on which they accepted large garbage items, like furniture, tires, lawn mowers, etc. On those days industrious folks would troll the city in their pickup trucks or conversion vans on the lookout for any item of value that had been carelessly discarded. Inevitably, Maude would have a few people who brought in lamps for appraisal, repair or sale.

She was busy trying, unsuccessfully, to explain to a woman best be described as Jerry Garcia's biggest fan that they typically did not deal with lava lamps and that she could offer her vintage "Peace" lamp for sale on eBay, when Christine came in the front door. The historian/antique dealer made no effort to suppress her mirth as she smugly listened to Maude trying politely attempting to explain how not all old items are valuable. "I honestly can't tell how much money you could get on E-Bay. Like any item, it depends on the condition of the lamp, how rare it was at the time it was originally made and what the current demand for the item is. Honestly, I don't have any experience with this type of lamp. Do you have a computer?" As the woman nodded that she did, Maude wrote down the web address for eBay on a neon orange sticky note and handed it to the old hippie. "Why don't you go online and do a search for lava lamps? That might give you an idea what yours is worth."

Christine was standing behind a cast iron Victorian floor lamp, her face hidden by a large fabric tassel shade, still laughing when the woman left the shop. With the only other customer in the store staring upward, apparently mesmerized by the glittering crystal chandeliers hanging from ceiling, Christine seized the opportunity to secure plans for lunch.

"Okay, but it has to be a quick lunch," Maude cautioned. "I've been trying to take look at the poorhouse records all week, but we have been swamped."

"Oh, on to something, are you?"

"I'm not sure. I stumbled across something in the journal. It may be nothing, but I just wanted to take a look at the inmate records for the early period and see if anything grabs my attention. It's just another rabbit hole, really."

"You and your rabbit holes!" Christine knew she wouldn't get anything more out of her friend until there was more to tell. That was always how it worked with Maude and her wild goose chases, cryptic in the beginning, and then gushing if she found what she was looking for. Christine was willing to wait. "Let's do lunch another day, then. I know you and you'll be wolfing down your salad and trying to rush me out the door to get a look at those records. But be warned: I want full disclosure, including why your back door is still locked!"

Maude laughed, knowing that it was still killing Christine that she could not figure out what Maude was up to behind locked doors. "You got it, thanks Christine. If I can get this done today, we can do lunch tomorrow."

"Unless whatever you find leads you deeper into the hole!" she teased.

By the time they had finished their conversation the other woman had chosen a lovely Victorian crystal chandelier for her dining room. It took another thirty minutes to complete the transaction and to arrange for

Don to come and install the piece.

Maude was thrilled that it was a full hour before her regular lunch break, giving her time to turn on her laptop and begin scrolling through the records. It did not take long to go through the first decade, as fewer inmates sought relief then than in later periods. She was pleasantly surprised when she found the records of three women she had read about in Ciara Nolan's journal. Bruna Wilmar had come to the almshouse as a widow in 1835 at the age of 52, and had been listed as "Carried Forward" each year after that. Mrs. Olsen, oddly with no first name listed, had come in June 10, 1840. She was 58 years old and was also listed as a widow. Her occupation was listed as "domestic", as was common for women. Continuing to scroll down the page, she then found Frederika Kaiser, whose age was recorded as 48, and was also a widow. Maude ruminated on how none of these women would be considered "old" today, but were certainly past their prime in early nineteenth century Buffalo where the average life expectancy was about 38 years old for women, owing to the high risk of childbirth and the constant threat of epidemic infectious diseases.

The fiscal year for the poorhouse ended September 30th each year, and the records would begin again, listing all of the inmates who had been carried forward from the previous year, meaning that they were still in residence. Having found some familiar names, Maude scrolled ahead to October of 1840 to see if the women were still there. Sure enough she found each woman with the notations "Carried Forward" and "OA" listed by each name. Maude took the latter notation to mean Orphan Asylum, as she had read that two women had been transferred there early in the fall of 1840. She was able to trace Bruna Wilmar until her death in 1849. The cause of death at the age of 68 was listed as "Debility and old age".

Finding three women who had been mentioned in another historical source (the journal) listed in the inmate records and accounted for through time gave Maude even more confidence in the accuracy of these documents. Any record is only as good as the person keeping it. These discoveries were yet more evidence in an elaborate system of cross-checking that indicated that, at least during this period, the Superintendent of the Poor for Erie County Poorhouse took his job seriously. Over the next hour, Maude found nothing else noteworthy in the records and turned off the laptop disappointed, yet not really surprised.

Chapter Twenty-Eight

When Sunday came around, Maude woke early in anticipation of an exciting day. She knew better than to wake Don before 9 a.m., as this was the only day he did not have to rise at dawn. Maude had never been able to really sleep in the way Don could, and she envied him. She was almost always up before he was on weekends and was content to read until he began to stir. This morning, though, she was unable relax in bed with her Nook. Although she managed to lie still on her back, her posture was a bit stiff, the muscles of her back and legs tense, as she considered what might happen when they got to the lab.

When two people share the same bed for a number of years, they grow accustomed to each other's habits and movements, particularly in the morning, when the slightest deviation from the norm can pull them from their dreams. If Maude had awoken and gone to the bathroom or padded around the bed for her Nook that she had fallen asleep reading the night before, Don would have slept through those familiar movements. However, this morning, with his wife lying still, almost rigid, he sensed her deep contemplation rather than her relaxed interest in whatever she was currently reading and woke with a groan. "What are ya doin'?"

"Sorry, I didn't mean to wake you," she said as she rolled over and kissed him on the tip of his nose.

Pulling her into his arms, he said, "I could hear you thinking in my sleep. Nervous about today?

"Not so much nervous as curious. I just want to get in there and see what happens. The suspense is killing me."

"You are out of your mind," he told her before giving her a proper good morning kiss that could have easily turned into something more with the house to themselves.

She pushed his wandering hands aside and reluctantly pulled away. "You seek to distract me, but I am not so easily redirected."

"I seek to enjoy a morning in bed, with you, without the boys barging in," he said as his lips traveled down her neck to just behind her ear, "and, yes you, are!"

The prospect of the day's adventure was no match for her husband's tender kisses and Maude easily gave in. It was after 11 o'clock before they were finally out the door. "Why are you turning here?" Maude asked Don, who had obviously intended to make a stop before continuing on to the lab.

"It's nearly lunch time and we haven't even had breakfast yet. Whatever might happen today, I don't want it complicated by low blood sugar. We'll hit the drive thru at Bagel Jay's and be back on our way."

"Good thinking." It was unlike Maude to forget to eat, and surely a sign that her thoughts were entirely occupied by burial number116. She was absolutely certain that this woman still had more to tell her, and that the skull figured significantly into the story. Maude ate her bagel in the remaining time it took to get to the lab. The truck hadn't even come to a complete stop and she was out the door, key in hand. She moved quickly out of the parking lot and down the corridor, leaving the doors along the way open for Don. Once at her destination, she immediately began filling the plastic tub

A Whisper of Bones

with warm water and gathering her tools.

Don followed, the paper bag containing his breakfast in hand, locking the door behind him. Taking in the aroma of damp earth and drying bones that seemed to have seeped into the walls since the burials had started coming in, he said, "I'm glad you're almost done with this. It's starting to smell like an old cemetery in here."

Maude was walking in the direction of the box that contained the skull of burial number 116. Her husband stopped her. "Wait. Aren't you forgetting something?" He said, picking up a box of latex gloves and handing them to her. "You are not touching that skull without gloves on."

"I know. I was just getting the box. Nothing is going to happen if I carry the box with my bare hands," Maude answered, snatching two gloves out with an intentional roll of her eyes. She had been patient with Don's concerns, but he was being ridiculous.

"Just wear the damned gloves, please."

Much to Don's relief and Maude's disappointment, the afternoon proved uneventful. Maude spent three hours carefully removing hunks of clay from the base of the skull and the teeth, alternating between a wooden skewer and a soft tooth brush. When she was finished she left the skull to dry. It was on the table in the lab, carefully balanced upside down on a roll of masking tape to protect the more fragile base from being damaged and to prevent it from rolling onto its side. While cleaning the bones of the face she had uncovered what she thought were recently healed fractures of the right temporal and zygomatic bones that made up the cheek bone, recent meaning around the time of the woman's death as opposed to earlier in her life. *These perimortem fractures may have been related to her death. That's something at least,* she thought. "Well, I guess that's it, then," she said to Don as she peeled off her gloves and threw then in the trash. "I'll leave it to dry overnight and come back and pack it up tomorrow."

His wife's discontent was evident as they exited the shop. Before they got in the truck, Don said, "Maude, look, I know you are disappointed." His comment was met with an expression that might just have been a glare. "I am sorry this didn't turn out the way you wanted, and I really do appreciate you stepping away from the skeletal analysis. I know it was not easy for you to do that."

Realizing she was behaving like a child, Maude rearranged her features and gave her husband a reassuring smile. "It's fine. There are enough records to keep me busy for the foreseeable future." She was disappointed but there was no sense in making a big deal about it. Marriage was full of compromises, after all. Don had willingly changed around his schedule over the last few months to allow her to participate in this project, so it was definitely her turn to give a little.

The next morning Maude arrived at the lab early to be sure she had enough time to pack up burial-number116 before she had to go into work. Placing her purse on the stainless steel table, she went to retrieve the box that housed the rest of burial number 116. Remembering her promise to Don, she went straight to the box of latex gloves on her desk before even removing the lid. With the skull in her hand, she took a final look at the perimortem trauma on the right side of the face before reaching for the piece of bubble wrap in which she had intended to wrap the fragile cranium. Before she could complete her task, she heard her cell phone ring and quickly placed the skull on the bubble wrap, stripped off her gloves and hurried over to the table to answer it. By the time Maude rummaged through her purse and found the phone, the ringing had stopped. She took a look at the call history to see who had trying to contact her. Strangely, there was no indication that she had just missed a call. "Weird," she said out loud as she put the phone down on the counter."We hardly ever get a signal in here."

Returning to the task at hand, Maude remembered that she still needed packing tape to secure the bubble wrap and insure the intact skull was not damaged if the box contents shifted. After searching a desk by the door, she spent a frustrating few minutes trying to peel the edge of the tape back from the roll and re-load it on the dispenser. "This would be a hell of a lot easier if people would just fold the sticky edge over when they are done using it," she complained to the skull on her desk.

Finally with her supplies ready she turned toward the table and reached for the skull, with her hand over the top and her fingers grasping down the bones of the side of the face. Her realization that she had taken off her gloves was overshadowed by an excruciating pain behind her eyes. She had the sensation of falling forward, and then searing pain as the side of her face made contact with hard wood. Then she felt disoriented, sitting in a hallway just outside of a kitchen. There were people around, fussing over her, but she had forgotten who they were. The pain was so intense.

When Maude came to she could still feel the pain on her cheek. She slowly lifted her head and realized that she had hit her face on the tape dispenser when she fell forward. Gingerly, she reached up and felt her cheek. It was beginning to swell, but she didn't think it was broken. Taking a minute to catch her breath, she noticed that the skull was on its side, still on the table. She had not yet actually picked it up and was relieved to see that it had not been damaged when it fell out of her hand. "That's more than I can say for my own skull," she said out loud as she slowly got up to go in the bathroom and assess the damage to her face. Running a wad of paper towels under the cold water, she gently padded her face while she looked at her reflection in the mirror. *That's not going to be pretty,* she thought as she ran the towels under the water again and wiped the rest of her face.

As she wrapped the skull, Maude began to ponder

the images from her vision. The fracture to the bones of the face likely occurred just before the woman's death, so it seemed reasonable to conclude that the severe pain behind the woman's eyes was somehow related to her death. A sharp pain behind the eyes could mean many things, though. On the serious end, the woman might have had a tumor, a stroke, an aneurysm, or a cerebral embolism. She might also have experienced an injury to her eyes, a severe sinus infection, or even a migraine. There was little evidence to rule any diagnosis out. It hadn't felt like a sinus infection, and she had no idea what it would feel like to experience the other conditions, any one of which could have been life-threatening under the right conditions.

Somehow the story seemed unfinished. Maude's previous visions had left her with an idea of how each skeletal pathology had occurred. In this case, the trauma to the bones of the face had been caused by the fall, but unlike all of the other times, there was nobody else who had contributed to the woman's injuries. There had to be more to it, but Maude was unsure how she could find out more now that the skeleton was finished. Reluctantly, she placed the skull in the box, deciding she would just have to wait until the skeleton had been completely analyzed.

Later that day, Maude slowly opened the back door to her shop and peered outside to see if the alley was empty. She didn't want Christine to see her and was not in the mood to explain the now very angry bruise on her face. Seeing that the coast was clear, she hurried out, opened the driver's side door of her SUV and placed her computer bag on the passenger seat. She was just about to climb in when she heard the familiar creak of the back door to the shop next door.

"What the hell happened to you?" Christine asked.

Shit! Maude thought, *I was almost in the clear.* "What, this?" she asked, pointing to her cheek. "Don and I had a fight last night. He looks worse!"

"Ha ha," Christine responded, stepping into the alley to get a closer look. "Another barroom brawl, no doubt." She laughed, answering sarcasm with the same. "Holy crap, Maude, that's quite a shiner."

"Yeah, I know, sadly the real reason isn't quite a dramatic as domestic violence or a bar room brawl. The bathroom door was stuck again, so when I used my super human strength to pull it open, I hit myself in the face, again." Maude had no trouble coming up with the story she had planned to tell people to explain her injury because she had actually done it before. Their building was old, and when the weather got warm and humid the bathroom door would get stuck. Don had told her after the first time she whacked herself in the face trying to open it to apply downward pressure to the door knob, rather than to just try and pull the door open and she never had trouble with it again. She counted on her feigned embarrassment at having done the same foolish thing twice to deter people from asking any more questions.

"Again? You've got to be kidding me! Why don't you have Don take that thing off of the hinges and re-plane it so you don't knock yourself unconscious next time?"

"Good idea. Clearly I am a danger to myself. Well, I've gotta run. It's my day to pick up the boys from camp. See ya later."

"Maybe you should wear a helmet? Be careful getting out of your car!"

Maude kept on her cheery smile until she exited the alley. "Shit!" she said out loud this time. With an exasperated sigh she pulled over and texted her husband knowing that Christine would be on the phone to Don within the next few minutes.

I fell at the lab, but I am fine. I have a pretty impressive bruise, though. Will tell you all about it tonight.

Chapter Twenty-Nine

March 7, 1841

Our friend has passed and I am determined that her death at least brings her the peace she did not know for most of her life. As I write this entry, a dangerous plot is afoot. Although our actions are the lesser of all the evil that has occurred, they are evil nonetheless. Patricia and I wait as the men sneak off into the night to dig a secret grave in the hopes that Mrs. Kaiser's eternal rest will go undisturbed. I wait anxiously for them to return because my role in this deception must also begin before dawn's first light.

Ciara put the journal aside and looked out the kitchen window, knowing that in the blackness of the night she would not see Michael and Rolland walking back from the potter's field, but she couldn't stop herself from checking periodically anyway. It was an institutional kitchen, not warm and inviting like hers at home. This one was built for efficiency, with a large cast iron stove and even larger counters for food preparation. There was a small table where the staff had their meals, but other than that, there was nothing about this space that invited those in it to sit down. Despite the impersonal nature of the room, Ciara waited there because it was the room furthest away from any of the children's dormitories or staff sleeping quarters and there was less of a chance that any of the goings on would disturb the rest of the orphanage. She did not hear the men approach but was relieved when her husband eased the door open, careful not to wake any in the house. "It's done, then?" She asked quietly.

"Aye."

"Will they notice where ye buried her?" Patricia asked.

"We were careful to put the sod back, and it looks as if we're in for heavy rain, so I think she'll be safe enough," Michael told her. "And have ye completed yer task?" He asked. Patricia and Ciara had wrapped what was essentially a log with a head of cabbage and a few branches attached in a burial shroud so that it could be taken out to the death house to await burial. In what little light was available during the predawn hours, the farmers tasked with digging the grave wouldn't notice it was not really Mrs. Kaiser, Ciara hoped.

"Aye, we did," Ciara answered. "'Tis outside by the door. Ye'll have to get Rolland to help ye carry her. I mean it."

The evening had taken its toll on his wife and Michael was very concerned that she did not look well. "The sun will be up in another hour or so. We'd best be on our way. Are ye up for it?" He asked, taking both of her hands in his.

"Aye, but I'll be that glad when our business is done."

It took no more than a few minutes for the men to load the dummy corpse into the carriage. Seeing them placing the would-be Mrs. Kaiser across the bench brought home the reality of what they were about to do. Lies, deception, breaking the law…Ciara had not actually considered that these inevitabilities were inherent in their plan to protect Mrs. Kaiser's final resting place. The truth of it staring her in the face as she stared at the figure lying in the back of the carriage turned her stomach and she was sick, right there outside the back door.

"Are ye all right, love?" Michael asked, coming to hold her as she leaned against the side of the building with one hand and holding her hair out of the way with the other. Taking his handkerchief out of his pocket and, he handed it to her as she slowly stood upright. "Ye don't have to do this."

"Aye, I'm fine, just a bit scared is all," her voice was steady and clear as she wiped her mouth and tucked the handkerchief into the pocket of her skirt. "And, yes, I do have to do this."

"Are ye sure?" Michael asked as he wiped the damp tendrils of hair away from her face. "I can send Rolland to the Big House."

"No, it's got to be me. Mrs. Rowan will not let anyone else in at this hour, least of all someone she does not know. I'm fine," she insisted, hoisting herself up into the front seat of the carriage.

They could see the outline of the Big House as they set out into what was left of the night. When the path forked, Ciara climbed down from the carriage and walked swiftly in the direction of the poorhouse and Michael and Rolland continued on to the death house. Their timing had been perfect, as the inmates had not yet risen for the day.

"And just where are ye sneaking off to in the middle of the night?" Ciara was startled, as she was so focused on the task at hand, she did not see the shadowy figure approach. Like before, she recognized the voice immediately. In all of the activity of the predawn hours, nobody had noticed Angus McLean's arrival. He had come up the path between the two asylums to the stable to put his horse away and was just leaving there when he noticed Ciara approaching the house. "And me thinkin' ye were a respectable married woman, yet here ye are, out when no decent woman should be out. And where are ye off to in such a hurry?"

Dressed all in black, she could barely see him in the shadows of dawn, but she could smell him as he came closer. Ciara began to panic both out of fear of the man approaching her and at how his presence would most certainly foil their plans. "Leave me be, Angus McLean. I've business at the Big House that won't wait." She hoped the harshness in her voice would not betray her anxiety. She knew if she screamed that Michael would come running, but that would most certainly bring unwanted attention from the almshouse.

"What business brings ye here at this hour? Whatever it is can surely wait while we get reacquainted. I seem to recall ye've a fondness for the stables, and me just back from a lonely journey.

Just ye come wi' me and let's have that kiss I've been waiting these long years for."

Panic turned to terror as he grabbed her, one hand clamped behind her head trying to push her face to his, while the other groped at her skirts. His putrid, hot breath assaulted her senses, bringing back every horrifying memory of what he had done to her years before. Her terror was instantly replaced with fury as she thrust her knee up into his gut as hard as she could. As he doubled over she pushed him to the ground and ran for the barn. "Why, ye filthy wee bitch!" He growled as he ran after her. Just inside the door she groped around quickly for whatever she could find to use as a weapon, knowing he was right on her heels. She grabbed the wooden handle of something, a pitchfork, maybe. Turning, she lunged forward, thrusting her weapon at the shadow figure running toward her with all her might. She heard a groan and felt the weight of the man as he fell with the object still embedded in his mid-section. She quickly dropped the handle and fell to her knees, vaguely registering the sound of his head hitting the edge of the mounting block before he hit the ground. Hearing footsteps approach, she tried to scramble back into the barn until she recognized the hushed tones of her husband calling. Struggling to push the words out between ragged breaths, she barely whispered, "I'm here, Michael." She tried again, taking a deep breath, "I'm here."

He had thought better of letting her walk to the Big House alone, and had doubled back to make sure she had reached her destination safely. Surveying the scene before him as he came around the barn, he fell to the ground running his hands gently probing along his wife's arms and torso, desperately trying to determine if she was injured. "Dear God, what's happened? Are ye hurt?"

Ciara pulled away, although her husband was reluctant to let her go. "McLean," she said, her voice surprisingly calm. "He came upon me as I was headed up to the Big House. Oh, Michael, what are we to do? He's sure to tell Mr. Proctor…"

"I don't think he'll be sayin' much of anything anymore," Rolland interrupted. He had followed Michael, thinking that if there was trouble, two men were better than one. "By the looks of it, he's dead."

"Oh, dear God, have I killed him?"

Michael helped his wife to stand, and then made sure that she was steady on her feet before he walked over to the body slumped on the ground next to the mounting block. Grabbing hold of the man's hair, Michael raised his head so he could feel for the carotid pulse in his neck. He left his fingers there for a full minute to be sure. "Aye, he's dead, and good riddance."

Ciara stood there, shaking, trying to reconcile what she had just done. Seeing her struggle, Michael took her hands in his and looked her squarely in the eye. "Now just ye listen to me, ye defended yerself. The man nearly killed ye the first time, and likely would have succeeded this time if ye hadn't done what ye did."

"I know, I know," she nodded in agreement. "He is truly evil and he deserves worse than death for the sins he has committed. But now what are we to do? How will we explain this to Mr. Proctor? He's sure to find out."

"He'll not find out if we act quickly," Rolland said

dispassionately. Looking out into the dawn, the light just beginning to emerge, he continued. "Give me a five minute lead and then the two of ye continue on the Big House as ye planned. By the time ye get the two men down here, I'll have McLean wrapped in the shroud. He's wasted away to practically nothing and will be more convincing as the widow than that log anyway." Not giving either of them a chance to argue, he pulled the pitchfork out of the body, heaved McLean up over his shoulder and headed off toward the death house.

As soon as he was out of sight, Ciara turned to her husband. "Michael, I don't know about this. I've killed a man. Self-defense or not, we've got to tell someone."

Michael was silent for a moment, considering what his wife had just said. He picked up the pitchfork, wiped it on the grass and replaced it in the barn. There would be a mess to clean up, but the rain that had just begun to fall would likely take care of that. He'd send Rolland down to make sure before the other men came to do their morning chores. Michael took his wife's arm and led her toward the fence so that they might speak away from the blood-soaked ground. "No, I don't think we do." Seeing her about to protest, he continued.

"Now just ye hear me out. Think about what this man has taken from us. He robbed us of a family of our own! Think about what he was about to do to ye, again! He was an evil man, Ciara, and to be sure no one will miss him, or he wouldn't have come back here. Nobody knows that he had returned, and after a few days, Proctor will assume McLean ran off with his money." Michael paused a moment, unsure if he should share his final thoughts with his wife. He took another deep breath before he continued. "The man is a criminal, and no mistake. Should Proctor do as we expect him to, it will be McLean on the dissecting table in Geneva, and it would serve him right. Can ye live with that?"

Ciara hadn't considered all that McLean had taken from her and what he could have taken had she not killed him. The city was a dangerous place, and she knew other women who had resorted to violence in order to defend themselves from men like Angus McLean. She looked at her husband with absolute certainty and said, "Aye, I can live with it." Without another word, they set off for the Big House. By the time they arrived at the back door, the rain was coming down hard.

"Are ye ready, then?"

"Aye," she answered and opened the door.

After some harsh words and more than a few threats, the two men who were critical to the completion of the final phase of their plan were reluctantly following Ciara and Michael to the death house. Annoyed at being dragged out before their breakfast, the two farmers were all too willing to let Dr. Nolan lift the body into the casket and for he and the teacher to load it on to the wagon. The heavy rain continued as they made their way out to the potter's field.

Ciara stood in the pouring rain vigorously rubbing her hands along her cold and wet arms to keep warm. Two equally drenched and shivering young men removed the casket from the wagon and tried to ease it into the muddy hole they had dug by the light of a single lantern. It was just dawn on Saturday morning and the poor lads could barely see what they were doing. It was difficult to maneuver the large wooden box on the slick ground and the men were not timid about expressing their annoyance at having to bury the body so soon after death.

"We've gone and dug the grave in the middle of

the night. Can we no' save the burial until after the storm has passed?" Thomas Mulligan, the larger of the two, complained after he had lost his footing on the wet ground for the second time and nearly dropped the casket.

"No!" Ciara's comment was punctuated by roar of thunder so well timed, it made both men shudder. "She'll have a decent burial, or at least what passes for decent 'round here. She was a good woman and deserves as much. Quit yer wailin' and get on with it!" and then another well timed burst of thunder, this time with lightening. If the men were back in the old country they would surely think her a witch! Ciara pulled her soggy shawl around her shoulders as she and Michael moved under the large oak tree thinking its few remaining leaves would provide some sort of shelter from the storm.

As the wind picked up, driving the rain directly into their eyes, the desire to get out of the weather overrode any fear of Ciara Nolan's wrath, supernatural or not. "Mr. Proctor says three days in the death house before they're put in the ground, just in case one of these poor sod's 'as got someone willin' to pay for a proper burial." Joseph Buxton argued hoping the mention of the Poorhouse Keeper's name would change her mind."Mr. Proctor will no' be pleased we didn't wait," Buxton continued.

More likely he was not pleased that the general good health of the inmates and the scrutiny of the Board had left him with precious few poor souls he could sell to the medical college, Ciara thought. "Never ye mind, Mr. Proctor," she said. "He'll be none the wiser unless one of you tells him." At present he was at his family hunting lodge in Williamsville. When he returned on Monday, everyone would have forgotten about poor Frederika Kaiser. "To be sure he'll make you dig her up so that she can *wait* her few days in the death house." Ciara placed special emphasis on the word wait to indicate to the two men that she knew full well there would be no period of waiting. Mrs. Kaiser would be dug up and sold if Proctor learned of her death.

The men nodded to each other as they took a minute to consider the miserable task of slogging through the mud and clay to exhume her body, which would be harder to take out of the grave than it was to put in, not to mention that, should they be caught, they'd likely be thrown in jail. "He'll no' hear about it from us, but should he notice this," Mulligan gestured toward the swamp that had been created by digging a grave in the pouring rain, "I'll be tellin' him 'twas you stood out here and forced us to do it."

"The more you should hope he doesn't," she replied. "For if I must, I will explain my reasons to Mr. Pratt and the Board of Directors, and where will ye come out of all this if I do?" While both Mulligan and Buxton lacked any formal education, they were smart enough to know that William Proctor would likely deny any wrong doing and point the finger at them. Without another word, the men completed their task.

Michael, who had been silent during the burial, made a note of the number on the stake hammered into the ground to mark the grave. That number, 10, was supposed to correspond to the burial record kept in the ledger in the Keeper's office. No headstones for those buried at the Erie County Almshouse. There was neither the time nor the money for such luxuries. Standing over the muddy grave, he prayed, "May you find the peace in Heaven you were denied here on earth, in the name of the father, and of the Son, and of the Holy

Ghost. Amen." As he said the words, both he and Ciara were looking across the field at where the real Mrs. Kaiser was buried. The farmers, eager to be out of the rain, didn't even notice as they hurried away. It was a small thing, but it was all they could do for this woman, as there would be no other acknowledgement of her passing.

Having waived the men on ahead, the Nolans would have to walk across the cemetery to the orphanage on the far side of the poor farm. As they proceeded, a bolt of lightning silently lit up the sky. Ciara looked up, taking it as sign from God that they had done right by this woman. While the rain had lessened a bit, still they were soaked through and frozen. It was a small price to pay to make sure that Mrs. Kaiser would finally have a place to rest in peace.

As the couple hurried across the field, they were unaware that they were being watched. Mrs. Rowan had seen them come in and drag the farmers out to the death house. She was paid well to provide the Keeper with useful bits of information, and he would certainly be interested in what had transpired this morning. "What on earth are you lot up to?" She mumbled to herself as she walked toward the Big House.

* * *

It was late Monday afternoon when William Proctor finally arrived at the Poorhouse. He hadn't even had time to remove his coat and hat before Mrs. Rowan was at his office door.

"Good afternoon to ye, sir. Did ye pass a pleasant few days in the country? To be sure, there's been plenty o' trouble here while ye were gone."

William had lost heavily at cards over the past few days and he was uninterested in whatever squabbles were currently causing problems among the inmates. He was more interested in whether McLean was back, and, more importantly, if he brought the money. "Mrs. Rowan, I'll hear whatever you've got to tell me later," he said as he turned toward the door. "I have a few things to see to that won't wait."

"Forgive me, sir, but I think ye'll be most interested in what I've got to tell ye," the matron insisted.

"Later, Mrs. Rowan," he repeated, and then he was walking in the direction of the Keeper's quarters before she had a chance to utter another word.

He climbed the stairs to his rooms, sniffing the air

for cheap whiskey and stale tobacco, the signs that McLean had returned. He opened the door calling out, "McLean!" There was no sign of him in the sitting room. He continued calling out as he proceeded through the kitchen, the dining room and the bedchamber. There was no sign of him. "I shall have a word with him about lingering in the taverns on the way back," Proctor said out loud as he left the Keeper's quarters. Halfway down the stairs he bellowed for Mrs. Rowan to come to his office immediately.

"Has McLean come back yet?" He asked as she came running in his office.

"I've not seen him, but I daresay, ye'll no' be worried about the likes of him once ye've heard what I've got to tell ye."

"Tell me what you know," he directed, becoming interested in what could be more important than McLean and his money.

"Well, just the other day I had to pull two of the inmates out of the women's dorm. Tryin' to shirk their chores, so they were, and them thinkin' as they could have a wee lie-in after havin' been up all night with the orphans! Short of help over there, they claimed. Well I just went right over there…"

"Get to the point, Mrs. Rowan," Proctor interrupted.

"Well, as I was just gettin' to that part. Seems they've been hidin' a sick inmate over there for quite some time. The woman died in the night, Friday, I think. And doesn't Mrs. Nolan and the Doctor come rushin' over here before the breakfast is even served and haulin' the two farmers out o' their beds, insistin' the woman be buried straightaway. Well, and didn't the three of us tell them the body's to stay in the death house for three days and ye'd see to her burial after that." Mrs. Rowan's voice was getting louder, her outrage evident. "I told ye as that woman would be trouble! I followed them out there, her and the doctor, and her shoutin' at the men to get on wi' it, while the sky thundered above her. If I didn't know better, I'd say she is a witch!"

"Was the death reported to Mr. Pratt?"

"Well, he hasn't been in today, but to be sure Dr. Nolan was in first this morning, came right into your office and wrote in the death book, so he did." Moving forward, Mrs. Rowan took the ledger off the shelf and opened it to the page where Mrs. Kaiser's death had been entered and turning the book so that the Keeper could see for himself. "Of all the cheek, bargin' into yer office like that!"

Proctor smiled as he noted that the woman's death recorded in the ledger. "Thank you, Mrs. Rowan that will be all." Handing her a coin from his pocket, he continued. "There's no need to trouble Mr. Pratt with this business at the orphan asylum. I will handle it."

After the matron left the office William shut the door and returned to his desk. He opened the desk drawer and pulled out a quill. He wrote "taken by cousin" in the ledger, leaving the book open so the ink could dry.

Chapter Thirty

Having completed his business at the poorhouse earlier that morning, Michael stopped at the orphanage to pick up his wife. It was time that they pay a call on Mrs. Farrell and bring her up to date on the events over the weekend. She listened, wide-eyed, as the Nolans gave a full report. "There's none here who will shed a tear over the death of that man, and no mistake." Looking at Ciara, she continued, "Don't ye fret for one minute over what you've done. There's a few women on Canal Street who've killed a man to save themselves, I'd wager, and nobody the wiser."

Ciara, feeling ill from the events of the past few days, answered, "'Tis not the killin' part that bothers me; 'tis the keepin' of this secret that wears on me. I can't even go to confession, for surely I'd have to tell Father Mertz the whole of it."

"Aye, Michael was right to tell no one. The Proctors are in tight with the constable. They've had to be with all the trouble their William causes. I'm sure they'd find a way to turn your story around if it suited them. Aye, 'tis a heavy load ye carry, but it will lessen in time."

"I hadn't even thought of that," Ciara said, stunned at the possibility that she might have been accused of murder.

"Well, it's as ye said," Michael explained, "If we went to the constable, ye'd have to tell him the whole of it. Proctor's family would not allow their son to be accused of such heinous crimes, and they've the money to see someone else pay for what he's done."

"Well, it's done, and only four of us who know, and sure enough we'll tell no one," Ciara said, effectively closing the discussion of the death of Angus McLean.

"I'm that sorry about poor Mrs. Kaiser. God bless you and yours for doin' what ye did to give her a peaceful place to rest for all eternity." Pausing to look at each of them, Colleen continued, "What's to be done now? Surely Mrs. Rowan has told Mr. Proctor there's been a death at the orphan asylum."

"The burial was listed in the death book as the widow Kaiser, but I doubt a written record of her passing will stop Proctor if he is desperate," Michael told her.

"Aye, and he is that. If the rumors are true, Mr. Proctor has gambled away all of his money. And what's likely to happen if he goes to the trouble of digging her up and finds his minion instead?" Colleen asked.

"Likely he won't," Ciara suggested. "He'll no' do the work himself, to be sure, and those two cowards saw Michael put a body into the coffin, so they've no reason to check."

"Well, you've protected your Mrs. Kaiser, and you've rid the world of a villain, but I don't see that we are any closer to putting a stop to Mr. Proctor's nefarious activities," Colleen told them "The only way to make any charge of wrongdoing against him stick would be to catch him in the act, which seems a nearly impossible task."

"What if we catch him along the road?" Ciara suggested. "He'll have a time explainin' a body in the back of his wagon."

"Maybe not," Colleen countered. "He's the Keeper of the Poor. Should anyone ask, he's transporting a dearly departed to their beloved kin for a proper burial.

Who would question him?"

"We can't just let it end here! He'll do it again, ye know he will. We've gone too far down this road to stop now," Ciara argued. "This has to end now!"

Michael heard in his wife's voice the anguish over all that had transpired over the past few days finally coming to a boil. She had convinced herself that killing Angus McLean was a small price to pay if she could stop Proctor once and for all. Michael had suspected the discussion with Mrs. Farrell would go in this direction, having thought things through many times since that night, and feared what this realization would do to his wife's fragile hold on her emotions. "Well, we've still got the death of the stable man, Buchman. I looked in the Death Book before I entered Mrs. Kaiser's name. It was never recorded. 'Twas Dr. Ferris who reported the death, to Mr. Pratt, no less, so I don't see how Proctor can lie his way out of trouble should someone come lookin' for the man."

"And just who would come lookin?" Mrs. Farrell asked. "I doubt we could get away with sendin' one of the servants again to claim him!"

"No, there's no need to send any of yer household

staff on another adventure," Michael told her. "I can suggest Dr. Ferris to add a few notes to Buchman's burial entry. He's very much in favor of better record-keeping and will go straight to Mr. Pratt when he realizes the death was never entered into the ledger. After that, Ferris and I can insist that it become the physician's job to record the deaths in the ledger. Surely ye can get them to agree with that?"

"Aye, I can do better than that. I can issue a formal reprimand to Proctor and insist that all deaths be reported by the attending physician directly to the Board," Colleen assured him.

Ciara was not pleased with the solution, but could offer no other alternative. "He'll find a way if he's as desperate as ye say."

"Aye, he might," Michael agreed, "But we've made it nearly impossible for him to continue on as he has. He is known for his dislike of any sort of work, so he may lose interest now that we've made it difficult for him."

"I hope yer right."

* * *

William Proctor held the reins in one hand as he

fished in the pocket of his coat for a pair of gloves, the cold night air being too much for bare hands. He dropped the reins, letting the horse find its way down the access road while he worked them on over his fingers. It was later than he had intended to leave, although it really didn't matter, as there was no money to stop at an inn to rest. McLean still hadn't arrived back at the poorhouse and Proctor had exhausted all of his available funds. He'd have to sleep rough on this trip, and that thought put him in a foul mood. There was a rifle resting on the bench beside him, William placed a hand on it to reassure himself that is was still there. *He'll be sorry that he tried to steal from me!* There was a good chance he would run in McLean on the road, and the Keeper was prepared to extract his money by force if necessary. To add insult to injury, Mulligan and Buxton initially refused to dig up the grave and he had to threaten to put them out of the poorhouse if they didn't. Listening to them grumble about the doctor and his wife forcing them out into a thunder storm without so much as a cup of tea made Proctor realize just what thorns in his side the Nolans had become. "I'll deal with the two of them when I get back," he said into the night.

The early spring weather conspired to make for a grueling four day trip to Geneva. Damp, chilly days gave way to frigid nights as the wagon rolled on toward the Finger Lakes. By the time William made it to the Geneva Medical College, he both looked and felt like one of the inmates in the lunatic asylum. He was cold, wet and starving and wanted to conclude his business as quickly as possible so he could enjoy a hot bath and whatever other hospitality his uncle had to offer. Pulling the wagon into the narrow alley behind the anatomy laboratory, he knocked on the door. The man who opened the door was unable to contain his shock at the disheveled looking vagrant on the other side of it.

"What the devil happened to you?" Dr. Standish asked not bothering to hide his disgust.

"I'd rather not talk about it. What I would like is my usual fee and directions to your rooms. I am in need of a drink after my long journey."

"You are in need of a good scrubbing," his uncle replied, "and you should burn those clothes before you set foot in my rooms."

"My fee, if you please, uncle."

"All in good time, I'll need to assess the condition of the specimen before I agree to your usual fee, which you well know."

William rolled his eyes and began unwrapping the burial shroud. He had the pulled enough of it aside to see that the hand that emerged belonged to a man rather than the woman Mrs. Rowan had told him about. Pulling the arm out further, he recognized the tattered coat of Angus McLean. Shoving it back into the shroud, he turned to his uncle. "Really, Uncle Standish, it's been a very long and tedious trip, kindly get my fee while I finish unwrapping the body. As you so delicately pointed out, I am in need of a bath and a change of clothes."

"Well, as you smell worse than the anatomical theater in summer, I will. But be warned: I will not pay full price for an amputee.

As soon as his uncle had left the room, William began to tear the shroud away from the body to expose the face. It was indeed McLean. "How the hell did you end up here?" He asked, half expecting McLean to answer. Mrs. Rowan had told him that the Nolans had insisted the body be buried right away. It must have been McLean they were burying. Could one of them have killed him? He didn't think the doctor had it in him and he had a hard time believing that his wife could get the better of Angus McLean. Then a thought suddenly occurred to him. "My money," he said out loud. He threw the shroud aside and began pawing through the man's pockets, ripping the fabric of the already battered coat as he searched. Not finding anything in the coat, he pushed the body to one side so that he could check the pants pocket. Sticking his hand in, he shouted, "Ah ha!" as he pulled out a wad of bills. Bringing a fist full of cash to his lips, he kissed it, and let out another maniacal laugh.

"Stand aside sir!" Proctor turned, eyes wide, grubby fist full of money, to find a man he did not recognize standing in the door shaking a fist at him.

The other man took in the scene; the shroud carelessly tossed on the floor, the body askew, the clothing torn, and repeated his command. "I say, stand aside, sir!"

Proctor adopted his typical expression of arrogant indifference. Stepping casually away from the body, he asked, "And just who are you?"

"I am Dr. Harold Crosby, Dean of Medicine, and you, sir, need to hand over the money you have just stolen off of this cadaver immediately!"

"Dr. Crosby, if you would kindly fetch Dr. Standish, I am sure he would be happy to tell you who I am."

Before the Dean could fire off an indignant reply, Dr. Standish came through the door, quickly pressing the money he had been holding into his pocket as he surveyed the situation. "What is going on here? Who is this man and how did he get in here?"

"I was just going to ask you the same question, Dr. Standish. He claims to know you."

"I do not know this man."

"I found him going through the pockets of this specimen. He found a considerable sum of money," the Dean reported.

"Have one of the orderlies tie him up and we'll call the constable," Standish replied.

"What!" William was furious that his uncle had denied him. "This is outrageous! I'll have you know…"

Standish interrupted before his nephew could say anything that would incriminate either one of them.

"Dr. Crosby, might I trouble you to fetch one of the orderlies so we can safely contain this scoundrel?" As soon as the Dean left the room, Standish held his hand up, demanding silence. "What the devil were you doing? You know better than to reveal our relationship to anyone here."

"Don't you recognize this man?" his nephew asked, outrage evident in his voice. "This is the very man who made a delivery to this laboratory just last week. He stole my money. I was merely trying to get it back when that man barged in."

Standish stared at his nephew in disbelief. "Did you kill this man? How could you have been such a fool as to bring him here! *That man* is the Dean of this college! How dare you jeopardize my career by implicating me in your devilish scheme?"

Before Proctor could reply, the Dean came back, accompanied by a rather muscular young man carrying a length of rope. "Mr. Wilbur, kindly secure this scoundrel and then take him to the constable. Tell the Chief that I'll be along shortly to explain the charges."

"You're having me arrested? This is an outrage!! Do you know who I am?" William continued shouting at the two physicians long after they had left the room, leaving him in the very capable and strong hands of young Mr. Wilbur.

Chapter Thirty-One

"Don't even tell try and tell me you hit your head on the bathroom door again," Don warned as he walked into their bedroom, ice pack in one hand and a tumbler of whiskey in the other.

"Of course I didn't." Maude placed the fragile journal on the bed, speaking quietly to be sure that the boys stayed glued to their Xbox in the next room. She wanted to discuss this with her husband without being interrupted or overheard. "I hit my head on the tape dispenser when I was packing up the skull this morning."

"What? How the hell…? Did you…?"

"Look," she interrupted, "I was wearing gloves and I took them off to answer the phone. Then I was so aggravated at the tape dispenser that I forgot to put them back on. I mean it; I really forgot," she insisted, scanning his expression for some indication of how he was processing this revelation.

"What happened?" Don asked, handing her the ice pack and taking a sip of the whiskey. He would reserve judgment until he had heard the whole story.

"I picked up the skull with my bare hands by accident, I swear. My fingers touched that fracture on her face and I fell forward and the tape dispenser broke my fall."

"What else happened? What did you see?"

"This time it was more about what I felt. I was sitting at my desk. At first I had an excruciating pain behind my eye. That's when I fell forward. She collapsed and banged the side of her face, I think. I saw a kitchen, but not the same one I was in earlier. There were people fussing all around me, I mean, her. I felt like I should know them, but I couldn't remember who any of them were. When I came to, the side of my face was throbbing. I remember thinking that was wrong. Whenever I come back, whatever pain she felt is gone. Then I realized that I hit my face." She gently rubbed the bruise, now angry shades of red and purple, hoping to elicit sympathy rather than anger.

"Maude, do you realize what might have happened

if you had been standing up?"

"But I wasn't. Besides, I may not have been injured at all if I hadn't been sitting there. Look, Don, I certainly did not intentionally touch that skull without gloves. I had every intention of packing it up and leaving campus. Anyway, it's done and I am fine. The entire skeleton is finished and I will not be working in the lab anymore."

Don stared at his wife, who looked almost comical lecturing him with one eye nearly swelled shut and made no attempt to suppress a laugh. "You do look like you were in a bar fight."

Laughing with him, she said, "Yeah, that's what Christine said!"

"So, what's next?" He knew that she would not let the mystery of burial number116 go even though the skeleton was safely packed up in the lab.

"Well, Brian had told me there were a few grave goods included with burials clustered around number 116, but he couldn't say off the top of his head if any of them were specifically associated with her. I guess I'll run over to campus tomorrow and take a look. I could also take a look in the mortality ledger and see if any deaths jump out at me, although if these are burials from an earlier period that were moved from the original poorhouse location I won't find anything. There was a resolution in the Erie County Board of Proceeding Report around 1840 that called for the use of a separate ledger to record all deaths at the poorhouse, but that book is long gone. We only have ledgers from the later decades of the nineteenth century."

"What is the likelihood you will find anything to give this woman some identity?" Don asked.

"Well, that depends on how you define the term identity. Am I likely to find out her name? No, I am not. We don't have any records that specifically document where the entire cemetery was located or any map that could identify specific burials. However, after cleaning this skeleton, I can tell you that this woman's life was not easy and that she experienced physical pain, likely constantly at the end of her life. Maybe it's not so important to know her name. Maybe she just wanted me to know her story."

Don held up his glass before taking the last sip. "Here's to you, number 116. I hope you're finally able to rest in peace."

The next afternoon Maude headed over to campus in the hopes of finding some artifact that would help her identify the woman whose tortured past she had shared. Brian was out in the field, so a graduate student escorted her to the far corner of the archaeology lab where the few grave goods associated with the excavated burials were laid out. Each item had been placed on a tray with an index card identifying the site number, the burial location number, the date it was found and various other notations, such as the location of the item within the burial. It was an interesting assortment of artifacts for a potter's field site. Maude noted a pair of shoes, two newspapers dated 1901 and 1903, men's trousers, a coat, a few rosaries and two bibles. Pointing to the upper left hand corner of the table, the student said, "They are arranged by burial location number starting from there. Be careful if you touch anything," and left Maude to examine the evidence alone.

The sight of the few possessions on the table, out of context, made Maude pause and consider the people who might have owned them. She looked closely at one of the newspapers, resisting the urge to touch the fragile, water stained pages. It looked to be written in

French, suggesting that its owner had stayed connected to his or her mother country. The dark trousers were worn at the knees and mended many times at the seams. The coat had the same well-worn appearance, likely having seen many years of use before its final service, protecting its owner for all eternity. She was surprised how small in size all of the clothing was. Even the shoes would not fit most adult men today. These were items likely very important to their owners during life, providing comfort and even protection when times got tough. Their importance would become more critical in death, as these common items had the potential to provide their owners with some identity: if not a name, perhaps a small part of their story, like their native language or the importance of faith in their lives.

Scanning the burial location numbers, Maude's heart skipped a beat when she saw a small bible labeled with the location number 116. Maude walked around the other side of the table to get a better look. The small book looked very old, its leather cover blistering and peeling from over a century of exposure to the destructive forces that work beneath the ground. Reaching in her pocket, she withdrew a single white cotton glove and put it on her right hand to protect the fragile pages from the naturally occurring oils on her hand. Very carefully she opened the book, not daring to lift the fragile cover any higher than was necessary to see the pages, many of which looked to be stuck together. She noted the writing on the first page was in German. Very carefully, she lifted up the cover just a tiny bit more (still only a few inches above the page) to see if there was a name inscribed on the page. Crouching down on her knees for a closer look, her head bent and turned in the direction of the book, she saw what she thought was an inscription on the inside cover. Daring to raise the cover just a hair more, she could see the first initial, "F", more clearly. She spent the next few minutes squinting, moving her face closer, then away from the page, trying to get a better look at the name. There were spikes in the first name that appeared to be a "d" and a "k", and the first initial of the last name was definitely a "K". Maude's eyes became as wide as saucers when she realized the name that had been inscribed in the bible. "Holy crap! It can't be her!" She said out loud.

"Who can't be her?" Maude had been so focused

on trying to read the name in the book that she hadn't noticed Brian come up behind her.

"What are you doing here? I thought you were in the field." Startled out of her discovery, Maude's question sounded more like an accusation.

"It started to rain, so we packed it in early. Find anything interesting?" He asked, pointing to the bible.

"I'll say. You are not going to believe who the owner of this bible is! I really just can't believe this," she went on, still shocked at her discovery.

"Well, don't keep me in suspense."

"I think it belonged to a woman named Frederika Kaiser. She was an almshouse widow who had been transferred to the orphan asylum in 1840 to help care for the children there. Brian, I have found several mentions of her name in both the inmate records and in the diary of the Buffalo Orphan Asylum's first Keeper." Gently lifting the cover of the bible again, she pointed to the name. "Here, look for yourself."

Brian leaned over the book for a closer look. "Looks more like "Fredenka" to me, but I can see how the "r" and the "i" could have run together."

"Don't you think that is a dot over the 'i'?"

Squinting and bringing his face as close to the book as he dared, Brian took a second look. "Well, it could be, but that doesn't prove definitively that the person buried with this bible was your Frederika Kaiser. She could have given it to this person, or this person could have stolen it."

"I know, I know, but we still have the demographic variables in the skeleton to compare with those from the records. If the age, sex, and ancestry match up, then it could be her, and that would mean that these burials are likely the ones that were transported from the Black Rock location."

"That would be really exciting. You should bring Jean up to date and then keep me informed once the students start working on the skeletons."

"Will do! I'll go downstairs now and see if she's in."

Maude was disappointed to get no response to her repeated knocks on Jean's office door. Checking her watch, she reached in her pocket and pulled out the key to the Physical Anthropology Osteology Lab where the cleaned burials were being stored. The graduate students would have gone out for lunch after they left the field, so she would have the room to herself. Opening the door, she was greeted with the familiar smell of embalming solution that always wafted in from the Comparative Primate Anatomy Lab next door. Maude walked into the room and turned on the lights near the chalk board. Boxes containing the already cleaned skeletons were stacked three high on the tables. *The students are working hard*, she thought. She went over and pulled the box containing burial number 116. Keeping her promise to Don, she did not open it.

For a long time, she just stood staring at the box with her hand on its lid. Finally, Maude said, "I know it's you. I'm sorry you had so many difficulties in your life." She was quiet again for a while, wanting to say something, but not knowing what. Finally, she placed both of her hands on the side of the box and said, "Thank you, Mrs. Kaiser, for sharing your story with me. I want you to know that I will do my very best to make sure that it's not forgotten." Giving the top of the box a final pat, she turned to leave.

Maude was just locking the door as she realized that she had forgotten to put the box back in the location she found it in and to turn off the lights. "What the…?" she exclaimed in disbelief as she pushed open the door of the empty lab to find the room dark and the box back where she had found it. "I'll be damned," she said under her breath as she exited the room and locked the door for the second time.

The lights had been turned off and the box was back where it belonged. Maude couldn't help but think that it was a sign from Frederika Kaiser that their time together had ended. As she continued out to her car, Maude started to think about how she would go about keeping her promise to the widow. So much about what she had learned about this woman's life came from her unusual connection to the skeleton. She couldn't very well publish a report of her supernatural experiences in the American Journal of Physical Anthropology. Putting her key in the ignition, the antique dealer/physical anthropologist smiled and said, "I always wanted to try writing a novel!"

Chapter Thirty-Two

March 10, 1840

There's sadness about the place with Mrs. Kaiser gone. I feel the loss of her in the pit of my stomach. Still, our minds cannot dwell on our grief as the demands of the children keep us focused. Somehow, wee Martha was right, and we've had three newborn babes brought to us in the last week, all with what Michael calls purulent opthalmia. The poor wee things are miserable with their red and swollen eyes. All three were born to prostitutes and all three were sent here by their mothers in the hopes of finding a better life than their wretched existence could provide. I shall remember these women in my prayers tonight in the hope that God will show them a better way. As for wee Martha, she has the rare gift of sight, I think. She's a special lass, and no mistake. I wonder what the future brings for her. Perhaps she knows already.

Life at the orphan asylum became a bit more subdued after the passing of Mrs. Kaiser. While the children had become accustomed to the transient nature of the staff, they felt her loss more keenly than others. Because she derived so much happiness in her care for them, her joy became infectious and it seemed that her renewed sense of hope spread throughout the institution. They would all miss her very much.

The Keeper of the Poorhouse had, presumably, left town without word earlier in the week, leaving Ciara an opportunity to make some changes in her staff. Without Mr. Proctor to protest, Ciara had secured Mrs. Loderick and Mrs. Munroe permanent positions and argued successfully to Mr. Pratt that if the other women were working nights at the orphanage, they should not be expected for morning chores at the Big House.

With four women staying in residence, in addition to the night nurses, there was no longer a reason for Rolland to spend as much time at the orphanage. However, he still came at the end of each day to see Patricia home. He watched as she issued last minute instructions to the evening staff with all the authority and confidence of the Keeper herself. It was then that it occurred to him that one day she might very well become the Keeper of the Orphan Asylum. He found himself surprised to realize how much that pleased him. It was time, he thought.

"What this, then?" Patricia asked, looking very impressed at the carriage parked out by the back door.

"Well, I thought it time I had a proper carriage to take ye about in, rather than that old rickety thing they keep behind the shed here." Rolland looked nervous as he helped her up on to the bench.

"'Tis a fine carriage indeed," she stated, "and I should be proud to ride in it wherever ye'd like to take me." She kissed him on the cheek and looked at him expectantly, wondering why they were not yet on their way. Rolland was silent for a moment while he gathered the courage to say what he wanted to say.

"Is there somethin' on yer mind? She asked.

"Aye, it's been on my mind for a time, but what with all that's gone on lately, I thought it could wait, but I don't want to wait anymore." Putting the reins down, he asked, "Will ye walk with me a while?"

"Aye," she agreed, allowing him to help her down from the carriage.

They had reached the orchards before he spoke again. Stopping just under one of the larger apple trees whose leaves were just starting to burgeon after the cold winter, he took her hands in both of his. "Patricia Sloane, I love ye with all my heart and I'd like to ask the doctor for yer hand in marriage, if ye'll have me."

Patricia smiled and squeezed his hands, nodding her head. "I love ye back, Rolland Thomas, and I'd be proud to be yer wife."

"Yer sure? I'll no' expect ye to leave the children, I want to be clear about that. I've got some money saved and, well ye can decide where ye'd like to live and …." His rambling ceased when soft cool lips met his. They kissed for a good long while, neither of them concerned with the cold evening air or the need to breathe it. When they finally parted, Rolland, overcome with joy, wrapped his arms tightly around her, picking her up off of the ground and swung her around until they were both dizzy. "Yer the prettiest lass in all of Buffalo and I do love ye so," he said, and then he was kissing her again, as the light of the day faded around them.

Having spent a considerable amount of time in the orchard, it was full dark by the time Rolland pulled into the long drive that lead to the Nolan's house. They were just coming up to the barn when Michael exited the house to meet them. "Mr. Thomas, I should hope ye have a reasonable explanation as to why yer bringin' the lass home in the middle of the night."

"Michael, don't ye be rude," Ciara chastised as she came up behind him. "Patricia come in the house with me and let the men have a word."

Patricia looked at her future husband and gave him an encouraging nod before following Ciara back in the house. The two were no sooner in the door when Ciara spun around with a conspiratorial grin and said, "Tell me everything, sister," knowing there had to be a reason the couple had taken so long to arrive.

"He wants to ask Michael for my hand in marriage!" Patricia couldn't wait to get home and tell her sister the good news and the first few words all tumbled out as one. "Is he truly cross that we are a bit late?"

Ciara gave her sister a quick hug and moved her closer to the window so that they could both watch the men as they talked. "I'm that happy for ye. He's no' so much mad as he is concerned for ye, and yer more than a bit late. We've finished our supper and Martha and Johnny are off to bed."

"We walked a bit in the orchard before we started

for home. I guess we lost track of the time. Did ye save some supper for us?" Patricia asked, suddenly becoming aware of the mouthwatering smells of ham and boiled potatoes.

Taking in her slightly swollen lips, Ciara guessed that they hadn't done much walking. "Aye, of course we did, set the table for the two of ye and I'll see to it."

Michael glared at the young man before him after the women had gone in to the house. "Just what are ye about keepin' her out this late?"

Rolland took a deep breath, looking at his accuser directly. "I'm that sorry, sir. We took a walk in the orchards for a wee while to discuss a few things. The time got away from us, is all. Surely ye know me to be an honorable man. I'd never do anything that would reflect on Patricia poorly."

"If I didn't think ye an honorable man, I'd have flattened ye the minute the women went in the house. See that ye get her home directly from now on."

"Yes, sir, I will. Dr. Nolan, there's another matter I wish to discuss with ye if ye will stay out with me here just a wee bit longer."

"As I'm not wearin' my coat, it had better be just a

wee bit longer. What's on yer mind, lad?"

"I asked Patricia to walk with me this evening because I had intended to ask ye for her hand in marriage and I thought it wise to make sure she'd have me first," Rolland explained, sheepishly.

"And?" Michael asked, charmed by the young man's humility.

"Aye, she will. She'll have me, aye," he repeated nervously.

"Do ye love her?"

"Aye, I do, sir," he answered more confidently this time.

"Ye know, the Sloane women are like no others. Ye'll no' have a wife at home to serve ye. Patricia will expect to continue on at the orphan asylum after she's wed. What are yer feelings on the matter?"

"I would not ask her to leave the children. We've discussed it, and as long as she wants to stay and care for the children, she'll get no argument from me."

"Have ye put some money away?"

"Aye sir. We'll no' be livin' on Pearl Street, but I believe I can take proper care of Patricia and make her happy."

Michael extended his hand toward the younger man and shook it heartily. "Yer a good man, Rolland Thomas, and if it's ye Patricia wants, I've no objection. However, I'll not have her married before she's turned eighteen. That's just over a year from now. Yer willin' to wait, I trust?"

Rolland shook the doctor's hand heartily. "Aye, I am, sir. Of course I am. Thank ye, sir. Ye've made me the happiest man in all the city."

Seeing the two men turn toward the house, Ciara and her sister quickly scrambled away from the window. The door opened and Michael came in first. "Patricia," he said, unable to keep the smile from spreading across his face, "the young lad has somethin' to ask ye!"

* * *

Sunday morning came with the usual flurry of activity as the Nolan family prepared to leave for church. Michael drove the carriage down Franklin Street, carrying Ciara and Patricia, while Charlie followed behind with Karyn and all of the younger children in the wagon. In the short ride, the occupants in the carriage reviewed the events of the week.

"I've been meanin' to ask ye: how's the woman

with the fits?" Patricia asked her brother-in-law.

"Not much improved, I'm afraid. 'Tis an interesting case, to be sure. I spoke with the woman who brought her in, and there's been no sickness or fever through the tenements all winter. I'll have to turn her over to Dr. Ferris' care for the next few days until we've seen the end of the opthalmia at the orphan asylum."

"Oh, the poor dears are miserable," Ciara added.

"I remember not too long ago Ferris telling me they had more than a few cases at the Big house," Michael added, too much of a gentleman to mention that the afflicted women were likely prostitutes.

"Dr. Ferris has become a fine physician," Ciara remarked. "Mrs. Munroe says he is very kind, unlike some of the other doctors who practice there."

"Aye, that he has. I'm impressed with his work at the poor farm as well. A stickler for recordkeeping is Ferris. To be sure he went straight to Mr. Pratt when he found no record of Mr. Buchman's heart attack in the death book. William Proctor will have that to answer for that when he returns."

"Aye, about that, do ye not find it strange that the

man has been gone all week?" Patricia asked.

At the mention of The Keeper's name, Ciara felt her gorge rise up. She immediately put her hand to her mouth and swallowed hard to keep everything down.

"Are ye not well, love?" Michael asked.

"Ach, I'm fine. The mention of that man's name just turns my stomach, is all," she answered. "I'd be pleased if he never comes back, but I don't believe he'll stay away for too long. William Proctor does as he pleases until the money runs out."

The carriage pulled up behind the church, just under the big sycamore tree. Over the years, as the children got older and the adults had become friendly with the other parishioners, the time before and after mass was spent visiting with friends and catching up on the news of the neighborhood. The big tree behind the church had become the accepted meeting place for everyone to regroup before heading home. Ciara looked pale as Michael helped her down from the carriage. Sending the others on ahead, he asked her, "Are ye sure yer well?"

"Aye, I'm fine." No sooner did the words leave her mouth then did she turn and wretch. Michael stood by, handkerchief at the ready for when she was done. He took in the swell of her breasts and realized that in all of the excitement of the past few weeks he hadn't noticed that her courses were late. As both a physician and her husband, Ciara's monthly cycle was something to which Michael was well attuned and, now that he was considering the topic, he noted that she was several weeks late. As she turned and reached for the handkerchief, she couldn't help but notice the huge grin spreading across her husband's face.

"What are ye gawkin' at?" she asked, somewhat annoyed by his amusement.

"I think maybe we'll be expectin' a new addition to the family in a wee while," he said, glancing down at her mid-section.

"What?" Looking down at her own waistline, Ciara ran her hand gently around her abdomen. She had been so worried about Mrs. Kaiser that she hadn't even thought about the fact that her courses were late. "Do ye think it's possible? Do we dare hope? Oh, Michael, are we havin' a baby?" Tears ran down her face as she flung herself into his arms.

"Aye, I think we are!" He said, taking her into his

arms. They were both so delighted with this unexpected revelation that each was reluctant to part from the other, fearing that the spell would end and their hearts would again be broken. Finally, the sound of the church bell beckoning them to mass pulled them away from each other. Arm in arm, they strolled toward the church to thank God for the most precious gift that finally had been bestowed upon them.

Epilogue

Buffalo, New York, April 18, 1841

To the Honorable Board of Directors, City and County Hall, Buffalo, N.Y.

Gentleman,

There is a subject that I must, once again, call to the attention of Your Honorable Body. Every effort has been made to locate the whereabouts of the Keeper of the Poor so that he may answer the charges brought against him by Your Honorable Body. None of said attempts have met with success. At present the almshouse is without daily management beyond the feeble efforts of the Matron, which, I would hope Your Honorable Body would agree, is unacceptable. I would respectfully request that Your Honorable Body advise me on this matter.

Very Truly Yours,
A. Pratt
Alfonse Pratt
Superintendent

A Whisper of Bones

Black Rock, New York, May 1, 1841

To Alfonse Pratt, Superintendent of the Poor, Black Rock

Dear Mr. Pratt,

It has come to our attention that the Keeper of the Poor has returned to Buffalo and has been under the care the highly esteemed physician, Dr. Reginald Standish, of Buffalo, since his arrival. Dr. Standish has come before this Board to speak on behalf of the Keeper, who, he informs us, has suffered great emotional and physical injury as a result of a case of mistaken identity in Geneva, New York. The doctor further testified that the Keeper is neither of sound mind nor of sound body, and to bring him before this Board to answer for his shortcomings in management of the almshouse, specifically with regard to recordkeeping and mismanagement, could, indeed, cause him irreparable harm. Upon the advice of his esteemed physician, the honorable Mr. Proctor has resigned his position as Keeper of the Poor effective immediately. It was the unanimous decision of this Board to give you, the Superintendent of the Poor, leave to submit a list of potential candidates to fill this now vacated position, said list to be presented to this Board in one weeks' time.

Very Truly Yours,
Colleen Farrell
**Board of Directors
for Indoor Poor Relief**

Author's notes

When you juggle owning a business, a scholarly research project and writing a book you need a great support network. To my husband, Bob, and my son, Charlie, I thank you for taking care of yourselves, the dogs, the house and the business when I needed you to. My profound thanks also goes to Julia, Stephanie, Claire, Ashley, and Lucy for holding down the fort at work when I needed them.

My novels are inspired by my scholarly work, and so I thank Drs. Joyce E. Sirianni and Douglas Perrelli for inviting me to join the Erie County Poorhouse Cemetery Project. It has been such a pleasure to work on this project. I have learned so much from the both of them and their research has inspired many parts of this book.

There were several historians who were incredibly generous in giving me both their time and their detailed knowledge of various aspects of Buffalo's history. Jennifer Liber Raines, from the Western New York Genealogical Society, is without a doubt the most gifted researcher I know. She provided me with countless municipal reports and period newspaper articles that helped me to understand where the Erie County Poorhouse existed in the public stream of consciousness. She has become a valued friend and colleague, and I will write many more books so that I can continue to work with her. Cynthia Van Ness, from the Buffalo History Museum, provided me with the municipal reports that helped me to understand the Buffalo Orphan Asylum, the City directories from the period that allowed me to incorporate real locations into the story, and a better understanding of how the religious controversies of the period impacted on the charitable efforts of its citizens. Charles Alaimo from the Buffalo and Erie County Public Library helped me navigate period maps of the city so that my characters could move about on foot, horseback or by carriage as they would have in 1840 Buffalo.

There is a real antique lamp shop located on Hertel Avenue in Buffalo, New York, called the Antique Lamp

Company and Gift Emporium. John and Sue Tobin, the owners of this wonderful establishment, were very gracious and accommodating in answering all of my questions about their business and about the specific lamps mentioned in this book. I am grateful for their support of both *Orphans and Inmates* and *A Whisper of Bones*.

For helping with the German translation I thank Bob Higgins and Jerry Scharf for allowing me to pester them with questions.

Buffalonians love their history and there are quite a few local history enthusiasts who were very helpful. They include Cindy and Paul Gorski from Explore Buffalo, Ian Edbauer and all of my friends from Buffalo and Western New York's Proud History, Chuck La Chiusa, who created Buffalo Architectural History (www.buffaloah.com), and Bill Coleman.

Thanks to Sally Algera from Erie County Medical Center for allowing me access to the original inmate records from the Erie County Poorhouse, and for helping to insure that these records found a home where they could be available to all those who might be interested in them.

Thanks to my readers, Bob Higgins, Casilda G. Lucas, Jennifer Liber Raines, Joyce E. Sirianni and Christine Hicks for helping me with everything from skeletal biology and local history to spelling and grammar.

About the Author

Rosanne Higgins was born in Enfield, Connecticut, however spent her youth in Buffalo, New York. Her experiences traveling in both the United States and in Europe as a child resulted in a love of history from an early age. She knew from the time she was in fourth grade that she wanted to be an Anthropologist and went on to graduate school at the University at Buffalo. Combining her two interests, she studied the Asylum Movement in the nineteenth century and its impact on disease specific mortality. This research focused on the Erie, Niagara, and Monroe County Poorhouses in Western New York. That research earned her a Ph.D. in Anthropology in 1998 and lead to the publication of her research.

www.rosannehiggins.com/blog.html
www.facebook.com/pages/Orphans-and-Inmates/516800631758088